W9-AOZ-072

Individual Pathways of Change

Individual Pathways of Change

Statistical Models for Analyzing Learning and Development

Edited by Peter C. M. Molenaar
and Karl M. Newell

American Psychological Association • Washington, DC

Published by
American Psychological Association
750 First Street, NE
Washington, DC 20002
www.apa.org

To order
APA Order Department
P.O. Box 92984
Washington, DC 20090-2984
Tel: (800) 374-2721;
Direct: (202) 336-5510
Fax: (202) 336-5502;
TDD/TTY: (202) 336-6123
Online: www.apa.org/books/
E-mail: order@apa.org

In the U.K., Europe, Africa, and the Middle East,
copies may be ordered from
American Psychological Association
3 Henrietta Street
Covent Garden, London
WC2E 8LU England

Typeset in New Century Schoolbook by Circle Graphics, Inc., Columbia, MD

Printer: United Book Press, Baltimore, MD
Cover Designer: Mercury Publishing Services, Rockville, MD

The opinions and statements published are the responsibility of the authors, and such opinions and statements do not necessarily represent the policies of the American Psychological Association.

Library of Congress Cataloging-in-Publication Data

Individual pathways of change : statistical models for analyzing learning and development / edited by Peter C.M. Molenaar and Karl M. Newell.
    p. cm.
  Papers presented at a conference held at The Pennsylvania State University, University Park in Sept. 2008.
  Includes bibliographical references and index.
  ISBN-13: 978-1-4338-0772-5
  ISBN-10: 1-4338-0772-6
  ISBN-13: 978-1-4338-0773-2 (e-book)
  ISBN-10: 1-4338-0773-4 (e-book)
  1. Developmental psychology—Congresses. I. Molenaar, Peter C. M. II. Newell, Karl M., 1945-
BF713.5.I54 2010
155—dc22

2009046232

British Library Cataloguing-in-Publication Data
A CIP record is available from the British Library.

Printed in the United States of America
First Edition

APA Science Volumes

Attribution and Social Interaction: The Legacy of Edward E. Jones

Best Methods for the Analysis of Change: Recent Advances, Unanswered Questions, Future Directions

Cardiovascular Reactivity to Psychological Stress and Disease

The Challenge in Mathematics and Science Education: Psychology's Response

Changing Employment Relations: Behavioral and Social Perspectives

Children Exposed to Marital Violence: Theory, Research, and Applied Issues

Cognition: Conceptual and Methodological Issues

Cognitive Bases of Musical Communication

Cognitive Dissonance: Progress on a Pivotal Theory in Social Psychology

Conceptualization and Measurement of Organism–Environment Interaction

Converging Operations in the Study of Visual Selective Attention

Creative Thought: An Investigation of Conceptual Structures and Processes

Developmental Psychoacoustics

Diversity in Work Teams: Research Paradigms for a Changing Workplace

Emotion and Culture: Empirical Studies of Mutual Influence

Emotion, Disclosure, and Health

Evolving Explanations of Development: Ecological Approaches to Organism–Environment Systems

Examining Lives in Context: Perspectives on the Ecology of Human Development

Global Prospects for Education: Development, Culture, and Schooling

Hostility, Coping, and Health

Measuring Patient Changes in Mood, Anxiety, and Personality Disorders: Toward a Core Battery

Occasion Setting: Associative Learning and Cognition in Animals

Organ Donation and Transplantation: Psychological and Behavioral Factors

Origins and Development of Schizophrenia: Advances in Experimental Psychopathology

The Perception of Structure

Perspectives on Socially Shared Cognition

Psychological Testing of Hispanics

APA Decade of Behavior Volumes

Contents

Contributors

Cindy S. Bergeman, PhD, University of Notre Dame, Notre Dame, IN
Steven M. Boker, PhD, University of Virginia, Charlottesville
Sy-Miin Chow, PhD, University of North Carolina, Chapel Hill
Conor V. Dolan, PhD, University of Amsterdam, Amsterdam, the Netherlands
Guillaume Filteau, PhD, University of North Carolina, Chapel Hill
Raoul P. P. P. Grasman, PhD, University of Amsterdam, Amsterdam, the Netherlands
Ellen L. Hamaker, PhD, Utrecht University, Utrecht, the Netherlands
Scott Hofer, PhD, University of Victoria, Victoria, British Columbia, Canada
Lesa Hoffman, PhD, University of Nebraska, Lincoln
S. Lee Hong, PhD, Indiana University, Bloomington
Michael D. Hunter, PhD, University of Virginia, Charlottesville
Brenda R. J. Jansen, PhD, University of Amsterdam, Amsterdam, the Netherlands
Jan Henk Kamphuis, PhD, University of Amsterdam, Amsterdam, the Netherlands
Shu-Chen Li, PhD, Max Planck Institute for Human Development, Berlin, Germany
Yeou-Teh Liu, PhD, National Taiwan Normal University, Taipei City, Taiwan
Eric Loken, PhD, The Pennsylvania State University, University Park
Gottfried Mayer-Kress, PhD, The Pennsylvania State University, University Park
Peter C. M. Molenaar, PhD, The Pennsylvania State University, University Park
Mignon A. Montpetit, PhD, Illinois Wesleyan University, Bloomington
John R. Nesselroade, PhD, University of Virginia, Charlottesville
Karl M. Newell, PhD, The Pennsylvania State University, University Park
Michael J. Rovine, PhD, The Pennsylvania State University, University Park
Katerina O. Sinclair, PhD, The Pennsylvania State University, University Park
Martin Sliwinski, PhD, The Pennsylvania State University, University Park
Maarten Speekenbrink, PhD, University College London, London, England
Cynthia A. Stifter, PhD, The Pennsylvania State University, University Park
Peter van Rijn, PhD, CITO, Arnhem, the Netherlands
Ingmar Visser, PhD, University of Amsterdam, Amsterdam, the Netherlands
Guangjian Zhang, PhD, University of Notre Dame, Notre Dame, IN

Series Foreword

In early 1988, the American Psychological Association (APA) Science Directorate began its sponsorship of what would become an exceptionally successful activity in support of psychological science—the APA Scientific Conferences program. This program has showcased some of the most important topics in psychological science and has provided a forum for collaboration among many leading figures in the field.

The program has inspired a series of books that have presented cutting-edge work in all areas of psychology. At the turn of the millennium, the series was renamed the Decade of Behavior Series to help advance the goals of this important initiative. The Decade of Behavior is a major interdisciplinary campaign designed to promote the contributions of the behavioral and social sciences to our most important societal challenges in the decade leading up to 2010. Although a key goal has been to inform the public about these scientific contributions, other activities have been designed to encourage and further collaboration among scientists. Hence, the series that was the "APA Science Series" has continued as the "Decade of Behavior Series." This represents one element in APA's efforts to promote the Decade of Behavior initiative as one of its endorsing organizations. For additional information about the Decade of Behavior, please visit http://www.decadeofbehavior.org.

Over the course of the past years, the Science Conference and Decade of Behavior Series has allowed psychological scientists to share and explore cutting-edge findings in psychology. The APA Science Directorate looks forward to continuing this successful program and to sponsoring other conferences and books in the years ahead. This series has been so successful that we have chosen to extend it to include books that, although they do not arise from conferences, report with the same high quality of scholarship on the latest research.

We are pleased that this important contribution to the literature was supported in part by the Decade of Behavior program. Congratulations to the editors and contributors of this volume on their sterling effort.

Steven J. Breckler, PhD
Executive Director for Science

Virginia E. Holt
*Assistant Executive Director
for Science*

Preface

The analysis of change in learning and development has long been an area of scholarly focus at Penn State, particularly in the Department of Human Development and Family Studies. A distinguishing feature of this research emphasis has been the integration of theory and methods in developmental systems—a perspective that has come to be known as *developmental systems theory*. Recently, a number of new approaches have been published from both theoretical and methodological perspectives. Our opening introductory chapter outlines these thematic influences. The general push is to the study of the individual over the life span in the many contexts of learning and development.

In this volume we bring together established and emerging scientists who lead the way in the development of innovative statistical methods to apply systems theoretical models to individual learning and developmental processes, ranging from mother–infant interaction processes to cognitive aging. This provides the reader with a state-of-the-art overview of the fundamental paradigm of developmental systems science.

This book was written in the wake of a conference titled "Individual Pathways of Change in Learning and Development" held at The Pennsylvania State University, University Park, in September 2008. The conference and book were supported by the Science Directorate of the American Psychological Association. Additional funding was provided from several units at Penn State, including the Social Science Research Institute, the College of Health and Human Development, the Department of Human Development and Family Studies, and the Department of Kinesiology. We appreciate very much the respective support from these organizations. Many individuals from Penn State contributed to running the conference meeting and determining the organization of the book, in particular, Eric Loken, Mike Rovine, and Nilam Ram. Thanks are also due to Dori Sunday and Brenda Wert for their superb organization of the conference details. Finally, and not least, we would like to thank all the participants for their many contributions to the conference and the book.

Individual Pathways of Change

Introduction

Peter C. M. Molenaar and Karl M. Newell

There exists a long tradition in theoretical psychology and theoretical biology that argues that developmental and learning processes should be analyzed at the level of intraindividual variation (time series data). A general denotation for this tradition is *developmental systems theory* (DST). Important contributions to DST include Wohlwill's (1973) monograph on the concept of developmental functions describing intraindividual variation; Ford and Lerner's (1992) integrative approach, which is based on the interplay between intraindividual variation and interindividual variation and change; and Gottlieb's (1992, 2003) theoretical work on probabilistic epigenetic development. Oyama, Griffiths, and Gray (2001) presented a compilation of recent contributions to DST in theoretical biology.

Although the tenets of DST are well established and have links to contemporary theory of dynamic systems and artificial neural networks (e.g., connectionism), most analysis efforts in learning and development still focus on data averaged across subjects. There is a growing realization of the limitations of this time-honored approach. For example, in the domain of learning it has been shown through simulation that learners who change as an exponential but with different individual exponents (or time scales) will approximate a power law when considered on a group-averaged basis (Newell, Liu, & Mayer-Kress, 2001). Examples such as this have helped reintroduce the need in a variety of domains for the analysis of the individual over time—an approach that is particularly fundamental to theory in learning and development.

The basic tenet of DST concerning the necessity of analyzing developmental processes at the level of time-dependent intraindividual variation has been recently vindicated by mathematical–statistical proof (Molenaar, 2004). It was shown that this necessity is a direct consequence of the so-called classical ergodic theorems that hold for any measurable stochastic process. These theorems specify the general mathematical conditions that have to be met by a dynamic process in order to guarantee that its structure of interindividual variation can be validly generalized to the subject-specific level of intraindividual variation (and vice versa).

The ergodicity conditions concerned are twofold: (a) the process has to be stationary, and (b) each person in the population (ensemble) has to obey the same dynamics (homogeneous population). For a Gaussian (normally distributed) stochastic process, stationarity implies that the mean function (level) of the process is constant in time (no trends or cycles) and that the sequential dependence of the process also is invariant in time (constant variance and sequential

3

correlation dependent only on relative distance between time points; cf. Hannan, 1970). If a Gaussian dynamic process obeys both conditions, it is called *ergodic*; if one or both conditions are violated, the process is called *nonergodic*. Only ergodic processes have lawful relationships between their structure of intraindividual variation and their structure of interindividual variation. For nonergodic processes, however, no a priori relationships exist between results obtained in an analysis of interindividual variation and results obtained in an analogous analysis of intraindividual variation.

The consequences of the classical ergodic theorems affect all psychological statistical methodology (e.g., Borsboom, 2005; Molenaar, 2004). Prime examples of nonergodic processes are developmental and learning processes, which almost always are nonstationary and hence nonergodic (violation of the first ergodicity condition of stationarity). In other words, the mean function, variance, and/or sequential dependencies of developmental and learning processes are, in general, time varying (cf. Molenaar, Sinclair, Rovine, Ram, & Corneal, 2009). For instance, stage transitions typically are characterized by transitory changes in variance and sequential dependencies (cf. Wagenmakers, Molenaar, Grasman, Hartelman, & van der Maas, 2005). Developmental and learning processes that obey different dynamic laws for different subjects (subject specificity) also are nonergodic (violation of the second ergodicity condition of homogeneity; cf. Molenaar, 2007). Analysis of these processes should be based on intraindividual variation, that is, single-subject or replicated time series analysis, in accordance with the basic tenet of DST.

The necessity that analysis of developmental and learning processes should be based on intraindividual variation poses new methodological challenges. There is a need to develop appropriate generalizations of standard statistical models used in the analysis of interindividual variation in order to be able to apply these models in the analysis of intraindividual variation (time series analysis). This is particularly the case for latent variable models, which constitute the state of the art in analysis of interindividual variation. Using the well-known classification of Bartholomew (1987), one can distinguish four classes of latent variable models:

1. Models in which both the observed variables and the latent variables are continuous. Time series analogues are linear and nonlinear state space models (e.g., Shumway & Stoffer, 2006).
2. Models in which the observed variables are categorical and the latent variables are continuous. Time series analogues are generalized dynamic models, including dynamic item-response theoretical models (e.g., Fahrmeir & Tutz, 2001).
3. Models in which the observed variables are categorical and the latent variables are categorical. Time series analogues are hidden Markov models (e.g., Elliott, Aggoun, & Moore, 1995).
4. Models in which the observed variables are continuous and the latent variables are categorical. Time series analogues are Markov jump models (e.g., Costa, Fragoso, & Marques, 2005).

In this book, new advanced statistical time series analysis techniques are presented and applied to developmental and learning processes. The book consists of four parts. Part I, "Life Span Development," addresses the modeling of developmental processes in early life, including weight change (Chapter 1), cognitive aging (Chapters 2 and 3), and mother–child interaction (Chapter 4). The chapters in Part II, "Dynamics of Learning," discuss the analysis of learning processes from various methodological perspectives, including different time scales (Chapter 5), the occurrence of discontinuities (Chapter 6), discrete change (Chapter 7), and educational process analysis (Chapter 8). Part III, "Modeling Issues," presents new approaches to modeling, including regime changes (Chapter 9), factor analysis of time series (Chapter 10), and dynamic systems modeling (Chapter 11). The book concludes with Part IV, "Reflections and Prospects," an intriguing description of the emerging fundamental paradigm within which this book's innovative work takes place (Chapter 12).

Although this book conceptually categorizes chapters according to the four topics just described, readers may also wish to conceptually categorize chapters according to class of dynamic latent variable model. Chapters 1, 2, 3, 5, 10, and 11 discuss models belonging to Bartholomew's first class of dynamic models, with continuous observed and latent variables. Chapter 8 discusses Bartholomew's second class of dynamic models, with categorical observed variables and continuous latent variables. Chapters 4 and 7 focus on dynamic models in which both the observed and latent variables are categorical. Chapters 6 and 9 complete the coverage of Bartholomew's classification scheme, addressing the dynamic models with continuous observed variables and categorical latent variables.

The statistical analysis of nonergodic time series with time-varying and/or subject-specific characteristics requires the use of advanced modeling techniques that have only recently become available. The chapters in this book provide an excellent coverage of important approaches to the analysis of nonstationary and/or subject-specific multivariate time series that are appropriate, in the sense indicated by the ergodic theorems, for the analysis of developmental and learning processes.

References

Bartholomew, D. J. (1987). *Latent variable models and factor analysis*. New York, NY: Oxford University Press..

Borsboom, D. (2005). *Measuring the mind: Conceptual issues in contemporary psychometrics*. Cambridge, England: Cambridge University Press.

Costa, O. L. V., Fragoso, M. D., & Marques, R. P. (2005). *Discrete-time Markov jump linear systems*. London, England: Springer-Verlag.

Elliott, R. J., Aggoun, L., & Moore, J. B. (1995). *Hidden Markov models: Estimation and control*. New York, NY: Springer-Verlag.

Fahrmeir, L., & Tutz, G. (2001). *Multivariate statistical modeling based on generalized linear models*. New York, NY: Springer-Verlag.

Ford, D. H., & Lerner, R. M. (1992). *Developmental systems theory*. Newbury Park, CA: Sage.

Gottlieb, G. (1992). *Individual development and evolution: The genesis of novel behavior*. New York, NY: Oxford University Press.

Gottlieb, G. (2003). On making behavioral genetics truly developmental. *Human Development, 46,* 337–355.

Hannan, E. J. (1970). *Multiple time series*. New York, NY: Wiley.

Molenaar, P. C. M. (2004). A manifesto on psychology as idiographic science: Bringing the person back into scientific psychology, this time forever. *Measurement: Interdisciplinary Research & Perspective, 2,* 201–218.

Molenaar, P. C. M. (2007). On the implications of the classical ergodic theorems: Analysis of developmental processes has to focus on intra-individual variation. *Developmental Psychobiology, 50,* 60–69.

Molenaar, P. C. M., Sinclair, K. O., Rovine, M. J., Ram, N., & Corneal, S. E. (2009). Analyzing developmental processes on an individual level using non-stationary time series modeling. *Developmental Psychology, 45,* 260–271.

Newell, K. M., Liu, Y.-T., & Mayer-Kress, G. (2001). Time scales in motor learning and development. *Psychological Review, 108,* 57–82.

Oyama, S., Griffiths, P. E., & Gray, R. D. (Eds.). (2001). *Cycles of contingency: Developmental systems and evolution.* Cambridge, MA: MIT Press.

Shumway, R. S., & Stoffer, D. S. (2006). *Time series analysis and its applications: With R examples.* New York, NY: Springer.

Wagenmakers, E. J., Molenaar, P. C. M., Grasman, R. P. P. P., Hartelman, P. A. I., & van der Maas, H. L. J. (2005). Transformation invariant stochastic catastrophe theory. *Physica D, 211,* 263–276.

Wohlwill, J. F. (1973). *The study of behavioral development.* New York, NY: Academic Press.

Part I

Life Span Development

1

Person-Specific Analysis of the Dynamics of Weight Change

Eric Loken

In a 2004 article in *Behavioral and Brain Sciences,* Seth Roberts noted the major historical accomplishments achieved by researchers who experimented on themselves (e.g., Ebbinghaus's memory studies, self-monitoring of insulin) and argued that self-experimentation was a neglected and underestimated source of new hypotheses for scientific inquiry. Many of Roberts's examples were concerned with the personal goal of achieving and maintaining weight loss, and he has since popularized a diet that attempts to readjust the body's equilibrium, or set point.

In this chapter, I too argue for the importance of self-study for understanding the dynamics of weight gain and weight loss. The argument here, however, comes from a different direction than Roberts's (2004). The reasoning I pursue in this chapter is that essential aspects of the dynamics of energy balance may well require that single subjects be studied. Traditional research designs used in the social sciences are, almost without exception, concerned with the variance between individuals. As Molenaar (2004) reminded us, only under certain strong assumptions about the stationarity of a process, and about the exchangeability of individuals in the population, can findings based on between-person variance be applied to inferences at the individual level. Molenaar contended that much of the data necessary for progress in social science have been neglected, and he advocated renewed attention to time series analysis in single-subject designs.

In what follows, I review Molenaar's (2004) discussion of ergodicity; examine the relevance for common research designs in nutrition; and offer a small, single-subject demonstration as an example of the kind of research that may be critical in making progress for the study of health behaviors and health outcomes.

A Call for Person-Specific Studies in Social Sciences

Molenaar (2004) appealed directly to theorems from physics and engineering to argue that social scientists are often doing the wrong thing in terms of data acquisition and data analysis. He stressed that only under specific conditions of exchangeability of individuals and the stationarity of a process was it permissible to draw conclusions about intraindividual variation from the study of interindividual variation. If these conditions fail to hold, then a process is non-ergodic, and analyses about the structure of between-person variation are not necessarily applicable at the individual level.

A simple intuitive example of ergodicity and the relevance of group-level data to making inferences about individual behavior is to think about a map of a college campus (this example is in part motivated by Tarko, 2008). Imagine that superimposed onto the map is a representation of the current distribution of people on campus. The map would look like a "heat map," or a topological map, where information (in this case, population density) is projected on top of the map's coordinates, showing for a given point in time the population density in classrooms, the library, dining halls, recreation facilities, and other campus areas.

Now imagine a similar map of a campus, but one for which the information projected is derived from tracing the path of a single individual moving around campus for a period of time. Would the two maps be similar? They almost certainly would not. The distribution of the group behavior at an instant in time is not descriptive of the behavior of an individual over a period of time. Unlike gas molecules in a box, people on a university campus are not interchangeable, and they do not really form a system that is in long-term equilibrium. Although there may be subgroups in a campus population that are highly similar (e.g., premed students flocking predictably to introductory science lectures), there is no sense in talking about an average person. There might be a "big man on campus," but there is no "average man on campus."

The discrepancy is not resolved by allowing that the individual person's trajectory be followed indefinitely to trace out a similar density map. It is true that, in the long run, the individual might end up visiting most of the popular parts of the campus; however, what is at issue is the proportion of time spent in specific locations, and there is no expectation that this should match up with the density of the population as measured in a snapshot in time. Neither does it help to say that we should be talking about the evolution of the group-density map over time. We can imagine tracking the population density and averaging its movements over time, but here too there is no expectation of a correspondence between an individual's density map and that of the population.

The inescapable point is that descriptions of, inferences about, and predictions regarding the behavior of an individual person on a campus are not necessarily improved by information about how the group behaves. Only under the assumption that all the people on campus are identical in their expected behavior patterns, and that the system as a whole is in a stationary state, is there a direct correspondence. We know full well that people carrying out activities on a university campus do not behave like gas molecules bouncing around in a closed system at constant temperature. Nevertheless, in the social sciences researchers often discuss and interpret findings on the basis of population- or group-level variance, as if they applied to explaining causal processes at the individual level.

The campus map example is meant only to be illustrative. A scatter plot of observations on any two variables, call them X and Y, also forms a two-dimensional map that represents the relative positions of people in a coordinate system defined by X and Y, but it does not automatically follow that, for any specific individual, a change in X is accompanied by a change in Y as given by the group-level covariance structure.

The problem here is not merely that observational data are correlational, whereas data gathered in experimentally controlled settings can support inferences about causation. It is true that experimental control allows for stronger inference about the average causal effect in the population of interest; however, *average* causal effects are by definition based on the *average* change of the group. To be sure, for humans there are very many ways in which change is highly uniform. Extreme calorie restriction or sleep deprivation can have predictable effects that generalize across people. There is no serious contention that anatomy and physiology are purely single-subject sciences, as it is of course true that average causal effects in many situations correspond well to what is observed at the individual level.

Nevertheless, there are limits to what is represented by average change. For example, a formula for energy balance of input = output, where input is measured as the calorie content of food consumed and output is measured as the calories expended, does need to be qualified by individual differences. One cannot infer an expected weight gain on the basis of an observed energy imbalance without accounting for individual variation in metabolic rates, patterns of consumption, and ability to process and digest various dietary components. Thus, a new diet supplement may be observed in an experimental paradigm to demonstrate a certain causal effect—let's say a net weight loss of 1 kilogram in 3 weeks—but this effect size represents the population average and might not correspond to the pattern seen in any individual. The population may divide neatly into responders and nonresponders—with the effect being null for 80% and a loss of 5 kg for the remaining 20% of the population. The average causal effect is important to estimate from a public health perspective, but it may have nothing whatsoever to do with the actual causal processes occurring at the individual level.

Molenaar's (2004) main example is based on personality research (Hamaker, Dolan, & Molenaar, 2005) in which the dominant five-factor model of personality posits underlying dimensions of Openness, Conscientiousness, Neuroticism, Extraversion, and Agreeableness (i.e., the Big Five). The model is based on data from lengthy personality inventories taken by millions of individuals, and the five-factor structure is completely inferred from an analysis of the variation between people. Building on the previous discussion, the questionnaire's items form a map, and people are positioned on that map relative to one another. The model seems to do a good job of describing the essential underlying structure because it accounts for the relative positioning of people on that map.

However, what does that mean at the level of the individual? Hamaker et al. (2005) analyzed data from people who answered personality inventories on 90 successive days. With those data it is possible to draw maps for individuals (analogous to following someone around campus over time), and Hamaker et al. found that the individual-level maps did not at all look like the common five-factor structure. So, although the Big Five may be useful in positioning someone relative to the population in a matrix of personality dimensions, it does not necessarily follow that a similar pattern of variation will emerge at the level of the individual.

The central thesis considered in this chapter is that weight change over time in individuals might have dynamics that are best seen by focusing on the time series variation of individuals. Just as Roberts (2004) found utility in tracking his weight and looking for associations with different aspects of his diet, it might be fruitful to look for longitudinal associations with many aspects of personal behavior, including exercise, sleep, and diet. Such associations, however, are unlikely to be observed in the standard types of research design undertaken in health and nutrition research.

Nutrition Research and the Study of Factors Associated With Weight Gain and Weight Loss

Nutrition research, especially at the behavioral level, seems to be overwhelmingly concerned with average models and with aggregating data across people. Recommendations for daily nutritional requirements are widely disseminated, but these are largely based on regression models that determine what is advantageous on average for a population. We are constantly advised of new research linking dietary elements to reduced or elevated risk for various health outcomes (although this advice sometimes reverses itself as new evidence comes in). There can be no doubt that a vast number of common dietary recommendations are indeed almost universally applicable for people, but one does not have to look far to find research examples that highlight the gap between population averages and person-specific processes.

A majority of the diet and lifestyle advice presented as scientifically validated comes from large-scale surveys, such as the oft-cited Nurses' Health Study (Colditz, Manson, & Hankinson, 1997), which has tracked more than 100,000 nurses since 1976. One research question (among many) examined in these data is the association between sleep and weight gain. Patel, Malhotra, White, Gottlieb, and Hu (2006) found that women who reported getting 5 or fewer hr of sleep each night gained significantly more weight over 10 years compared with women who reported getting 7 hr of sleep per night. The net effect over 10 years was approximately 0.7 kg (the precise estimate varied depending on the covariance adjustments made). This is an interesting finding relating sleep and weight gain, and the prospective nature of the data is valuable. However, the net effect of 0.7 kg over 10 years represents a population average. It is probably not meaningful to divide that number by 10 and conclude that there is a relative weight increase of 70 g per year. Neither is it appropriate to infer that the net change for individuals who sleep 5 or fewer hours per night would be 70 g per year if they changed to sleeping 7 hr per night. The population average is an estimate derived only from the population means—in this case, between two groups of women who reported different sleeping habits—and it says very little about the dynamic association between sleep and weight gain for individual women.

However, it can be very easy to slide from an analysis of population effects to inferences regarding individual-level effects. Consider, for example, the following statement from a call for proposals by the National Institutes of Health to take a bioengineering approach to the study of energy balance:

> Assessment of human energy balance, the net difference between energy intake (by diet) and expenditure (by work and heat), is a key component of obesity research, prevention, and treatment. The importance of accurate measurement of states of energy balance can be appreciated by considering average weight gain in middle-aged adults (~10 lb/decade). This significant gain in weight results from very small, persistent excesses of intake over expenditure of approximately 0.3% of the daily calorie consumption. This imbalance is well below the level of perception for most individuals. (National Institutes of Health, n.d.)

It actually does not follow from the fact that the population average weight gain is 10 pounds (4.5 kg) per decade that the process of weight gain in individuals "results from very small, persistent excesses of intake over expenditure of approximately 0.3% of the daily calorie consumption." The excess could take the form of one indulgent meal per year and still have the same net effect, on average, on energy balance, and a single large meal is an event well above the perception process for individuals. This is not to defend the idea that weight gain over a decade is attributable to one yearly meal with excessive consumption; the point is that it is improper to infer, because the population average energy imbalance appears to be as little as 10 calories per day, that the search must begin for an imbalance of 10 calories per day in the energy intake and expenditure of individuals. The population average (where *average* here is taken both across people and over time) is not necessarily representative of the process at the individual level.

Despite quibbling with the specific passage just quoted, I actually agree that bioengineering approaches can be very useful in the study of the dynamics of weight change. One promising tool borrowed from bioengineering is the statistical modeling of systems. Although methods for forecasting, optimal control, and feedback are widely used in engineering, physics, and economics, time series methods have not played a significant role in psychology and other social science fields. The vast majority of research conducted at the human, behavioral level on nutrition, diet, exercise, and weight change, for example, is carried out using methods of analysis (analysis of variance, growth curves, factor analysis, mixture models) that analyze variance *between* persons rather than variance *within* persons.

Single-subject designs are not entirely absent in nutrition and health research. Tarasuk and Beaton (1991) specifically attempted to model within-person variance in diet assessments of energy intake. They collected 1 year's worth of daily estimates of energy intake for 29 participants. They modeled the time series by including period effects for day of week as well as effects for the time during which the participants were also being monitored for weight. Tarasuk and Beaton then also checked whether first-order autoregressive terms were needed to capture day-to-day covariance. Their study is frequently cited in the diet assessment literature as demonstrating the need for both weekend and weekday assessments, the need to address nonindependence of residuals if assessments are on contiguous days, and the need to do several assessments to properly estimate "typical" energy intake.

Less frequently discussed are the insights Tarasuk and Beaton (1991) drew by comparing the between-individual and within-individual patterns. They reported tremendous heterogeneity in the sample with regard to the appropriate predictive model for daily fluctuations in energy intake. In the average time series (averaging energy intake across participants on each day) there was a significant pattern of higher consumption on Friday and Saturday, and less consumption on Monday and Tuesday, but although many participants exhibited something close to this pattern no single participant had exactly this trend in his or her data. This provides yet another example of how the group trend may not describe the trend of any individual.

In other studies that have collected intensive measurements of weight change or energy intake there has been an unfortunate tendency to aggregate the data both across people and across time. Racette et al. (2008), for instance, conducted an experimental intervention to assess the effects of calorie restriction and exercise on weight. Their sample of 48 participants was measured daily for 2-week sessions at baseline and at several other times during the yearlong intervention. A recent finding was that, on average, participants ate more on Saturdays, exercised less on Sundays, and tended to gain weight between assessments on Friday and Monday (Racette et al., 2008).

Interesting as the result is, the analysis requires doubly aggregating the data, both across all participants and within participants by averaging to 7-day intervals. Both these steps make sense only under the dual assumptions that the participants are exchangeable and that the process of weight change is stationary. The first assumption is suspect, if only for the reason that the weekly cycle is substantially different across people (because, e.g., people have very different work and family commitments). The second assumption is violated if there are any trends among the individuals in terms of net weight gain and weight loss (and, possibly, multiple such periods per individual). By analogy back to the map example for ergodicity, it is as if the researchers were trying to draw the average map for the average person's week on campus.

Whether a specific person tends to eat more on Saturdays, or exercise less on Sundays, is a relatively easy fact to establish by gathering enough data on that person. (Note that identifying the problem of weekend weight gain on a person-specific basis is perfectly sensible, because the problem can be resolved only on a person-specific basis anyway.) However, daily measurements of weight, exercise, sleep, and diet could be used for much more than merely identifying such simple patterns. Multivariate time series at the individual level could be used to identify person-specific processes, such as lagged associations between sleep and weight, or—by analogy to a technical analysis of stock market fluctuations—channels of resistance and support whereby "breakouts" of weight gain or loss are associated with certain combinations of diet and exercise. The possibilities for uncovering hidden dynamics between behaviors and weight status are greatly enhanced if sufficient data are gathered at the individual level and if the focus of analysis becomes within-person variation rather than between-person variation.

A Simple Example of Tracking Weight and Sleep

Believing that time series data might be useful in the study of energy balance, I collected pilot samples of the data I feel are necessary to explore properly contingencies between behaviors and weight status at the level of the individual. Three participants tracked their weight and sleep with daily measurements for 80 to 120 days. Participants tried as much as possible to weigh themselves at the same time of day (usually immediately after rising in the morning). Sleep duration was also recorded on waking each morning. One participant recorded the days on which he went for a 7- to 10-mile run. An investigation of energy balance ideally would contain even more information, both in length of the study and in the level of detail. In future work I will continue to record weight and sleep data but also add daily data about diet and exercise. What is shown in the following paragraphs is intended as "proof of concept" that even simplified experiments can yield interesting results.

The data for each participant were bivariate time series. The top panel of Figure 1.1 depicts data from a late-30s man gathered over a period of 82 days, for which weight and nightly sleep have been centered at zero by subtracting the mean (with no loss of generality). As a first pass at such data one can examine lagged correlations between sleep and weight status. For each of the three participants I regressed weight onto sleep for the previous night and for several nights previous (to investigate the lagged relationships). These regressions violate the independence assumption because of the time correlations; nevertheless, they give a first pass at the magnitude of the within-person associations that might be observed (see Table 1.1 for the coefficients).

All three participants showed negative correlations extending back at least to the 2nd night before data collection. For the man, the association dropped off decisively after 2 nights. For Female A, a graduate student in her mid-20s, there were modest associations for 4 nights. For Female B, a mother in her late 30s nursing twins, the correlations seemed to become greater in magnitude going farther back in time. The regression diagnostics for this participant showed clear nonlinearity with curvature in the partial plots. For space reasons, those partial plots are not shown here, but the patterns were striking. Quadratic terms improved the fit. However, this participant also had general upward and downward trends in weight over the period of study, and this is nonstationary behavior of the time series that requires additional modeling.

One can already draw some important conclusions from these simple regressions. First, longitudinal data within the same individual can yield valuable information regarding possible associations between behavior and weight. As discussed in the previous section, theory and experimental evidence do in fact suggest a link between sleep and body weight. However, to find a similar result with such a simple study design—collecting coarse, self-report data over a period of months—suggests that there is indeed much to be learned from this recommended approach.

Second, there appears to be heterogeneity of processes. All three participants had a negative association between sleep and weight, but the dynamics are different for each person. Male A may have a pattern in which lags greater than 2 are irrelevant. Female B may have a very complex pattern of autocorrelations,

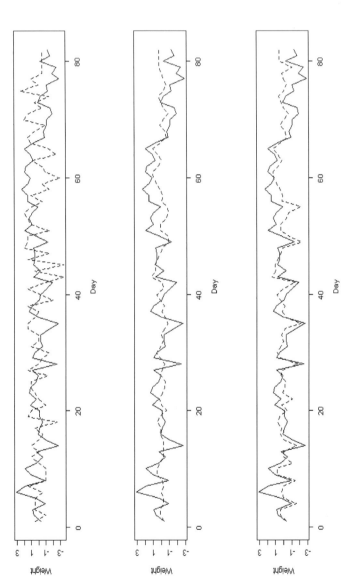

Figure 1.1. Three plots illustrating the success in predicting daily weight from recent sleep history. In each panel, the solid line is the daily weight in pounds, centered at 0 for the series. Top panel: Daily measures of sleep in hours, centered at zero (dotted line; $r = -.24$). Middle panel: Predicted weight based on previous nights of sleep (dotted line; $r = .35$). Bottom panel: Predicted weight now including the indicator for the previous day's run (dotted line; $r = .51$).

Table 1.1. Regressions of Weight Status Onto Nightly Sleep

Time	Female A	Female B	Male A
Previous night	−.227*	−.255*	−.245*
2 nights prior	−.148	−.173	−.260*
3 nights prior	−.270*	−.395*	.049
4 nights prior	−.177	−.438*	.044
5 nights prior		−.512*	
R^2	.15	.18	.13
Series length (days)	85	112	82

*$p < .05$.

and Female A's pattern may be different yet. This heterogeneity is exactly what is at issue in the person-specific approach I advocate. Not only would complex, lagged associations over time be impossible to identify in most traditional research designs (i.e., with data from many participants with a few time points each), but also the underlying processes are often likely to be specific to the individual. If the time series are nonergodic, then aggregation will distort what is happening at the individual level. This is why it seems prudent to conduct an in-depth analysis of within-person variance before pooling data.

As an example of the more involved time series–based analyses, consider the time series of Male A. Following Box and Jenkins (1976), I calculated a transfer function to describe the dynamic association between sleep and weight. I started by examining the cross-correlations at successive lags. The largest correlations are between weight status and sleep the previous two nights (as already shown in Table 1.1). With all the other cross-correlations of much lower magnitude, the pattern is consistent with a model in which sleep "causes" change in weight status. (The quotation marks surrounding *cause* remind us that establishing causation is difficult but that at least there is a strong suggestion of a direction of effect.)

Lag	−5	−4	−3	−2	−1	0	1	2	3	4	5
$r =$	.03	0	.03	0	−.26	−20	.05	.01	−.10	.02	0

Box and Jenkins recommended prewhitening the input series and then estimating the cross-correlations again between the input and output series. (*Prewhitening* refers to removing the observed time pattern in the input sequence and applying that same transformation to the response function. The net effect is that the transfer function is easier to construct as a function of the input data.) In this case, the sleep schedule showed very little autocorrelation, so the prewhitening had very little effect, and the autocorrelation structure was similar to that just displayed. The coefficients for the transfer function are then estimated on the basis of the cross-correlations and the variances of the series. The result is a transfer function that predicts the value of the output series (weight status) as a function of the previous observed values in the input series (sleep).

Figure 1.1 contains three plots illustrating the success in predicting daily weight from recent sleep history. In each plot, the solid line represents the daily weight measurement, where the mean for the series has been subtracted. The top plot is just the raw time series for sleep (dotted line) and weight (solid line). The correlation here is −.24. The second plot shows the predicted weights from the transfer function based on the cross-correlations between the series (and their lags). The dotted line represents the predicted weight, and it clearly begins to track the weight function more closely, with a positive correlation of .35. Finally, the bottom plot adds in an impulse function for whether the person ran 7 to 10 miles the previous day. Note now the improved correlation between the predicted to the observed time series (here, $r = .51$).

The degree of correspondence between the predicted and actual weight sequences is impressive considering the relatively crude and incomplete nature of the data. The data are considered crude because they rely simply on the self-report of sleep duration, a protocol that might not be considered acceptable in large-scale experiments. The advantage of the person-specific approach, however, is that most of the bias or measurement error cancels out on a within-person basis, and it is possible for signal to emerge from the noise (see de Castro, 2006, for a similar argument with regard to short sequences of diary studies in nutrition research). The data are considered incomplete because they contain only a specific measure of exercise and because they do not include any information on diet or energy intake. It is hardly risky to predict that the modeling of weight time series will improve with the inclusion of more information.

In summary, extended longitudinal data of daily self-reports appear to be a promising way to demonstrate associations between sleep and weight status. These series can reveal overall patterns that are consistent with the research literature from between-person research designs (i.e., a global tendency for sleep and weight status to exhibit negative correlations). However, these series can also reveal more specific information on the process and dynamics, and they can reveal the level of heterogeneity from person to person in the dynamics.

One can see a parallel between this pilot work and a study in the public health literature conducted by Monnet et al. (2001) that examined the connection between antimicrobial use and bacterial resistance in hospitals. Typical studies are conducted by aggregating data across a sample of hospitals and looking for concurrent relationships. Monnet et al. pointed out that such designs are not good for estimating lagged relationships between antimicrobial use and the emergence of resistant bacteria (because the correlation can take a year to develop, and the lags may be heterogeneous across the population). Furthermore, multiple confounding factors associated with the prevalence of resistant bacteria need to be controlled for in large-scale, between-hospital studies, and the plausibility of the regression assumptions necessary to construct such models may account for inconsistent results in estimating the correlation of interest. Monnet et al. argued that gathering time series data on single hospitals affords another opportunity to study the connection between use and resistance. Using monthly hospital data, they estimated transfer functions to model resistance as a function of use, and they showed decent forecasting of the future rise of resistant bacteria. What they did not mention was the possibility then of optimizing the use of antimicrobials to prevent problems associated with an unchecked rise in resistant bacteria. Such control models might represent an ultimate goal for the study of the dynamics of weight change at the individual level.

It is important not to oversell matters at this stage. All I have shown thus far is that a single sequence of daily weight change can be predicted with daily information on sleep and exercise. The model is quite simplistic in assuming a single direction of "cause" and in incorporating only a small amount of relevant information. Obviously, the measure of exercise is crude (only gym exercise that occurred once or twice per week was recorded), and to this point no information on diet has been included. Furthermore, analyses of the two female time series indicates that menstrual cycle contributes significantly to the daily weight variance. This means that a whole set of periodic confounds (workweek, holidays, seasons, menstrual cycles) would need to be considered to make the models generalize across longer chains of observations and across more people. Replicating this kind of study across a larger sample is necessary not because it is assumed that people will share the same patterns but to validate the presumption that some regular pattern of systematic covariation among behavior and health indicators can be modeled. To the degree that these systematic patterns manifest themselves regularly, and show a correspondence to theoretical models of energy balance, or prove amenable to optimization, the person-specific approach to studying energy balance will be validated.

A further limitation is that there is a need to establish the theoretical significance of daily weight change. What is the underlying cause of changes, over 24 hr, in body weight? What, exactly, is being measured? The motivation for taking daily measures was mostly that it is a convenient time scale for which to ask people to gather data. It is also obviously a natural scale for measuring sleep (and, to some degree, diet), and is probably the most natural scale for intervention (e.g., it seems like it would be easier for individuals to set daily behavior goals rather than weekly goals). However, body weight can change only so much over 24 hr, and the change may well be dominated by variations in hydration. As with any time series analysis, the proper time scale of measurement is an important consideration.

Discussion

Converging ideas and methodological advances from a variety of areas are pointing to a new paradigm in social science. From one direction, Roberts (2004) stressed the importance of self-experimentation as a source for generating new hypotheses. Self-experimentation, he argued, is flexible and efficient, and it has greater potential for the discovery of unanticipated associations between behaviors and outcomes. From another direction, Molenaar (2004) challenged many of the accepted research paradigms in social science, arguing that statistical models from engineering and the physical sciences might be more appropriate. Both perspectives emphasize the intensive study of individual-level variation. Molenaar's advocacy for time series and systems analysis adds a more rigorous methodological approach to the perspective; Roberts's designs were typically focused on simple associations discovered with sequential A-B-A–type designs. The ergodicity arguments indicate that single-subject analyses are not just an underused luxury for social science but instead may be an indispensable tool for examining the dynamics of change.

Although the convergence of ideas as presented here is new, the main message has been delivered before. Researchers of learning have long grappled with the problem of reconciling developmental curves based on individual-level performance with developmental curves estimated from group means (Estes, 1956). Robinson (1950) described the *ecological fallacy* by showing that the state-to-state association between proportion of immigrants and literacy rates was opposite to the individual- (person-) level associations between immigration status and literacy. In some areas of social and economic science there does exist an established tradition of research at both the between- and within-person levels. One example is finance, in which stocks exhibit behaviors related to market-wide forces and exhibit unique features. The specific time series of an individual stock can be modeled with attention to price levels of resistance and support, seasonality specific to that stock, and fundamental business conditions particular to the company. A technical analyst might use certain general tools and concepts across stocks (moving averages, resistance levels), but the analysis has to proceed in a stock-specific manner because pooling data would distort the findings unless all the stocks in the sample were undergoing identical processes and were in perfect phase.

The main thesis of this chapter is that health and weight researchers should not be too quick to aggregate their data when their hypotheses concern intraindividual variation. This caution seems simple enough, but nonetheless it is repeatedly violated in published literature. I mentioned the work of Racette et al. (2008) earlier in this chapter because individual data were aggregated across a sample in an attempt to determine systematic weekly variation in consumption and energy expenditure. Recently, Bray, Flatt, Volaufova, Delany, and Champagne (2008) studied lags across multiple days in a corrective response to overconsumption. They were specifically looking for multiday lags between overconsumption and later compensating undereating at the individual level. With data from 20 participants, who each completed two 7-day food intake records, they tested autocorrelations at lags of 1 through 5 days. They centered the data for each participant and then created pairs of scores for days separated by the desired lag. (For example, for their test of the 3-day lag they said they had 160 pairs of scores. Each participant contributed four pairs of lagged scores per week, and aggregating over 20 participants yields 160 data pairs.)

The problem with the analysis is that these data do not form a chain of 160 data points with which to estimate an autocorrelation function. To estimate correlations with up to 5-day lags from 7-day sequences of observation requires at least two major assumptions. The first is that 7-day sequences can yield reliable autocorrelations unimpaired by edge effects (or weekend effects—after all, consider Racette et al.'s findings about weekend and weekday mean differences). The second assumption is that the 20 participants are exchangeable members of a population with identical lag patterns and who are all in phase with one another. Neither assumption seems particularly likely to hold.

A better analysis of lagged self-corrective patterns in consumption behavior would require individual-level time series of the sort described in this chapter. Gathering such data is at once easy and demanding. Recording weight and an estimate of hours slept takes approximately 30 s per day. Adding in a daily diary of food consumed takes much more time. Recent trends in research methods and technology, however, suggest that things will become much easier in the future. Researchers are finding that one of the most common habits of people who succeed in losing weight and then maintain the weight loss is daily weighing.

Self-knowledge is increasingly recognized as playing a role in motivation and self-regulation, although by no means is this automatically sufficient to bring about behavior change.

However, technological advances are also going to make data gathering even less effortful. Scales and pedometers will easily record readings for multiple days, and these can be uploaded to computers. New Web-based programs already make it increasingly easy to track dietary intake. It is clear that in the near future streams of continuous data on individuals will be easy to gather. This is already the case for monitoring specific body processes such as glucose level, heart rate, body temperature, motor activity, brain activation, and many other physiological variables. However, behavioral variables, such as sleep, physical activity, and dietary intake, can also be easily measured and recorded. I hope that such data will be used creatively to reveal dynamic associations between behavior and health and ultimately suggest strategies for optimal control.

There is an exciting convergence occurring in the social sciences with increasing interest in single-subject designs and self-experimentation, awareness of the necessity for single-subject data to support the logic of scientific inference regarding the dynamics of change, and the availability of methods for the collection of continuous individual-level data. Soon there will be a more widely shared understanding that nutritionists and behavioral scientists can look to engineering for the statistical models necessary to analyze person-specific data.

References

Box, G. P., & Jenkins, G. M. (1976). *Time series, forecasting and control.* New York, NY: Holden-Day.

Bray, G. A., Flatt, J. P., Volaufova, J., Delany, J. P., & Champagne, C. M. (2008). Corrective responses in human food intake identified from an analysis of 7-d food-intake records. *Journal of Clinical Nutrition, 88,* 1504–1510. doi:10.3945/ajcn.2008.26289

Colditz, G. A., Manson, J. E., S. E. (1997). The Nurses' Health Study: 20-year contribution to the understanding of health among women. *Journal of Women's Health, 6,* 49–62.

de Castro, J. M. (2006). Varying levels of food energy self-reporting are associated with between-group, but not within-subject, differences in food intake. *Journal of Nutrition, 136,* 1382–1388.

Estes, W. K. (1956). The problem of inference from curves based on group data. *Psychological Bulletin, 53,* 134–140. doi:10.1037/h0045156

Hamaker, E. L., Dolan, C. V., & Molenaar, P. C. M. (2005). Statistical modeling of the individual: Rationale and application of multivariate stationary time series analysis. *Multivariate Behavioral Research, 40,* 207–233. doi:10.1207/s15327906mbr4002_3

Molenaar, P. C. M. (2004). A manifesto on psychology as idiographic science: Bringing the person back into scientific psychology, this time forever. *Measurement: Interdisciplinary Research & Perspective, 2,* 201–218.

Monnet, D. L., López-Lozano, J.-M., Campillos, P., Burgos, A., Yagüe, A., & Gonzalo, N. (2001). Making sense of antimicrobial use and resistance surveillance data: Application of ARIMA and transfer function models. *Clinical Microbiology & Infection, 7,* 29–36. doi:10.1046/j.1469-0691.2001.00071.x

National Institutes of Health. (n.d.). *Bioengineering approaches to energy balance and obesity (R21)* (Funding Opportunity Announcement). Retrieved November 17, 2009, from http://grants.nih.gov/grants/guide/rfa-files/RFA-HL-07-007.html

Patel, S. R., Malhotra, A., White, D. P., Gottlieb, D. J., Hu, & F. B. (2006). Association between reduced sleep and weight gain in women. *American Journal of Epidemiology, 164,* 947–954. doi:10.1093/aje/kwj280

Racette, S. B., Weiss, E. P., Schechtman, K. B., Steger-May, K., Villareal, D. T., Obert, K. A., . . . Washington University School of Medicine CALERIE Team. (2008). Influence of weekend lifestyle patterns on body weight. *Obesity, 16,* 1826–1830. doi:10.1038/oby.2008.320

Roberts, S. (2004). Self-experimentation as a source of new ideas: Ten examples about sleep, mood, health, and weight. *Behavioral and Brain Sciences, 27,* 227–262. doi:10.1017/S0140525X04000068

Robinson, W. S. (1950). Ecological correlations and the behavior of individuals. *American Sociological Review, 15,* 351–357. doi:10.2307/2087176

Tarasuk, V., & Beaton, G. H. (1991). The nature and individuality of within-subject variation in energy intake. *American Journal of Clinical Nutrition, 54,* 464–470.

Tarko, V. (2008). *What is ergodicity?* Retrieved from http://news.softpedia.com/news/What-is-ergodicity-15686.shtml

2

Neuromodulation of Fluctuations of Information Processing: Computational, Neural, and Genetic Perspectives

Shu-Chen Li

Since the dawn of the cognitive revolution in the 1940s, principles of information processing at the brain, cognitive, and computational levels and their interactions are considered to be central to understanding behavior (see Gardner, 1985, for a historical review). This notion is, in general, shared by researchers of cognition working in a variety of related fields, ranging from neuroscience, psychology, artificial intelligence, linguistics, anthropology, and philosophy. In line with this general notion a few theoretical developments emerged and then foreshadowed the themes addressed in this chapter. The field of *cybernetics* focuses on understanding the control of and communication mechanisms in the operations of mechanical machines, electronic computers, or the nervous system and suggests that processes of self-regulatory systems are inherently dynamic and variable (Wiener, 1948/1961). The development of *information theory* at approximately the same time treats variability as an intricate part of the information transmission process in digital or other types of communication systems (Shannon, 1949). Also put forth was the insight that simple binary digital computational principles may bear a minimal resemblance to communications between the on-and-off firing of neurons (von Neumann, 1958).

Together with the Zeitgeist in psychology at that time, these strands of theoretical endeavors have pushed forward the cognitive revolution and provided new perspectives for considering cognition as the processing and computation of information by natural or artificial systems. Traces of these approaches' influence on cognitive psychology throughout the 5 decades following the cognitive revolution are easily identifiable in prominent concepts such as capacity limit (Miller, 1956; Posner, 1966), working memory (Baddeley, 1986), information filtering (Broadbent, 1958), and controlled and automated information processing (Schneider & Shiffrin, 1977; Shiffrin & Schneider, 1977). However, unlike the concepts of capacity, memory storage, or cognitive control, the phenomenon of information processing being inherently dynamic and variable, with transient fluctuations, has not been one of the main themes of cognitive research until recently. To this end, in this chapter I review recent theoretical and empirical research on understanding the roles of variability in information processing,

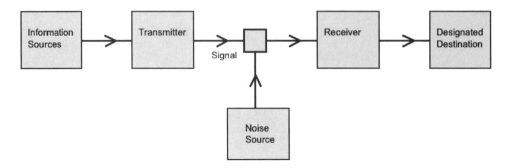

Figure 2.1. A schematic diagram based on Shannon's (1949) general communication system.

particularly in relation to neuromodulatory processes affecting random processing variability.

Information Processing in the Presence of Noise

In 1949, Claude E. Shannon published an article titled "Communication in the Presence of Noise," in which he proposed that a general communication system consists in essence of five components and that together their operations transmit information from its sources to a designated destination (see Figure 2.1). During the transmission process, or at the end of the receiving terminal, the signal may be perturbed by noise, which affects the capacity of the transmission channel (Shannon, 1949).

Specifically, if the noise has the properties of white Gaussian noise[1] with power N in the band W, then the capacity (C) of a channel with an average transmission power, denoted as P, can be defined as follows:

$$C = W \log_2 \frac{P+N}{N}.$$

From this equation it is obvious that the ratio between the power of the to-be-transmitted information (signal power) and the power of the noise (noise power) is an important factor that affects the capacity of information processing. Thus, to understand information processing in humans or machines, knowledge about how noise affects processing capacity and by which noise is regulated is indispensable. In Shannon's (1949) original diagram of a general communication system (see Figure 2.1), only external noise (i.e., noise source external to the transmission channel) is highlighted. However, other sources of noise, such noise in the information itself, as well as noise intrinsic to the transmission process (i.e., unreliable transmitters or receivers), are other potential sources of noise.

---

[1] Formulas relating channel capacity to other types of noise were also derived in Shannon's (1949) article.

Noise in Neuronal Signal Transmission and Neuromodulation

The central nervous system is a communication system with an enormous complexity: The brain is estimated to have approximately 100 billion nerve cells, and on average each of these nerve cells communicates with 1,000 other neurons. Although whether these intercellular communications across the synapses of the neurons was electrical or chemical in nature underwent a long period of debate from the 1930s to the 1960s, the current consensus is that over 99% of the synapses in the brain use chemical transmissions involving neurotransmitters (Greengard, 2001). A prominent source of intrinsic variability of neural information processing is *synaptic noise*. Synaptic noise arises, in part, from fluctuations of postsynaptic activations reflecting stochastic neurotransmitter releases (e.g., that are due to irregular firings of afferent neurons). Recent empirical and theoretical findings show that synaptic background noise is of critical importance for neuronal gain control (see Destexhe, Rudolph, & Paré, 2003; Stein, Gossen, & Jones, 2005).

Various transmitter systems are important for signal transmissions in the brain, with clear implications for cognition and behavior (for reviews, see Harris-Warrick & Marder, 1991, and Marder & Thirumalai, 2002). The specificities of the different transmitter systems (e.g., acetylcholine, noradrenaline, serotonin, dopamine, glutamate) and their influences on cortical processes and cognitive functions differ as well. However, at an abstract level many of their computational effects can be captured as dynamic regulatory mechanisms of adaptive systems, including regulating the signal-to-noise ratio of neural information processing (see Doya, Dayan, & Hasselmo, 2002, for reviews of recent computational works).

Although the mechanisms of noise or fluctuations of information processing per se have not been the main research focus of cognitive psychology, over the past decade research at neurophysiological (e.g., Huk & Shadlen, 2005; Philiastides, Ratcliff, & Sajda, 2006), neuroimaging (e.g., Heekeren, Marrett, & Ungerleider, 2008), and behavioral (e.g., Ratcliff, Gomez, & McKoon, 2004) levels has converged on the view that perception and cognition are gradual processes of evidence accumulation amidst noisy sensory information and signal processing (for reviews, see Bogacz, 2007; Gold & Shadlen, 2007; and Smith & Ratcliff, 2004). A variety of formal sequential sampling models have been devised to account for the dynamics of evidence accumulation underlying memory and decision behavior at various levels (e.g., Bogacz, 2007; Ratcliff et al., 2004; Usher & McClelland, 2001). Although evidence accumulation models of perceptual decisions usually assume noisy signal processing, with only a few exceptions (e.g., Lo & Wang, 2006; Seung, 2003) noise is commonly treated as a primitive and modeled as a Gaussian random variable without further specifications of how neurobiological mechanisms may affect the properties of noise and its functional consequences. In the following sections I review evidence on aging-related declines in dopaminergic modulation and increased processing fluctuations in older adults. These findings and theoretical studies of dopamine's noise tuning roles together suggest that neuromodulation of the signal-to-noise ratio of information processing has consequences for how the quality of information is represented during transmission (representation distinctiveness) and has implications for processing fluctuation and capacity.

Increased Processing Noise and Suboptimal
Dopaminergic Modulation During Aging

The efficacy of various neurotransmitter systems (e.g., the catecholiminergic and cholinergic systems) wanes during normal aging (e.g., Disterhoft & Oh, 2006; Grachev, Swarnkar, Szeverenyi, Ramachandran, & Apkarian, 2001; see Bäckman, Nyberg, Lindenberger, Li, & Farde, 2006, for a review). Of particular interest here is the dopaminergic system. Different aspects of the dopaminergic system, such as postsynaptic D2 receptor (Kaasinen et al., 2000) or presynaptic transporter (Erixon-Lindroth et al., 2005) binding mechanisms, decline during normal aging. On the one hand, dopaminergic modulation declines during aging, and on the other hand, aging is also related with an increase in performance variability (see MacDonald, Nyberg, & Bäckman, 2006, for reviews). For instance, within-person performance fluctuations (e.g., from trial to trial or session to session in reaction time or memory tasks) increase with advancing age for a variety of cognitive functions (e.g., Li et al., 2004), indicating decreases in processing robustness in late life. Conversely, during child development performance fluctuations decrease as brain and cognitive functions mature (see Figure 2.2, top panel). It is critical to note that age-related differences in within-person fluctuations are not simply an artifact of mean-level differences, because these are routinely partialed out in the analysis of within-person variability. At a cognitive level, performance fluctuations are thought to reflect momentary lapses of attention, a failure to exert executive control (West, Murphy, Armilio, Craik, & Stuss, 2002). Furthermore, longitudinal data demonstrate that older adults who exhibit higher within-person fluctuations declined more in executive functioning over several years than their more stable counterparts (see Figure 2.2, bottom panel; Lövdén, Li, Shing, & Lindenberger, 2007).

In the early 1990s, dopamine's role in regulating the signal-to-noise ratio of neural information processing was first highlighted in a theory of cognitive deficits in persons with schizophrenia. In this context, dopamine's noise regulation effect was modeled by the gain parameter of the sigmoidal activation function of neural networks (Cohen & Servan-Schreiber, 1992; Servan-Schreiber, Printz, & Cohen, 1990). This theory was later extended to account for the effects of deficient dopaminergic modulation in the aging brain on a wide range of commonly observed cognitive aging deficits (Li & Lindenberger, 1999; Li, Lindenberger, & Sikström, 2001).

The neuromodulation of cognitive aging model captures aging-related decline in dopaminergic neuromodulation by stochastically attenuating the gain control (G) of the sigmoidal activation function that models presynaptic to postsynaptic input–response transfer (see Figure 2.3A). With large inputs, a direct consequence of reducing the slope of the activation function is increased within-network random activation variability (see Figure 2.3B). This, in turn, leads to increased performance variability in simulated aging networks with attenuated G (see Figure 2.3C). In contrast, if G is increased to excessive values, the activation function becomes a step function, and activation variability depends critically on the amplitudes of inputs. Activation variability is markedly reduced with large positive or negative inputs and increased with intermediate inputs. Neurons with

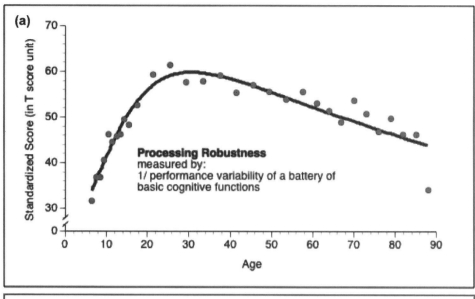

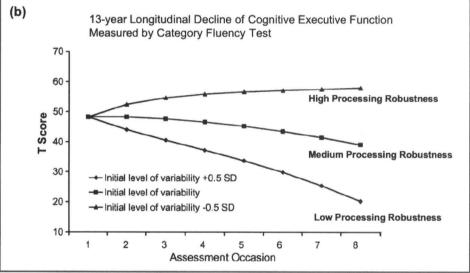

Figure 2.2. Top panel: Life span age differences in processing robustness as measured by the inverse of fluctuations in cognitive reaction times. Older adults and children show less robust processing. From "Transformations in the Couplings Among Intellectual Abilities and Constituent Cognitive Processes Across the Lifespan," by S.-C. Li, U. Lindenberger, B. Hommel, G. Aschersleben, W. Prinz, and P. B. Baltes, 2004, *Psychological Science, 15,* p. 158. Copyright 2004 by Blackwell. Adapted with permission. Bottom panel: Individual differences in processing robustness predict 13-year longitudinal decline in executive functioning measured by the category fluency test. From "Within-Person Trial-to-Trial Variability Precedes and Predicts Cognitive Decline in Old and Very Old Age: Longitudinal Data From the Berlin Aging Study," by M. Lövdén, S.-C. Li, Y. L. Shing, and U. Lindenberger, 2007, *Neuropsychologia, 45,* p. 2834. Copyright 2007 by Elsevier Science. Adapted with permission.

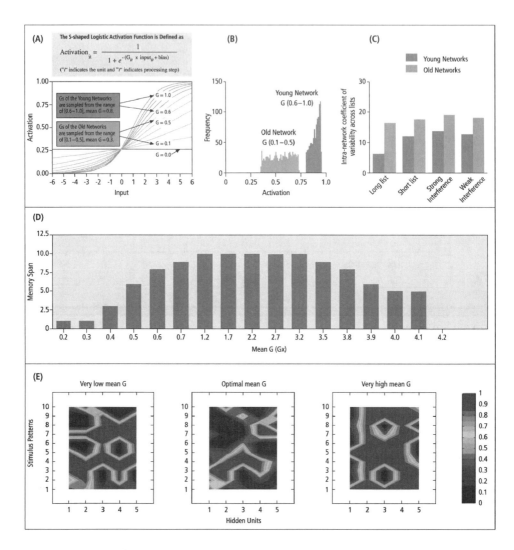

Figure 2.3. Modeling deficient neuromodulation in aging. (A) Simulating aging-related dopamine modulation by reducing stochastic gain tuning. Reduced gain tuning increases (B) random activation variability and (C) performance variability in simulated old networks. From "Aging Cognition: From Neuromodulation to Representation," by S.-C. Li, U. Lindenberger, and S. Sikström, 2001, *Trends in Cognitive Sciences, 5,* pp. 482, 485. Copyright 2001 by Elsevier. Adapted with permission. Stochastic gain tuning captures the inverted-*U* function relating dopamine modulation and functional outcomes of (D) memory performance and (E) distinctiveness of activation patterns. From "Integrative Neurocomputational Perspectives on Cognitive Aging, Neuromodulation, and Representation," by S.-C. Li and S. Sikström, 2002, *Neuroscience and Biobehavioral Review, 26,* p. 800. Copyright 2002 by Elsevier. Adapted with permission. G = gain control.

excessive gain modulation thus act as a high-pass filter, detecting only strong inputs while losing amplitude discriminability past a given threshold (Wolfart, Debay, Le Masson, Destexhe, & Bal, 2005). These properties of stochastic G tuning predict an inverted-U function (see Figures 2.3D and 2.3E) relating the levels of dopaminergic neuromodulation, neuronal representation distinctiveness, and cognitive outcomes such as working memory capacity that have been confirmed empirically (Arnsten, 1998; Goldman-Rakic, Muly, & Williams, 2000; Mattay et al., 2003). In summary, both deficient and excessive neuromodulation hamper neural information processing and result in less distinctive neuronal representations and compromised functional behavioral outcomes.

Neurobiological and Genetic Findings Supporting Dopamine's Noise Regulation Role

Like the computational studies, animal studies have shown that dopamine receptor reductions as observed during aging not only slow down the animal's performance but also increase performance variability (MacRae, Spirduso, & Wilcox, 1988; Schultz et al., 1989). In a first attempt to directly link dopamine to processing fluctuations, MacDonald Cervenka, Farde, Nyberg, and Bäckman (2009) measured extrastiatal D2 binding in the anterior cingulate, frontal cortex, and hippocampus in a group of middle-aged individuals. Processing fluctuation was assessed in terms of within-person variability in reaction time during episodic memory retrieval and concept formation. Systematic negative correlations between D2 binding and processing fluctuation across all three brain regions (rs ranged from −.30 to −.45) were found. Thus, these data indicate that, even within normal ranges, reduced availability of dopamine may result in more fluctuating behavior. On a related note, prefrontal broadband noise derived from electroencephalogram was also increased in patients with schizophrenia (Winterer & Weinberger, 2004), a pathological condition marked by dysfunctional dopaminergic neuromodulation.

Furthermore, recent evidence from genomic behavior and genomic imaging approaches also suggest a link between deficit dopaminergic modulation and processing noise. For instance, polymorphisms of the gene coding for catechol-O-methyltransferase (COMT), which catabolizes dopamine in the frontal cortex, are systematically related to performance variability. Relative to monozygotic carriers of the met allele of COMT, the degradation rate of dopamine in the synaptic cleft is about 3 to 4 times faster in monozygotic carriers of the val allele, who also show higher levels of performance variability during perceptual processing (Winterer & Weinberger, 2004). It has also been recently shown that val carriers' disadvantage in information processing speed is magnified in individuals with lower dopaminergic function, such as older adults (Lindenberger et al., 2008; Nagel et al., 2008). Individual differences in the COMT genotype recently were found to be predictive of blood-oxygen-level-dependent signal and noise characteristics in the prefrontal cortex in functional magnetic imaging studies (Winterer et al., 2006).

An Outstanding Question: Does Dopamine Affect Stochastic Resonance and Rate of Evidence Accumulation?

In addition to neuromodulation of intrinsic noise there are external noise sources, as outlined in Shannon's (1949) diagram of a general communication's system. In the context of information processing with subthreshold sensory stimuli, *stochastic resonance* (SR) denotes the phenomenon that optimal levels of noise are beneficial for detecting and transmitting weak signals in nonlinear physical and biological systems (e.g., Collins, Chow, & Imhoff, 1995; Simonotto et al., 1997; for a review, see Moss, Ward, & Sammoza, 2004). A basic aspect of SR (*threshold SR*) results from the interaction among a response (or activation) threshold, a subthreshold stimulus, and input noise. Consider the example of a hardly recognizable image of Big Ben with most of its pixels degraded below a certain threshold of gray scale (see Figure 2.4, left panel). In this case, with an optimal amount of random noise added to the gray scale the subthreshold image gradually emerges above the threshold and becomes visible (see Figure 2.4, middle panel). However, if more noise is added the image blurs again (see Figure 2.4, right panel).

More recently, the effect of suboptimal dopaminergic modulation altering the interactions between extrinsic neuronal noise and perceptual noise has been demonstrated computationally. Specifically, Li, von Oertzen, and Lindenberger (2006) used the stochastic gain-tuning model of neuromodulatory aging to simulate experimental effects observed in paradigms of subthreshold perceptual processing. Less efficient neuromodulation in aging neurobiological systems as modeled by reducing G from optimal to suboptimal levels yielded activation functions with less steeper slopes described earlier. Neural networks with attenuated system gain modulation reacted to input noise less effectively, resulting in SR functions with lower and right-shifted peaks (see Figure 2.5). These findings suggest that noise added to weak signals continues to yield beneficial effects in suboptimally modulated systems. However, the benefits of SR are affected in three major ways: (a) The absolute peak of SR is reduced, (b) the range in which

Figure 2.4. Optimal levels of noise in gray scale help in detecting a subthreshold image of Big Ben. From "Visual Perception of Stochastic Resonance," by E. Simonotto, M. Riani, C. Seife, M. Roberts, J. Twitty, and F. Moss, 1997, *Physical Review Letters, 78,* p. 1186. Copyright 1997 by the American Physical Society. Adapted with permission.

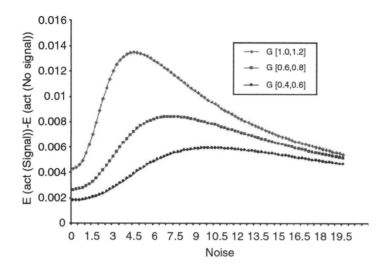

Figure 2.5. Different levels of stochastic gain modulation, simulating aging-related differences in neuromodulatory gain control (G), result in stochastic resonance functions that differ in peak stochastic resonance magnitude and the extent of right shift of the peak. From "A Neurocomputational Model of Stochastic Resonance and Aging," by S.-C. Li, T. von Oertzen, and U. Lindenberger, 2006, *Neurocomputing, 69,* p. 1555. Copyright 2006 by Elsevier. Adapted with permission.

noise operates optimally is reduced, and (c) more external noise is required to reach the peak of the SR function (Li et al., 2006).

SR has recently attracted much attention in research on aging because of its promising utility in attenuating the functional consequences of older adults' deficits in sensory and sensorimotor functions. For instance, keeping balance while standing is an important basic sensorimotor function that declines substantially during aging (Huxhold, Li, Schmiedek, & Lindenberger, 2006) and often is associated with serious negative consequences, such as falls. It has recently been shown that subthreshold electromechanical noise delivered through shoe insoles (Harry, Niemi, Priplata, & Collins, 2005) reduces older adults' body sway while standing. To counter the adverse consequences of declining neurosensory and neurocognitive functions through the benefits of noise, researchers need formal theories that capture interactions among different sources of noise to provide mechanistic explanations and make predictions. For instance, the intriguing prediction that aging systems require more input noise to benefit from SR was recently empirically verified (Wells, Ward, Chua, & Inglis, 2005).

Finally, relating back to early theoretical concepts underlying the field of cybernetics developed in the 1940s (Wiener, 1948/1961), the *Wiener process,* also known as *Brownian motion* (which was mathematically proved by Wiener in 1923), characterizes the continuous stochastic process that is implemented in a range of sequential sampling models of perceptual and simple cognitive decisions, such as the diffusion model (see Smith & Ratcliff, 2004, for a review). Thus far, the rate of evidence accumulation captured by the diffusion model's drift rate has been taken to reflect the quality of perceptual information integration (Gold & Shadlen, 2007; Heekeren et al., 2008; Smith & Ratcliff, 2004). This has been demonstrated in studies that manipulated task parameters to affect the quality of sensory information, such as extrinsic noise levels in static or moving (Heekeren, Marrett, Bandettini, & Underleider, 2004; Philiastides et al., 2006; Ratcliff, Hasegawa, Hasegawa, Smith, & Segraves, 2007) visual stimuli and exposure duration (Britten, Shadlen, Newsome, & Movshon, 1992). A stimulus with high sensory quality (e.g., clearer visual images or stronger motion signals) results in faster evidence accumulation. Holding extrinsic noise in the stimuli constant, in light of the empirical evidence relating dopaminergic modulation and processing noise and computational findings showing that suboptimal stochastic gain regulation would result in higher random processing fluctuation and less distinctive representations, one can make a conjecture relating dopaminergic modulation and the rate of evidence accumulation. As illustrated in Figure 2.6, aging or individual differences in genotypes affect dopaminergic modulation, which in turn would affect the signal-to-noise ratio of neural information processing with subsequent impacts

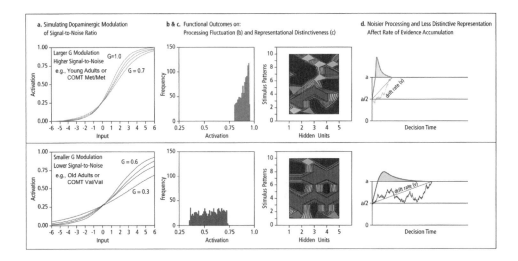

Figure 2.6. Schematic diagram relating the functional effects of dopaminergic modulation of neuronal noise to processing characteristics of evidence accumulation. (a) The role of dopamine (DA) in affecting neuronal signal-to-noise ratio is modeled by the gain parameter (G) of the sigmoidal activation function (Li et al., 2001; Servan-Schreiber et al., 1990). The neuronal input–response mapping functions of individuals with optimal dopaingeric modulation because of advantageous DA genotype (or being young) is captured by steeper activation functions with higher G and signal-to-noise ratio. (b) G modulation of signal-to-noise ratio results in less random activation variability in networks simulating optimal DA modulation and greater variability in networks simulating suboptimal DA modulation. (c) The internal stimulus representations are more distinctive (with fewer units overlapping in representing different stimuli) in networks with optimal DA modulation than in networks with suboptimal DA modulation. (d) Evidence accumulation theories of perceptual decision postulate that a higher drift rate of the evidence accumulation process reflects higher stimulus representation quality. COMT = catechol-O-methyltransferase.

on the quality of perceptual representations and the rate of information accumulations. This conjecture, however, awaits future empirical testing.

Conclusion

Classical theories of information processing in natural and artificial systems posit that variability is an intrinsic aspect of information processing. The brain, being an adaptive system, involves complex communications between 10^{11} neurons and external environmental inputs. The current consensus in the field indicates that these communications are predominately neurochemical in nature and are regulated by neurotransmitters. Converging evidence from neurocomputational studies and studies of older individuals and persons with schizophrenia suggest that dopamine affects the signal-to-noise ratio of neural information transmission with consequences on processing fluctuations and capacity of the neurocognitive system. Recent progress in genomic research has opened new avenues for investigating individual differences in genetic predispositions of the neuromodulatory mechanisms affecting how the brain processes noisy time-varying signals, which underlie perception and cognition.

References

Arnsten, A. F. T. (1998). Catecholamine modulation of prefrontal cortical cognitive function. *Trends in Cognitive Sciences, 2,* 436–447.

Bäckman, L., Nyberg, L., Lindenberger, U., Li, S.-C., & Farde, L. (2006). The correlative triad among aging, dopamine, and cognition: Current status and future prospects. *Neuroscience and Biobehavioral Reviews, 30,* 791–807. doi:10.1016/j.neubiorev.2006.06.005

Baddeley, A. (1986). *Working memory.* New York, NY: Oxford University Press.

Bogacz, R. (2007). Optimal decision-making theories: Linking neurobiology with behaviour. *Trends in Cognitive Sciences, 11,* 118–125. doi:10.1016/j.tics.2006.12.006

Britten, K. H., Shadlen, M. N., Newsome, W. T., & Movshon, J. A. (1992). The analyses of visual motion: A comparison of neuronal and psychophysical performance. *Journal of Neuroscience, 12,* 4745–4765.

Broadbent, D. E. (1958). *Attention and communication.* London, England: Pergamon Press.

Cohen, J. D., & Servan-Schreiber, D. (1992). Context, cortex, and dopamine: A connectionist approach to behavior and biology in schizophrenia. *Psychological Review, 99,* 45–77. doi:10.1037/0033-295X.99.1.45

Collins, J.-J., Chow, C. C., & Imhoff, T. T. (1995, July 20). Stochastic resonance without tuning. *Nature, 376,* 236–238. doi:10.1038/376236a0

Destexhe, A., Rudolph, M., & Paré, D. (2003). The high-conductance state of neocortical neurons *in vivo. National Review, 4,* 739–751. doi:10.1038/nrn1198

Disterhoft, J. F., & Oh, M. M. (2006). Learning, aging, and intrinsic neuronal plasticity. *Trends in Neurosciences, 29,* 587–599. doi:10.1016/j.tins.2006.08.005

Doya, K., Dayan, P., & Hasselmo, M. E. (Eds.). (2002). Computational models of neuromodulation [Special issue]. *Neural Networks, 4*(6).

Erixon-Lindroth, N., Farde, L., Robins Wahlin, T. B., Sovago, J., Halldin, C., & Bäckman, L. (2005). The role of the striatal dopamine transporter in cognitive aging. *Psychiatry Research: Neuroimaging, 138,* 1–12. doi:10.1016/j.pscychresns.2004.09.005

Gardner, H. (1985). *The mind's new science: A history of the cognitive revolution.* New York, NY: Basic Books.

Gold, J. I., & Shadlen, M. N. (2007). The neural basis of decision making. *Annual Review of Neuroscience, 30,* 535–574. doi:10.1146/annurev.neuro.29.051605.113038

Goldman-Rakic, P. S., Muly, E. C., & Williams, G. V. (2000). D1 receptors in prefrontal cells and circuits. *Brain Research Reviews, 31,* 295–301. doi:10.1016/S0165-0173(99)00045-4

Grachev, I. D., Swarnkar, A., Szeverenyi, N. M., Ramachandran, T. S., & Apkarian, A. V. (2001). Aging alters the multichemical networking profile of the human brain: An *in vivo* H-1-MRS study of young versus middle-aged subjects. *Journal of Neurochemistry, 77,* 292–303.

Greengard, P. (2001). The neurobiology of dopamine signaling. *Bioscience Reports, 21,* 247–269.

Harris-Warrick, R. M., & Marder, E. (1991). Modulation of neural networks for behavior. *Annual Review of Neuroscience, 14,* 39–57. doi:10.1146/annurev.ne.14.030191.000351

Harry, J., Niemi, J. B., Priplata, A. A., & Collins, J. J. (2005). Balancing act: Noise is the key to restoring the body's sense of equilibrium. *IEEE Spectrum Online.* doi:10.1109/MSPEC.2005.1413729

Heekeren, H. R., Marrett, S., Bandettini, P. A., & Ungerleider, L. G. (2004, October 4). A general mechanism for perceptual decision-making in the human brain. *Nature, 431,* 859–862. doi:10.1038/nature02966

Heekeren, H. R., Marrett, S., & Ungerleider, L. G. (2008). The neural systems that mediate human perceptual decision making. *Nature Reviews Neuroscience, 9,* 467–479. doi:10.1038/nrn2374

Huk, A. C., & Shadlen, M. N. (2005). Neural activity in macaque parietal cortex reflects temporal integration of visual motion signals during perceptual decision making. *Journal of Neuroscience, 25,* 10420–10436. doi:10.1523/JNEUROSCI.4684-04.2005

Huxhold, O., Li, S.-C., Schmiedek, F., & Lindenberger, U. (2006). Dual-task postural control: Aging and the effects of cognitive demands in conjunction with focus of attention. *Brain Research Bulletin, 69,* 294–305. doi:10.1016/j.brainresbull.2006.01.002

Kaasinen, V., Vilkman, H., Hietala, J., Någren, K., Helenius, H., Olsson, H., . . . Rinne, J. (2000). Age-related D2/D3 receptor loss in extrastriatal regions of the human brain. *Neurobiology of Aging, 21,* 683–688. doi:10.1016/S0197-4580(00)00149-4

Li, S.-C., & Lindenberger, U. (1999). Cross-level unification: A computational exploration of the link between deterioration of neurotransmitter systems and dedifferentiation of cognitive abilities in old age. In L.-G. Nilsson & M. Markowitsch (Eds.), *Cognitive neuroscience of memory* (pp. 104–146). Toronto, Ontario, Canada: Hogrefe & Huber.

Li, S.-C., Lindenberger, U., Hommel, B., Aschersleben, G., Prinz, W., & Baltes, P. B. (2004). Transformations in the couplings among intellectual abilities and constituent cognitive processes across the lifespan. *Psychological Science, 15,* 155–163. doi:10.1111/j.0956-7976.2004.01503003.x

Li, S.-C., Lindenberger, U., & Sikström, S. (2001). Aging cognition: From neuromodulation to representation. *Trends in Cognitive Sciences, 5,* 479–486. doi:10.1016/S1364-6613(00)01769-1

Li, S.-C., Oertzen, T. von, & Lindenberger, U. (2006). A neurocomputational model of stochastic resonance and aging. *Neurocomputing, 69,* 1553–1560. doi:10.1016/j.neucom.2005.06.015

Li, S.-C., & Sikström, S. (2002). Integrative neurocomputational perspectives on cognitive aging, neuromodulation, and representation. *Neuroscience and Biobehavioral Review, 26,* 795–808.

Lindenberger, U., Nagel, I. E., Chicherio, C., Li, S.-C., Heekeren, H. R., & Bäckman, L. (2008). Age-related decline in brain resources modulates genetic effects on cognitive functioning. *Frontiers in Neuroscience, 2,* 234–244.

Lo, C.-C., & Wang, Y.-J. (2006). Cortico-basal ganglia circuit mechanism for a decision threshold in reaction time tasks. *Nature Neuroscience, 9,* 956–963. doi:10.1038/nn1722

Lövdén, M., Li, S.-C., Shing, Y. L., & Lindenberger, U. (2007). Within-person trial-to-trial variability precedes and predicts cognitive decline in old and very old age: Longitudinal data from the Berlin Aging Study. *Neuropsychologia, 45,* 2827–2838. doi:10.1016/j.neuropsychologia.2007.05.005

MacDonald, S. W. S., Cervenka, S., Farde, L., Nyberg, L., & Bäckman, L. (2009). Extrastriatal dopamine D2 receptor binding modulates intraindividual variability in episodic memory and executive functioning. *Neuropsychologia, 47,* 2299–2304.

MacDonald, S. W. S., Nyberg, L., & Bäckman, L. (2006). Intraindividual variability in behavior: Links to brain structure, neurotransmission, and neuronal activity. *Trends in Neurosciences, 29,* 474–480. doi:10.1016/j.tins.2006.06.011

MacRae, P. G., Spirduso, W. W., & Wilcox, R. E. (1988). Reaction time and nigrostriatal dopamine function: The effects of age and practice. *Brain Research, 451,* 139–146. doi:10.1016/0006-8993(88)90758-5

Marder, E., & Thirumalai, V. (2002). Cellular, synaptic and network effects of neuromodulation. *Neural Networks, 15,* 479–493. doi:10.1016/S0893-6080(02)00043-6

Mattay, V. S., Goldberg, T. E., Fera, F., Hariri, A. R., Tessitore, A., Egan, M. F., . . . Weinberger, D. R. (2003). Catechol-O-methyltransferase val(258)-met genotype and individual variation in he brain response to amphetamine. *Proceedings of the National Academy of Sciences USA, 100,* 6186–6191. doi:10.1073/pnas.0931309100

Miller, G. A. (1956). The magical number seven, plus or minus two: Some limits on our capacity for processing information. *Psychological Review, 63,* 81–97. doi:10.1037/h0043158

Moss, F., Ward, L. M., & Sammoza, W. G. (2004). Stochastic resonance and sensory information processing: A tutorial and review of application. *Clinical Neurophysiology, 115,* 267–281. doi:10.1016/j.clinph.2003.09.014

Nagel, I. E., Chicherio, C., Li, S-C., von Oertzen, T., Sander, T., Villringer, A., . . . Lindenberger, L. (2008). Human aging magnifies genetic effects on executive functioning and working memory. *Frontiers in Human Neuroscience, 2,* 1–8.

Philiastides, M. G., Ratcliff, R., & Sajda, P. (2006) Neural representation of task difficulty and decision making during perceptual categorization: A timing diagram. *Journal of Neuroscience, 26,* 8965–8975.

Posner, M. I. (1966, June 24). Components of skilled performance. *Science, 152,* 1712–1718. doi:10.1126/science.152.3730.1712

Ratcliff, R., Gomez, P., & McKoon, G. (2004). A diffusion model account of the lexical decision task. *Psychological Review, 111,* 159–182. doi:10.1037/0033-295X.111.1.159

Ratcliff, R., Hasegawa, Y. T., Hasegawa, Y. P., Smith, P. L., & Segraves, M. A. (2007). Dual diffusion model for single-cell recording data from the superior colliculus in a brightness-discrimination task. *Journal of Neurophysiology, 97,* 1756–1774.

Schneider, W., & Shiffrin, R. M. (1977). Controlled and automatic human information processing: I. Detection, search, and attention. *Psychological Review, 84,* 1–66. doi:10.1037/0033-295X.84.1.1

Schultz, W., Studer, A., Romo, R., Sundstrom, E., Jonsson, G., & Scarnati, E. (1989). Deficits in reaction times and movement times as correlates of hypokinesia in monkeys with MPTP-induced striatal dopamine depletion. *Journal of Neurophysiology, 61,* 651–668.

Servan-Schreiber, D., Printz, H. W., & Cohen, J. D. (1990, August 24). A neural network model catecholamine effects: Gain, signal-to-noise ratio and behaviour. *Science, 249,* 892–895. doi:10.1126/science.2392679

Seung, H. S. (2003). Learning in spiking neural networks by reinforcement of stochastic synaptic transmission. *Neuron, 40,* 1063–1073. doi:10.1016/S0896-6273(03)00761-X

Shannon, C. E. (1949). Communication in the presence of noise. *Proceedings of the IRE, 37,* 10–21. doi:10.1109/JRPROC.1949.232969

Shiffrin, R. M., & Schneider, W. (1977). Controlled and automatic human information processing: II. Perceptual learning, automatic attending, and a general theory. *Psychological Review, 84,* 127–190. doi:10.1037/0033-295X.84.2.127

Simonotto, E., Riani, M., Seife, C., Roberts, M., Twitty, J., & Moss, F. (1997). Visual perception of stochastic resonance. *Physical Review Letters, 78,* 1186–1189. doi:10.1103/PhysRevLett.78.1186

Smith, P. L., & Ratcliff, R. (2004). Psychology and neurobiology of simple decision. *Trends in Neuroscience, 27,* 161–168.

Stein, R. B., Gossen, E. R., & Jones, K. E. (2005). Neuronal variability: Noise or part of the signal? *National Review, 6,* 389–397. doi:10.1038/nrn1668

Usher, M., & McClelland, J. L. (2001). On the time course of perceptual choice: A model based on principles of neural computation. *Psychological Review, 108,* 550–592. doi:10.1037/0033-295X.108.3.550

von Neumann, J. (1958). *The computer and the brain.* New Haven, CT: Yale University Press.

Wells, C., Ward, L. M., Chua, R., & Inglis, J. T. (2005). Touch noise increases vibrotactile sensitivity in old and young. *Psychological Science, 16,* 313–320. doi:10.1111/j.0956-7976.2005.01533.x

West, R., Murphy, K. J., Armilio, M. L., Craik, F. I. M., & Stuss, D. T. (2002). Lapses of intention and performance variability reveal age-related increases in fluctuations of executive control. *Brain and Cognition, 49,* 402–419. doi:10.1006/brcg.2001.1507

Wiener, N. (1961). Cybernetics, or control and communication in the animal and the machine (2nd ed.). Cambridge, MA: MIT Press. (Original work published 1948)

Winterer, G., & Weinberger, D. R. (2004). Genes, dopamine and cortical signal-to-noise ratio in schizophrenia. *Trends in Neurosciences, 27,* 683–690. doi:10.1016/j.tins.2004.08.002

Winterer, G., Musso, F., Vucurevic, G., Stoeter, P., Konrad, A., Seker, B., . . . Weinberger, D. L. (2006). COMT genotype predicts BOLD signal and noise characteristics in prefrontal circuits. *NeuroImage, 32,* 1722–1732. doi:10.1016/j.neuroimage.2006.05.058

Wolfart, J., Debay, D., Le Masson, G., Destexhe, A., & Bal, T. (2005). Synaptic background activity controls spike transfer from thalamus to cortex. *Nature Neuroscience, 8,* 1760–1767. doi:10.1038/nn1591

3

Modeling Retest and Aging Effects in a Measurement Burst Design

Martin Sliwinski, Lesa Hoffman, and Scott Hofer

Researchers who study human development are interested in how psychological, physiological, and behavioral phenomena change over time in aging individuals. In fact, Baltes and Nesselroade (1979) identified the primary objective of longitudinal developmental research as the "direct identification of intraindividual change" (p. 23). However, this goal is complicated by the possibility that observable change in any given individual may reflect the joint influences of multiple processes. For example, observable decreases in memory performance over time (i.e., with increasing age) may reflect the complementary effects of declining vascular health and the progression of Alzheimer's dementia (Sliwinski, Hofer, Hall, Buschke, & Lipton, 2003; Sliwinski, Lipton, Buschke, & Stewart, 1996). In contrast, observable change in cognitive performance may reflect a mixture of competing influences, such as aging-related declines that are partially or completely offset by performance gains attributable to repeated testing (i.e., retest or practice effects).

The purpose of this chapter is to examine a novel approach to decompose age (decline) and retest (gains) effects in longitudinal data. Specifically, we argue that conventional longitudinal designs consisting of repeated and widely spaced single measurements are significantly limited in their ability to disentangle multiple time-dependent processes, such as practice gains and age-related declines in cognition. We present an alternative approach that relies on the longitudinal measurement burst design (Nesselroade, 1991) and a nonlinear measurement model that represents cognitive performance as a function of previous experience and latent potential (i.e., asymptotic performance).

Retest Effects in Aging Research

The term *retest* (or *practice*) *effects* refers to performance gains that result from repeated exposure to testing procedures or materials. There is considerable evidence to indicate that repeated administration of the same or similar cognitive

---

This research was supported in part by Grants AG12448, AG026453, and AG026728 from the National Institute on Aging.

tests results in improved performance (e.g., Horn, 1972), and several studies have demonstrated significant retest gains after testing intervals of 5 to 10 years (e.g., Salthouse, Schroeder, & Ferrer, 2004; Schaie, 1996; Thorndike, Bregman, Tilton, & Woodyard, 1928). Because many longitudinal studies have retest intervals well less than 10 years, the potential durability of retest-related practice gains complicates the statistical analysis of developmental and maturational influences on cognitive performance. Failure to consider the influence of retest effects can lead to the inaccurate characterization of the rate and pattern of cognitive change (Salthouse et al., 2004) as well as confound attempts to study predictors of and correlations among estimates of change (Ferrer, Salthouse, McArdle, Stewart, & Schwartz, 2005; Wilson, Bienias, & Bennett, 2006). These rather serious consequences have prompted researchers to examine and try to correct for possible retest effects in longitudinal data.

Traditional longitudinal designs consist of widely spaced measurement occasions, often separated by long intervals (typically between 1 and 7 years). This type of design confounds the influence of repeated testing (i.e., practice) and aging on performance because the difference between any two scores from adjacent occasions reflects both the passage of time (and, presumably, aging) and increased exposure to testing (i.e., Occasion 1, Occasion 2, Occasion 3, etc.). If performance were to improve as a function of retest (because of practice) but decrease as a function of time (because of aging), then the observed performance would reflect the combined influence of these two competing latent processes. One approach to disentangle retest from aging has been to compare a control group (e.g., Schaie, 1965; Thorvaldsson, Hofer, Berg, & Johansson, 2006) that was tested only one time but at the same age as a comparison group that was tested multiple times as part of a longitudinal study. This experimental approach works well for quantifying the average retest effects in the population, but it cannot distinguish between retest and age effects in any given individual, which complicates both intraindividual and interindividual analyses of change.

An alternative approach (McArdle & Anderson, 1990; McArdle & Woodcock, 1997) involves statistically partialing the effects of age and retest occasion. This statistical approach has been used in numerous studies and is an increasingly popular analytic model for separating age and retest effects in longitudinal data (e.g., Ferrer, Salthouse, Stewart, & Schwartz, 2004; Ferrer et al., 2005; Ghisletta, McArdle, & Lindenberger, 2006; McArdle, Ferrer-Caja, Hamagami, & Woodcock, 2002; Rabbitt, Diggle, Smith, Holland, & McInnes, 2001; Salthouse et al., 2004; Wilson et al., 2006). The idea behind this approach is to include separate terms that capture both maturational influences (i.e., aging) and practice effects (i.e., retest occasion) in the analytic model of intraindividual change:

$$Y_{ti} = b_{0i} + b_{1i}(\text{age}_{ti}) = b_{2i}(\text{occasion}_{ti}) + r_{ti}, \quad (3.1)$$

where Y_{ti} is the cognitive performance for person i at time t, b_{0i} is the intercept for person i, b_{1i} is the linear age (or time in study) slope, and b_{2i} is the linear retest (practice) effect for person i. The estimate b_{1i} is the age effect partialed or statistically controlled for the effect of occasion (retest). We refer to this model as the *age + occasion retest model*. This approach will accurately recover population parameters for retest and age effects if its assumptions are reasonably met.

One set of assumptions is general to the underlying statistical model used for estimating the parameters of interest in longitudinal settings (e.g., the mixed model). The other set of assumptions pertains to the underlying conceptual model that allows interpretation of the estimated parameters as reflecting separable retest (practice) and age effects. It is this second set of assumptions that we examine in this chapter.

Retest effects in longitudinal studies could reflect several types of influences. Performance gains across repeated testing might reflect habituation to a type of "white coat" phenomenon resulting in a relief of general testing anxiety. Individuals might also become better at test taking, which would produce a generalized improvement across all cognitive tests, or they might become more proficient only at taking the specific tests in the longitudinal assessment battery. Also, as is the case for many longitudinal studies, individuals might learn the specific content of tests that repeat the same items across repeated assessments. For simplicity, we assume that retest effects in longitudinal studies reflect some type of learning of general test-taking skill, specific testing procedures, or testing material.

The age + occasion retest model requires that there be some variability in the interval between testing occasions, or else the longitudinal effects for age (time) and retest would be completely collinear. By introducing variability in the duration of follow-up it becomes possible to estimate the longitudinal effect of retest, which depends solely on the occasion variable (without respect to the actual interval), and the longitudinal effect of age, which depends solely on the interval between testing occasions. Thus, the age + occasion approach assumes that practice effects are invariant across different retest intervals. This raises the question of whether it is plausible to assume equivalent performance gains between two testing occasions that were separated by either a few days or a few decades.

It seems likely that retest effects would to some extent depend on the interval between testing occasions. At least one study, which had retest intervals ranging from a few days to a few decades, suggested that the magnitude of retest effects does diminish as the interval between testing occasions increases (Salthouse et al., 2004). One reason for diminishing practice effects with increasing retest intervals is that they are offset by the influence of aging. Another reason might be that the benefits of practice dissipate over time, independent of the influence of aging. Also, as Salthouse et al. (2004) suggested, this loss of performance gains across time may be an important component of retest effects in longitudinal studies. However, if retest effects do diminish as a function of time, then the age effect in the age + occasion retest model becomes difficult to interpret. This effect (b_{1i} from Equation 3.1) could reflect aging (as is its usual interpretation), but it could also reflect a type of forgetting (i.e., the time-dependent loss of retest gains) or some combination of both aging and forgetting. In skill acquisition studies forgetting, as evidenced by loss of previously demonstrated performance gains, is observed over intervals as short as 1 day (e.g. Newell, Mayer-Kress, & Lui, 2006; Rickard, 2007), and the magnitude of this loss may depend on the interval between assessments (Anderson, Fincham, & Douglass, 1999). A further complication is that there might be individual differences in the amount and rate of time-dependent forgetting (MacDonald,

Stigsdotter-Neely, Derwinger, & Backman, 2006) that would complicate analysis of individual differences in estimates of age-related change obtained from the age + occasion retest model.

This discussion of the conceptual assumptions of the age + occasion retest model is not meant to imply that the results from any given application of this model are incorrect; instead, it is intended to highlight the complexity of disentangling multiple time-dependent processes that drive intraindividual cognitive change. The age + occasion retest model addresses this complexity by representing intraindividual change as a function of two competing processes: (a) aging, which is measured by the passage of time, and (b) retest, which is measured by the number of testing occasions. We now present an alternative approach that relies on the longitudinal measurement burst design (Nesselroade, 1991) and a formal measurement model that represents cognitive performance as a nonlinear function of both testing experience and latent potential (i.e., asymptotic performance).

Modeling Changes in Performance and Latent Potential

Performance differences across long as compared with short retest intervals may reflect both increased aging influences and diminished retest influences (e.g., due to forgetting). One approach to addressing this confound is to use a mix of very closely spaced retest intervals to model practice effects and longer intervals to model age-related changes. This type of longitudinal design is referred to as a *measurement burst* (Nesselroade, 1991; Sliwinski, 2008), and it consists of repeated bursts of closely spaced measurements. This measurement burst design is in contrast to conventional multiwave longitudinal designs, which consist of widely spaced single measurements. In the present study, a "burst" consisted of six measurement occasions that occurred within a 10-day period. A day or two separated occasions within each burst, and each burst was repeated every 6 months for 2 years, yielding up to 30 observations for each individual. We hypothesized that overt performance on a speeded cognitive task would improve across sessions within bursts, because of the benefit of practice, but that estimates of individuals' latent potential (i.e., their asymptotic or best level of performance) would reveal slowing across bursts, because of aging (i.e., senescence, involution).

To represent this hypothesis mathematically, we begin with a model that represents response time (RT) as a negative exponential function of practice occasions:

$$RT_{ti} = a_i + g_i \exp[-r_i (\text{occasion}_{ti})] + e_{ti}. \qquad (3.2)$$

The first part of this equation, a_i, refers to a person's *asymptotic* response time, which is his or her fastest RT (or latent potential) given unlimited practice. The second part, $g_i \exp[-r_i(\text{occasion}_{ti})]$, reflects that portion of the observed response time, RT_{ti}, that is attributable to his or her experience. The r_i parameter is the rate of learning or improvement across repeated measurement occasions, and the g_i, or *gain* parameter, refers to the difference between an individual's initial performance with no practice and his or her estimated asymptotic performance. Other functions (e.g., power, hyperbolic) could also have been used, but the negative exponential has provided consistently better fits to our data than alternative functions.

Figure 3.1A shows what such a learning function might look like for data collected from a measurement burst design. The points on the graph connected by a line are from the same burst and separated by 1 day, whereas adjacent points that are not connected by a line come from different measurement bursts and are separated by approximately 6 months. The function in Figure 3.1A depicts a situation in which learning is not disrupted by the interval between bursts because an individual picks up on the first session of a burst exactly where he or she should be given where he or she left off on the last session of the previous burst. There is also a common asymptote across bursts, signifying that an individual's latent potential remains constant across the study's duration.

Figure 3.1B shows a slightly more complicated but perhaps more realistic situation in which individuals exhibit some forgetting (i.e., slowing) from the last session of the previous burst to the first session of the current burst. The practice gains on bursts after the first session reflect a recovery of what was lost during the interburst interval as well as performance gains that reflect a continuation of learning that occurred during earlier bursts. One way to model this situation would be to fit separate learning functions to data from each burst (see Rickard 2007). This would imply that there is a single learning process that transpires across bursts but would allow the learning rate to vary from burst to burst. Another approach would assume that the learning function for all bursts after the first reflects two processes: (a) continuous learning and (b) a recovery or warm-up effect. The result would be a rate of improvement during follow-up bursts that is faster than could be predicted by a single exponential learning function. This can be represented mathematically by a double negative exponential function:

$$\text{RT}_{ti} = a_i + g_i \exp\left[-r_i\left(\text{occasion}_{ti}\right)\right] + \left(\text{Burst}_{kj} > 1\right)$$
$$\times g_i^* \exp\left[-ri_i^*\left(\text{occasion}_{tki}\right)\right] + e_{ti}. \quad (3.3)$$

This equation stipulates that RT is a function of a person's asymptote plus two different learning/retest processes. The first, conveyed by the term $g_i \exp[-r_i(\text{occasion}_{tki})]$, reflects how a person's RT decreases as a function of the total amount of practice he or she has received on that task. The second process, conveyed by the term$(\text{Burst}_{kj} > 1) \times g_i^* \exp[-r_i^*(\text{occasion}_{tki})]$, is a warm-up' process, which operates only during follow-up bursts (i.e., bursts > 1) and indicates that a person's RT starts off higher on the first session of a new burst and then decreases rapidly (i.e., a warm-up effect).

For a real life example of such dual-process learning consider a middle-aged adult who takes up cross-country skiing. During her first season, she displays considerable and rapid improvement in her skiing ability, perhaps indexed by the time taken to complete a local trail. Then spring arrives, the snow melts, and 9 months pass before she can resume skiing. When she resumes skiing the following winter, she is a bit rusty and not quite as fast as she was at the end of the

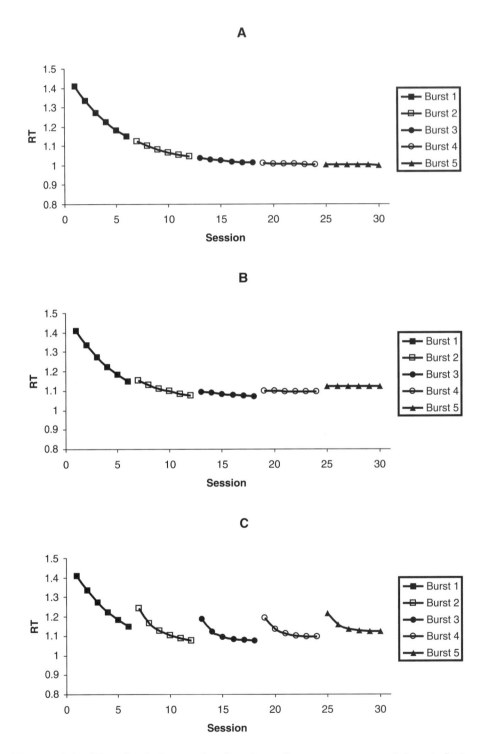

Figure 3.1. Hypothetical practice functions for a measurement burst design. RT = response time.

previous season. With practice, however, she quickly recovers the skill that was "lost" during the off-season and then continues to improve upon her best time. After a substantial temporal disruption in practice, performance becomes a function not only of the total amount practice (i.e., the cumulative practice) but also of how much practice has recently occurred (i.e., local practice).

Another complication may be overlaid on performance gains attributable to cumulative and local practice, namely that another process operates during the interval that separates measurement bursts. To follow our example, although our novice skier is becoming more skilled every season, as reflected in her performance, her potential or maximal speed might be decreasing across seasons because she is aging. Figure 3.1C shows the expected pattern of RTs if there were dual-process learning (i.e., cumulative learning and local warm-up effects) along with an upward drift in asymptote to signify age-related slowing that manifests across bursts. Assuming change in asymptote is a linear function of aging, the function would be:

$$\text{RT}_{ti} = a_i + \Delta a_i \left(\text{burst}_{kj}\right) + g_i \exp\left[-r_i\left(\text{occasion}_{ti}\right)\right] + \left(\text{Burst}_{kj} > 1\right)$$
$$\times g_i^* \exp\left[-r_i^*\left(\text{occasion}_{tki}\right)\right] + e_{ti}. \quad (3.4)$$

This equation adds the term $\Delta a_i(\text{burst}_{kj})$, which conveys the amount by which the asymptote changes from one burst to the next. The "fast" change that occurs across sessions within bursts conveys information about retest learning and relearning (the r and r^* parameters, respectively), whereas the "slow" change that occurs across bursts (Δa_i) reflects the effects of aging, senescence or involution.

The Present Study

The present study used a measurement burst design in which each burst consisted of six sessions that were repeated every six months for a period of 2 years. As depicted in Figure 3.2, the measurement burst design allows modeling of performance changes across different time scales. Performance change within each burst reflects fast practice gains, whereas change across bursts reflects the slow effects of aging. Performance change within follow-up bursts (i.e., bursts >1) reflects two processes: (a) cumulative learning and (b) local warm-up effects.

The first objective of this analysis was to determine whether a double negative learning function can describe the retest effects observed in an intensive measurement burst study. If the data follow the pattern depicted in Figure 3.1A, then a double learning function would not be necessary because there would be no forgetting or relearning processes. However, if the pattern of results resembles either Figure 3.1B or Figure 3.1C, that would imply that retest effects depend on the actual interval between occasions and would rule out use of the age + occasion retest model. The fit of a double negative exponential function will be compared with the fit of multiple single negative exponential functions fit to each measurement burst.

The second objective was to test the hypothesis that, despite retest-related improvements in observed performance, asymptotic performance shows age-

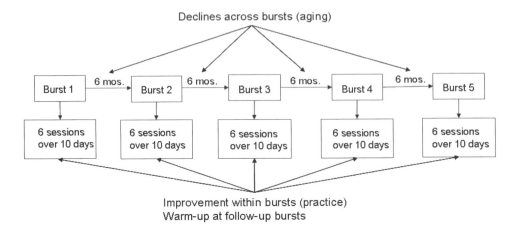

Figure 3.2. Different cadences of change in a measurement burst design. mos. = months.

related declines (i.e., slowing). This prediction implies results that follow the pattern depicted in Figure 3.1C and is grounded in research on cognitive training and testing-the-limits (Kliegl, Smith, & Baltes, 1989). Older adults maintain the ability to improve performance through practice; however, despite this preserved cognitive plasticity advancing age may result in diminished latent potential or reserve capacity. Detecting significant slowing in asymptotic speeded performance would be consistent with age-related reductions in latent potential.

Method

SAMPLE. One hundred sixteen older adults were recruited for participation in a longitudinal study of health and cognition through advertisements in local newspapers and flyers posted in senior centers. All older adults had intact mental status and were compensated $10 for each completed session. The average age was 80.23 (*SD* = 6.30, range: 66–95), the average years of education was 14.9 (*SD* = 2.40), and there was a higher percentage of women than men (72% vs. 28%, respectively).

PROCEDURE AND STIMULI. Participants were given a brief introduction to the study, and the experimenter obtained informed consent as approved by the Syracuse University institutional review board. Participants were told that they were taking part in a study that was examining health and cognition in adulthood. They were scheduled to visit the research site six times within a 14-day period. The research site was a rented apartment at a local senior residence. Half of the sessions (each lasting 1 hour) for each participant were scheduled before 11:00 a.m., and half were scheduled after 1:00 p.m. These bursts of daily measurements were repeated every 6 months, for a 2-year period, yielding up to five bursts of 30 daily assessments.

We examined performance on number comparison speed task, which required participants to compare two strings (three digits in length) to determine whether the same digits were in each string, regardless of their order. In the first session of each burst, sufficient practice trials for all tasks were provided until participants become comfortable with each procedure. Approximately 10 warm-up trials were given before commencement of each task during Sessions 2 through 6. Participants performed a block of 40 trials at each session. Participants were told to press the "/" key if the two digit strings were a match and to press the "z" key if there were a nonmatch. The next number string appeared 500 milliseconds after each response. Participants were instructed to be both fast and accurate. A high-resolution monitor controlled by a Pentium IV–based computer displayed the stimuli. The average RT from correct trials served as the dependent measure for this task. Accuracy was very high (mean proportion correct = .96) and did not significantly change across session within bursts or across bursts, so only RT data were analyzed. A computer-based vision check was administered to verify that all participants could identify test stimuli within video displays of 10.4° of visual angle.

Results

The RTs for each session and burst averaged across all individuals are displayed in Figure 3.3. Connected points belong to sessions obtained within the same burst, and there is approximately a 6-month gap between the last session of one burst and the first session of the following burst. The pattern of average RTs shows a decelerating rate of improvement across sessions within bursts

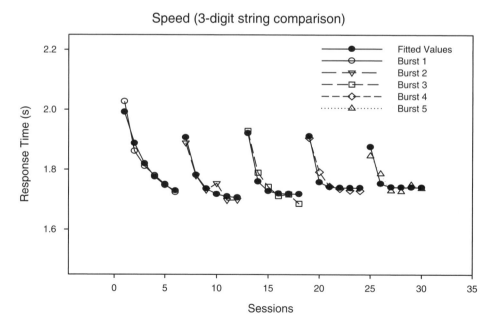

Figure 3.3. Observed and fitted values for average response time for the number comparison.

but exhibits slowing at the first session of each new burst, producing a scalloped retest pattern across bursts. This pattern demonstrates that the duration between occasions influences retest effects, making the age + occasion retest model unsuitable for these data.

We next compared the fit of the double negative exponential model (Equation 3.4) with that of single negative exponential (Equation 3.2). Preliminary model fitting indicated that the best-fitting single negative exponential model allowed all parameters (a, g, and r) to vary across bursts. The best-fitting double negative exponential constrained the parameters r, g, and r^* to be constant across bursts and allowed g^* and a to vary linearly across bursts.

We fit both models using nonlinear mixed modeling implemented by the PROC NLMIXED routine in SAS. Parameters that entered the model linearly (a, g, and g^*, and Δa) were specified as random, but the rate parameters (r and r^*) were constrained to be fixed to facilitate estimation and convergence of the mixed model. Although there is no formal significance test for comparing non-nested models, the double negative exponential fit better than the single according to both the Akaike information criterion (−1,222 vs. −1,207) and Bayesian information criterion (−1,190 vs. −1,174). There are no established guidelines for assessing meaningful differences in comparative fit indices, but Raftery (1995) suggested that a 10-point difference in the Bayesian information criterion constitutes "very strong" evidence in favor of the model with the more negative value.

Figure 3.3 represents the average of the fitted values obtained from the double negative exponential, which closely approximates the observed average values across all 30 sessions. Two different time scales are conveyed in this plot: (a) data points that are connected by a line occur on adjacent days, and (b) adjacent data points not connected by a line are separated by approximately 6 months. Fast change (within bursts) is described by the two rate parameters (r and r^*), and slow change (across bursts) is described by the Δa parameter. The estimated parameters for the double negative exponential model are shown in Table 3.1. The two rate parameters ($r = 0.17$, $SE = 0.011$, and $r^* = 3.44$,

Table 3.1.   Fixed and Random Effects Estimates from Dual-Exponential Fit

Parameter	Estimate	SE
a	1.500	0.048
Δa	0.054	0.007
g	0.560	0.043
r	0.172	0.011
g^*	1.060	0.007
r^*	3.450	0.141
Var(a)	0.200	0.028
Var(g)	0.115	0.023
Var(g^*)	0.187	0.056
Var(Δa)	0.054	0.001

Note.   For all values, $p < .01$.

$SE = 0.144$) reflect the cumulative learning rate across all sessions and the rate of warm-up related improvement at follow-up bursts, respectively. The asymptote was estimated to be 1.500 seconds ($SE = 0.048$) at the first burst and significantly increased ($\Delta a = 0.053$, $SE = 0.007$) across the follow-up bursts. These results indicate that, on average, asymptotic speed was slowing by about 53 milliseconds across every 6-month interval separating the measurement bursts. However, the significant variance component for the Δa parameter (var[Δa] = .003, $p < .001$) implies significant individual differences in the rate at which asymptotic speed slowed across the bursts. All values of Δa greater than 0 indicate slowing, so dividing the difference between 0 and the average Δa value of 0.053 by the square root of the variance component yields a z score of −0.92, implying that approximately 82% of individuals would be expected to exhibit asymptotic slowing, assuming a normal distribution of the random Δa effects.

As a final step in the analyses we correlated the random Δa effects with age and sensorimotor functioning, both of which are thought to relate to the rate of slowing in older adults. Age was positively associated with Δa ($r = .29$, $p < .01$), indicating that older individuals exhibited more rapid slowing. There was a strong negative correlation ($r = -.40$, $p < .01$) with a composite sensorimotor variable (a z-score average of visual acuity and grip strength). These correlations are in the expected direction and consistent with the a priori expectation that cognitive slowing would be accelerated in older individuals and in those with poorer sensorimotor function (MacDonald, Dixon, Cohen, & Hazlitt, 2004).

Discussion

The present results question the validity of a key assumption underlying age + occasion retest models, namely, that retest (i.e., practice) effects are invariant across different time intervals. They also support the utility of both measurement burst designs and the dual-exponential learning function as a model of clustered-practice effects that occur in measurement burst designs. The data summarized in Figure 3.2 clearly show within-burst speedup, across-burst loss of practice gains, and warm-up effects at follow-up bursts. The double-exponential learning model represents such clustered-practice effects by specifying two learning functions, one that describes cumulative learning and a second that describes local warm-up effects that result after a temporal delay between practice opportunities. These data are also similar in form to multisession learning data presented by Rickard (2007), which tend to show within-session learning, across-session forgetting, and a rapid warm-up effect at follow-up sessions. Additional research is required to determine whether a double-exponential learning model can also describe learning and warm-up effects in other contexts (e.g., multisession skill acquisition paradigms).

There are several noteworthy limitations of the present analyses. First, only six sessions per burst might not have been sufficient to bring each individual close to his or her asymptotic performance. Inspection of individual plots indicated that this was the case. Therefore, the present results depend on the accuracy of the extrapolation the model made for each individual asymptotic performance. Second, we aggregated across trials within each session and examined practice effects for the average RT across sessions, ignoring microlearning across trials within sessions. Consequently, the present analyses did not characterize microlevel (within-session) learning effects, which could have distorted the characterization of learning across sessions, within a given burst. For example, the warm-up effect might have been fully contained within the first dozen trials on the first session of follow-up bursts.

As intensive measurement designs become more prevalent, researchers will need to incorporate more dynamic measurement models that explicitly represent the role of time and repeated measurements. If cognitive performance is variable and does change across time, then a useful measurement model must specify how performance changes (e.g., exponentially with repeated measures), which aspects of cognitive function remain invariant (e.g., asymptote or latent potential), and the time scale over which change and invariance obtains (e.g., Newell et al., 2006). Most studies of learning and development have examined changes across fixed intervals and thus have not considered the importance of time scale for characterizing changes that are due to learning and development. One exception Newell, Mayer-Kress, and Lui's (2001) work, which provided a general theoretical framework for understanding motor learning and development across different time scales. Although consistent with Newell et al.'s argument for the importance of time scale, the present approach is purely descriptive. Equations 3.2 through 3.4 provide a simple measurement model that may be usefully applied to performance data that exhibit long-term (e.g., development) changes in parameters that are invariant in the short term (e.g., asymptotic performance). Future research is required to develop integrated theoretical accounts of short-term learning and long-term development (or aging) along the lines described by Newell et al.

Intensive measurement designs offer advantages over conventional single-shot prospective longitudinal designs, such as improved precision for tracking intraindividual change and estimation of changes in asymptotic performance. Processing capacity or latent potential, as indexed by asymptotic performance, might prove to be an especially sensitive marker of aging effects. However, a noteworthy limitation of the present study was the need to constrain r and r^* as fixed to obtain model convergence. In practice, learning rates will likely vary across individuals and within individuals across time. Future studies should consider including more within-burst sessions to facilitate estimation of person-specific learning rates as well as across-burst changes in rates. Despite this limitation, the analyses described in this chapter illustrate the utility of measurement burst designs and the dual-exponential learning function for separating retest performance gains, warm-up effects, and aging declines in asymptotic performance. Thus, the pairing of multiburst designs and informative measurement models may offer an especially useful approach for separating local and global developmental processes that operate across very different time scales.

References

Anderson, J. R., Fincham, J. M., & Douglass, S. (1999). Practice and retention: A unifying analysis. *Journal of Experimental Psychology: Learning, Memory, and Cognition, 25,* 1120–1136. doi: 10.1037/0278-7393.25.5.1120

Baltes, P. B., & Nesselroade, J. R. (1979). History and rationale of longitudinal research. In J. R. Nesselroade & P. B. Baltes (Eds.), *Longitudinal research in the study of behavior and development* (pp. 1–39). New York, NY: Academic Press.

Ferrer, E., Salthouse, T. A., McArdle, J. J., Stewart, W. F., & Schwartz, B. S. (2005). Multivariate modeling of age and retest in longitudinal studies of cognitive abilities. *Psychology and Aging, 20,* 412–422. doi:10.1037/0882-7974.20.3.412

Ferrer, E., Salthouse, T. A., Stewart, W. F., & Schwartz, B. S. (2004). Modeling age and retest processes in longitudinal studies of cognitive abilities. *Psychology and Aging, 19,* 243–259. doi: 10.1037/0882-7974.19.2.243

Ghisletta, P., McArdle, J. J., & Lindenberger, U. (2006). Longitudinal cognition–survival relations in old and very old age: 13-year data from the Berlin Aging Study. *European Psychologist, 11,* 204–223. doi:10.1027/1016-9040.11.3.204

Horn, J. L. (1972). State, trait and change dimension of intelligence. *British Journal of Educational Psychology, 42,* 159–185.

Kliegl, R., Smith, J., & Baltes, P. B. (1989). Testing-the-limits and the study of adult age differences in cognitive plasticity of a mnemonic skill. *Developmental Psychology, 25,* 247–256. doi:10.1037/0012-1649.25.2.247

MacDonald, S. W. S., Dixon, R. A., Cohen, A., & Hazlitt, J. E. (2004). Biological age and 12-year cognitive change in older adults: Findings from the Victoria Longitudinal Study. *Gerontology, 50,* 64–81. doi:10.1159/000075557

MacDonald, S. W. S., Stigsdotter-Neely, A., Derwinger, A., & Backman, L. (2006). Rate of acquisition, adult age, and basic cognitive abilities predict forgetting: New views on a classic problem. *Journal of Experimental Psychology: General, 135,* 368–390.

McArdle, J. J., & Anderson, E. (1990). Latent variable growth models for research on aging. In J. E. Birren & K. W. Schaie (Eds.), *The handbook of the psychology of aging* (3rd ed., pp. 21–43). New York, NY: Plenum Press.

McArdle, J. J., Ferrer-Caja, E., Hamagami, F., & Woodcock, R. W. (2002). Comparative longitudinal structural analyses of the growth and decline of multiple intellectual abilities over the life span. *Developmental Psychology, 38,* 115–142.

McArdle, J. J., & Woodcock, R. W. (1997). Expanding test–retest designs to include developmental time-lag components. *Psychological Methods, 2,* 403–435. doi:10.1037/1082-989X.2.4.403

Nesselroade, J. R. (1991). The warp and woof of the developmental fabric. In R. Downs, L. Liben, & D. S. Palermo (Eds.), *Visions of aesthetics, the environment, and development: The legacy of Joachim F. Wohlwill* (pp. 213–240). Hillsdale, NJ: Erlbaum.

Newell, K. M., Mayer-Kress, G., & Lui, Y. (2001). Time scales in motor learning and development. *Psychological Review, 108,* 57–82. doi:10.1037/0033-295X.108.1.57

Newell, K. M., Mayer-Kress, G., & Lui, Y. (2006). Human learning: Power laws or multiple characteristic time scale? *Tutorials in Quantitative Methods for Psychology, 2,* 29–39.

Rabbitt, P., Diggle, P., Smith, D., Holland, F., & McInnes, L. (2001). Identifying and separating the effects of practice and of cognitive ageing during a large longitudinal study of elderly community residents. *Neuropsychologia, 39,* 532–543. doi:10.1016/S0028-3932(00)00099-3

Raftery, A. E. (1995). Bayesian model selection in social research (with discussion). *Sociological Methodology, 25,* 111–196. doi:10.2307/271063

Rickard, T. C. (2007). Forgetting and learning potentiation: Dual consequences of between-session delays in cognitive skill learning. *Journal of Experimental Psychology: Learning, Memory, and Cognition, 33,* 297–304. doi:10.1037/0278-7393.33.2.297

Salthouse, T. A., Schroeder, D. H., & Ferrer, E. (2004). Estimating retest effects in longitudinal assessments of cognitive functioning in adults between 18 and 60 years of age. *Developmental Psychology, 40,* 813–822. doi:10.1037/0012-1649.40.5.813

Schaie, K. W. (1965). A general model for the study of developmental problems. *Psychological Bulletin, 64,* 92–107. doi:10.1037/h0022371

Schaie, K. W. (1996). *Intellectual development in adulthood: The Seattle Longitudinal Study*. New York, NY: Cambridge University Press.

Sliwinski, M. J. (2008). Measurement-burst designs for social health research. *Social and Personality Psychology Compass, 2,* 245–261. doi:10.1111/j.1751-9004.2007.00043.x

Sliwinski, M. J., Hofer, S., Hall, C. B., Buschke, H., & Lipton, R. (2003). Modeling memory decline in older adults: The importance of preclinical dementia, attrition and chronological age. *Psychology and Aging, 18,* 658–671. doi:10.1037/0882-7974.18.4.658

Sliwinski, M., Lipton, R. B., Buschke, H., & Stewart, W. F. (1996). The effect of pre-clinical dementia on estimates of normal cognitive function in aging. *Journal of Gerontology: Psychological Sciences, 51B,* P217–P225.

Thorndike, E. L., Bregman, E. O., Tilton, J. W., & Woodyard, E. (1928). *Adult learning*. New York, NY: Macmillan.

Thorvaldsson, V., Hofer, S. M., Berg, S., & Johansson, B. (2006). Effects of repeated testing in a longitudinal age-homogeneous study of cognitive aging. *Journal of Gerontology: Psychological Sciences, 61B,* P348–P354.

Wilson, R. S., Li, Y., Bienias, J. L., & Bennett, D. A. (2006). Cognitive decline in old age: Separating retest effects from the effects of growing older. *Psychology and Aging, 21,* 774–789. doi:10.1037/0882-7974.21.4.774

4

Modeling Mother–Infant Interactions Using Hidden Markov Models

Michael J. Rovine, Katerina O. Sinclair, and Cynthia A. Stifter

When a child experiences discomfort, one of the important roles of parents is to respond properly by soothing that distress. Not responding properly to distress over a long period of time may increase the child's risk of disease. In addition, parents who properly respond to an infant's distress help to create an environment conducive to the child's positive mental health and may ultimately create an environment that enhances the infant's ability to emotionally self-regulate (Davidov & Grusec, 2006; Roberts & Strayer, 1987). The ability to respond properly to infant distress may improve with experience, with the overall quality and the degree of improvement varying from parent to parent. In this case, we expect that by looking at parent–infant interactions we can see differences in the initial quality of soothing, the change of soothing strategies, and the eventual quality of soothing.

Researchers generally observe mother–infant interactions by collecting *time series data,* that is, observing mother and infant behaviors over a length of time. When several infant and parent behaviors are collected, the result is a multivariate time series, with observations in the series representing the occurrence of behaviors within a specific time frame. By collecting such data investigators have the opportunity to show not only near-simultaneous occurrences of behaviors but also lagged relationships between behaviors. For example, does the infant's behavior at a particular observation lead to a parent's response at some later time? Does the parent's response, in turn, lead to a change in the child's behavior? With this kind of data we can model the dynamics of a process.

A number of different methods exist for modeling multivariate time series. Because we are modeling dichotomous variables that represent either the presence or absence of a mother's soothing behavior along with an ordered categorical variable representing the level of the infant's distress, we will concentrate on methods appropriate for modeling dynamic processes for discrete variables. Researchers frequently select statistical methods that pool across

This research was supported by National Science Foundation Grant DHB 0527449. We thank Peter C. M. Molenaar, Karl Newell, Ingmar Visser, John R. Nesselroade, Michael W. Browne, Kathleen Gates, and Siwei Liu for comments on earlier versions of this chapter.

the whole time series, resulting in a single summary statistic that loses the dynamic flavor of the data. We use this approach, which is typified by Yule's Q statistic, to describe the most basic approach to the analysis of categorical time series data.

After describing this approach, we present a method that results in a richer description of the interaction, the *hidden Markov model* (HMM). This method has the advantage of allowing the dynamics of the process to be described through a set of states that represent probabilities of behavior for the parent and infant, with movement from one state to another representing a change in the process. We begin with a model that hypothesizes common states across all parent–infant pairs. It is possible, however, to derive different states for different pairs. We describe a practical method for determining whether the common model describes the individual. Finally, we present a truly person-specific approach that allows all parameters of the model to apply to all individuals. Because we use the R program depmix (Visser, 2005) to estimate HMMs, we use the parameterization of this program throughout this chapter.

Describing the Relationship Between Maternal Soothing and Infant's Reactivity

When describing any interaction, the questions we are interested in can be generally described as follows:

- What are the characteristics of the interaction?
- What are the dynamics of the system?
- What statistical model can best be used to describe these dynamics?

As an example, we use data gathered by Jahromi, Putnam, and Stifter (2004). To study the differences in soothing strategies in a stressful situation, they observed 150 healthy infants as part of a longitudinal study of emotional regulation. Infants and their mothers were videotaped during a routine inoculation that occurred either in their pediatrician's office or at a local health clinic. Immediately following the inoculation the infant was given to the mother, who was then free to soothe the infant in any manner she chose.

Data were coded by trained observers. Infants were scored every 5 seconds on their level of crying (degree of distress) on a 4-point scale (3 = *high intensity*, 2 = *moderate intensity*, 1 = *low intensity*, 0 = *none*). Mothers were also scored every 5 seconds on the presence (scored as 1) or absence (scored as 0) of different soothing behaviors. Co-occurring and mutually exclusive behaviors were combined to yield six categories of behaviors: (a) touching or affection, (b) distraction or face-to-face contact, (c) holding and rocking, (d) feeding or pacifying, (e) vocalizing, and (f) caretaking. These behaviors were selected not only for their substantive interest but also because they exhibited enough variability to allow modeling. Each dyad was observed 48 times or until the child exhibited no crying behavior for a period of 20 seconds.

We are interested in the selection of comforting strategies, the success of those strategies, and whether a mother can adjust her strategy on the basis of the infant's response. To give an indication of how these questions can be approached, we present simple imaginary data in Figure 4.1. Here the infant begins the series at the highest level of distress. After two observation periods, the mother tries Behavior 1 and maintains that behavior until the child exhibits less distress at Observation 12. Then the mother tries a second behavior. After an additional seven observation periods, the child's level of distress drops again. That level is maintained for an additional three observation periods, until the child's distress reaches 0, the lowest possible value. As one can see, such data can suggest which behaviors are effective, which might not work, whether maintaining a behavior can have an eventual effect, whether combinations of behaviors are more effective than individual behaviors, and whether the mother can switch from an ineffective behavior to an effective behavior. These represent characteristics that can be used to describe the dynamics of the interaction.

Such data typically have been modeled with techniques that require one to collapse the data across the time series and, often, to pool the results of those collapsed series across dyads. Such approaches are based on the notion of *sequential analyses* described by Bakeman and Gottman (1997) and are often realized by lagging the data and calculating a single summary statistic for the resulting contingency table (e.g., Yule's Q). We describe this approach and consider it the starting point to describe a more dynamic approach to modeling this data.

A Sequential Approach

Bakeman and Gottman (1997) suggested indicating the strength of the sequential relationship by indicating the odds that one event is associated with another

Sample Data

Infant's level of distress	3	3	3	3	3	3	3	3	3	3	3	2	2	2	2	2	2	2	2	2	1	1	1	0	0
Maternal behavior 1	0	0	1	1	1	1	1	1	1	1	1	1	0	0	0	0	0	0	0	0	0	0	0	0	0
Maternal behavior 2	0	0	0	0	0	0	0	0	0	0	0	0	0	0	1	1	1	1	1	1	1	1	1	1	1

Distress   3 – most distressed   to   0 – least distressed

Behavior   1 – performs behavior   0 – doesn't perform behavior

Figure 4.1.   Hypothetical mother–infant interaction data.

occurring at the previous occasion (at Lag 1). If we consider the data like those presented earlier we would be interested in whether the performance of a particular behavior at one observation (time t) leads to a decrease in the level of distress at the next occasion (time $t + 1$). We can calculate this for each behavior by constructing the table shown in Figure 4.2.

In the table depicted in Figure 4.2, X represents the mother performing a certain behavior at time t, and Y represents a shift in the level of distress at the following occasion. The $X = 1$, $Y = 1$ cell represents the target cell, with large values in that cell showing a successful application of the behavior. In such an analysis every observation would be included in the table. This approach tends to pick up relationships described by a shift in one variable followed by a shift in the other variable within the space of a specific lag. For the relationship to show up, the number of possible shifts in the outcome has to be large relative to the number of occasions. For the crying behavior we consider, most typically only three shifts would occur (3 to 2, 2 to 1, and 1 to 0), although it would be possible for crying to increase at some point and then decrease. As an example, we computed a Yule's Q table and coefficient for the first 10 cases in our data set relating touching or affection (one of the most frequently occurring behaviors) and face-to-face contact or distraction (typically one of most effective behaviors) to crying. The results are shown in Figure 4.3. In this figure it is easy to see that the association coefficients are greatly attenuated by disproportionate frequencies in the table. As a result, there will be limited variability in the coefficients. In

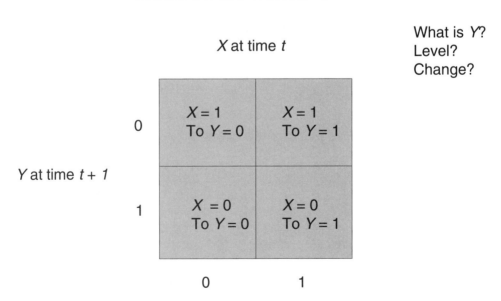

Figure 4.2.   Contingency table with lagged relationships between two behaviors.

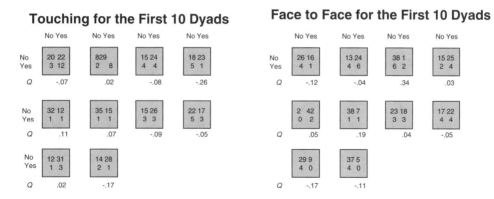

Figure 4.3. Yule's Q contingency tables and coefficients for touching and face-to-face contact for the first 10 dyads separately: touching (left panel) and face-to-face contact (right panel).

addition, this approach does not account for the duration of the behavior. An addition to the target cell could result from either a behavior that was briefly exhibited or a behavior that was steadily maintained, as long as each was followed by the shift in the outcome. So, duration really has no influence on the target cell but will instead inflate the $(1, 0)$ count (i.e., behavior performed, but no shift in distress). Alternatively, one could use an event-based approach that concentrates on shifts in infant distress and the behaviors that immediately precede that shift, ignoring the number of preceding observations in which the same behaviors were used without the change occurring. This would solve the problem of an inflated $(1, 0)$ cell but would still fail to account for a shift in distress resulting from a continually maintained soothing behavior.

Indeed, there are at least three situations in which a behavior could influence an outcome but no indication would show up in the Yule's Q frequencies: The change in y falls more than one observation period beyond the occurrence of x; the change in y requires an extended amount of the behavior x and, as a result, falls far past the observation in which x is first seen; x occurs briefly and is accompanied by a simultaneous change in y.

The following items summarize the problems of the sequential approach to multivariate time series based on categorical variables:

- The associations between each behavior and the outcome are summarized in a single number that cannot adequately describe a dynamic relationship.
- The effect on the relationship of the duration of each behavior is lost because it registers only when it leads almost immediately to a change in the outcome.
- The benefit of maintaining a behavior that ultimately leads to a positive (or negative) outcome is lost.
- The sequence requires a number of changes in the outcome to create enough variability to result in a meaningful statistic.

Although Yule's Q could be calculated separately for each dyad, its use in sequential modeling often requires that the data be pooled across individuals. However, aggregating across individuals creates conceptual problems because pooling assumes a common model in which the same process describes each mother–infant pair equally well. In addition, the pooled data retain the same problems because of disproportionately small cell sizes. For example, the pooled contingency tables relating touching and face-to-face contact to crying for the first 10 cases appear in Figure 4.4. The disproportionate cell sizes greatly attenuate the value of Q. Although there are transformations that could be used to stabilize the coefficient (Leinert, von Eye, & Rovine, 1987), better methods are available.

Genuine time series approaches exist in which the order of the process (here, the appropriate lag for predictors) can be determined for categorical data (Fahrmeir & Tutz, 1994). Although such methods represent an improvement over the method just described, they are still basically regression methods and may tell us little about the dynamics of the interaction. Here we suggest an alternative approach based on the HMM.

The Hidden Markov Model

Hidden Markov modeling was developed by Baum and his colleagues (e.g., Baum & Petrie, 1966; Baum, Petrie, Soules, & Weiss, 1970) in the late 1960s to provide probabilistic models for discrete Markov chains. Many of the early applications were related to speech processing (i.e., Baker, 1975; Jelinek, Bahl, & Mercer, 1982). Visser, Raijmakers, and Molenaar (2002) described some of the history of its use in psychology. Frühwirth-Schnatter (2006) provided examples of its use in modeling movement and economic time series data.

Considering our desire to model the dynamics of a set of categorical observed variables, we suggest that the hidden Markov approach has some distinct advantages over other methods. It is multivariate and can accommodate a large number of variables. By defining a set of states that represent combinations of variable

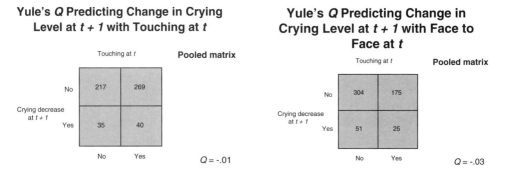

Figure 4.4. Yule's Q contingency tables and coefficients for touching and face-to-face contact pooled across the first 10 dyads: touching (left panel) and face-to-face contact (right panel).

probabilities we can follow dyads across time by observing the sequence of states through which each passes. This makes the model quite tractable and relatively straightforward to interpret.

To introduce these models, we first consider a simple situation. We observe an infant and mother dyad interacting. Over the course of the interaction the infant shows a certain degree of distress that we can categorize. To sooth the child, the mother engages in some subset of behaviors from a larger domain of soothing strategies and is assessed regarding which behaviors from that domain occur. These observations form a multivariate time series.

Suppose that we assume a set of hidden or latent (unobserved) states exist. In each state, we might expect the infant most likely to be at a certain level of distress. Given that level of distress, the mother is likely to use each possible soothing strategy with a particular probability. The dyad remains in this state for a certain amount of time. At the end of the time, the likely level of the child's distress changes, and with that change come changes in the probability of the mother using each of the possible soothing strategies. She may continue with the same strategies or possibly try some others. This new level of distress and accompanying behaviors may represent the transition to a different state. The HMM can be used to estimate this sequence of latent states from the observed series.

Each state is defined by the probability of each behavior (for both mother and infant) occurring; an example of a three-state model is shown in Figure 4.5. The probabilities show how likely the infant is at a particular level of distress along with the probability that the mother is performing each of the possible behaviors. According to this figure, the baby in this state is most likely to be at the highest level of distress while the mother is using both soothing and rocking. As an example of a state shift consider the move from State 1 to State 2. Here we see that the infant is less distressed and the mother has stopped soothing but continues to rock the child. Finally, the dyad could move to State 3, in which the child is most likely to exhibit no distress and the mother is most likely to use neither of the soothing strategies.

Each of these states represents a probabilistic statement: the likelihood of these behaviors occurring. That means that a child described as being in the first state is most likely at the highest level of distress but could (with some smaller probability) be in one of the lower levels of distress. The mother in the first state is most likely using both strategies but could with some small probability be using both strategies or neither strategy.

Assume that these three states represent a good description of the behaviors of the dyad at different times. We can then describe the probability that a dyad moves from one state to another. For the three states just described, a matrix of these probabilities might appear, as in Figure 4.5D. The probability in each cell represents the chance of changing states from one time to the next. The diagonals represent the probability of staying in the same state. The probabilities along each row sum to 1 because, according the model, the dyad has to change to one of the three possible states. All things considered, the dyad is most likely to remain in a particular state instead of changing states from one observation to the next. That is a reflection that the child will stay at a certain level of distress for a number of observations while the mother uses a set of soothing strategies

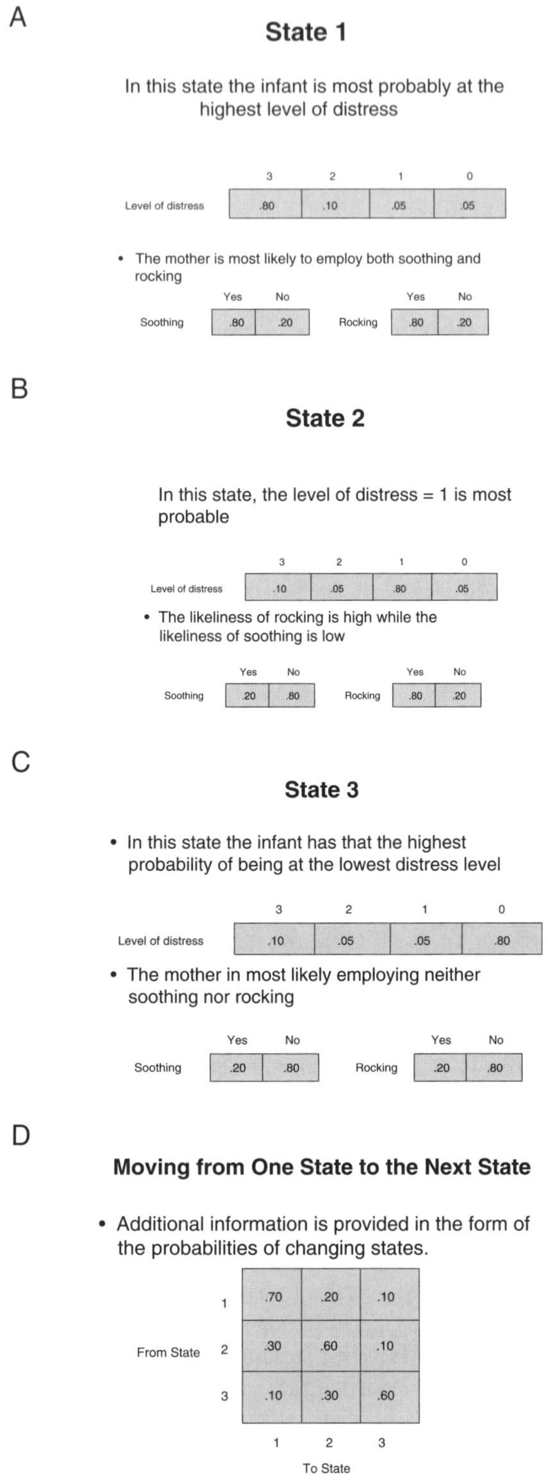

A

State 1

In this state the infant is most probably at the highest level of distress

	3	2	1	0
Level of distress	.80	.10	.05	.05

- The mother is most likely to employ both soothing and rocking

	Yes	No			Yes	No
Soothing	.80	.20		Rocking	.80	.20

B

State 2

In this state, the level of distress = 1 is most probable

	3	2	1	0
Level of distress	.10	.05	.80	.05

- The likeliness of rocking is high while the likeliness of soothing is low

	Yes	No			Yes	No
Soothing	.20	.80		Rocking	.80	.20

C

State 3

- In this state the infant has that the highest probability of being at the lowest distress level

	3	2	1	0
Level of distress	.10	.05	.05	.80

- The mother in most likely employing neither soothing nor rocking

	Yes	No			Yes	No
Soothing	.20	.80		Rocking	.20	.80

D

Moving from One State to the Next State

- Additional information is provided in the form of the probabilities of changing states.

From State	1	2	3
1	.70	.20	.10
2	.30	.60	.10
3	.10	.30	.60

To State

Figure 4.5. A possible three-state model. Panel A: State 1; Panel B: State 2; Panel C: State 3; Panel D: transition matrix.

that might eventually result in decreased distress. Remember that the first state is the most distressed state and the last is the least distressed state.

The model can be used to generate the sequence of states for each dyad, which suggests the number of observation periods spent in each of the states. An example of a sequence of states is shown in Figure 4.6. In this figure, one can see that the child remains in the highly distressed state for roughly one quarter of the observation period, then quickly moves from the moderately distressed to the lowest level of distress.

This alternative conceptualization represents the hidden Markov approach to the analysis of sequential categorical longitudinal data. In this model, the *states* represent certain combinations of behaviors that are likely to co-occur. When the child is likely to cry at a certain level, the mother is likely to use certain strategies. The *transitions* among the states indicate a dynamic process. For example, if the child is crying at a certain level, and the mother is performing these behaviors, the transition matrix will indicate the probability that the child might move to a different state. This new state will also suggest the likely behaviors the mother will use. The *trajectory* of the states indicates changes from state to state and duration of time spent within each state.

To understand the flexibility of HMMs one can compare them with a discrete model, the *Markov chain model*. In a Markov chain model infant distress would define a given state. For our example, any infant in a high distress level would be in the first state, and any infant without distress would be in the last state. For these models, the probabilities of behaviors in each state are not estimated; they are determined. The model only estimates the transition probabilities (i.e., the probabilities of changing from one state to another) along with the probability of starting in each state (i.e., the starting vector). For two variables—the child's distress and whether the mother uses a particular behavior to try to soothe the child—the state now represents some combination of these two variables. A child can be at one of four levels of distress, and at each level the

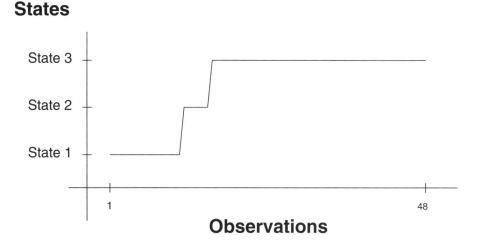

Figure 4.6. An example of a sequence of states for a dyad.

mother may or may not use that strategy to try to soothe the child, resulting in eight defined states and an estimated set of transition probabilities.

The HMM extends this model by allowing the definition of the state to be probabilistic. Whereas in the discrete model a state was defined by infant distress level and maternal behaviors, the HMM definition of the state posits the probability of being in any of the four distress states along with the probability of a soothing behavior. For each state, the probabilities of the each of the behaviors would be estimated as part of the model.

In the HMM (Rabiner, 1989) a system is presumed to have N distinct states: $S_1, S_2, \ldots, S_N$. The state that an individual is in at time t is q_t. Like the discrete first order Markov chain, the probability of being in the current state, S_j, coming from the previous state, S_i, is the transition probability:

$$a_{ij} = P(q_t = S_j | q_t - 1 = S_i).$$

The a_{ij} are collected in the (N,N) dimensional matrix A.

This set of probabilities describes the transition between any two observations across the whole series of observations. The defining characteristic of the first-order Markov process is that the information about the probability of currently being in a particular state depends only on knowledge of the prior state.

Each state is described by a set of observed variables that can take on any of a set of discrete (or continuous) values. Consider only a set of discrete observed variables. If there are m_1 possible values for Variable 1, m_2 for Variable 2, up to m_p for Variable p, then the number of observations symbols is $M = m_1 + m_2 + \ldots + m_p$. Given M observation symbols per state, the observation symbol probability distribution in state j is

$$b_{kj} = p(v_k \text{ at } t | q_t = S_j),$$

where v_k represents the particular symbol (e.g., the value of the categorical variable). The b_{kj} are collected in the (M,N) dimensional matrix B.

If $\pi_i = P(q_1 = S_i)$ is the probability of starting in a particular state S_i, then the parameter vector (vec) for the model is

$$\lambda = [\text{vec}(A), \text{vec}(B), \pi],$$

where $vec(matrix)$ creates a vector from a matrix by concatenating the columns of the original matrix. Given this set of parameters, we then find the set of λ that make the probability of observing the data most likely.

A THREE-STATE HIDDEN MARKOV MODEL FOR THE MOTHER–INFANT DATA. To demonstrate the HMM we begin with a three-state model based on the 6-month inoculation data. A common model was estimated for 141 mother–infant pairs (at this assessment, data for nine pairs were missing). The estimates from the model appear in Figure 4.7. The parameter estimates include a set of initial probabilities π (the probability of starting in each state); the transition matrix, A (the probability of moving between states); and the loading matrix, B (the probability of each behavior occurring in a particular state).

The Three State Model

	State 1	State 2	State 3
Initial Probabilities	.93	.03	.05
Infant Distress Level			
High Intensity	.73	.00	.13
Moderate intensity	.18	.25	.08
Low intensity	.05	.43	.30
None	.05	.32	.49
Maternal Soothing Behaviors			
Touching/Affection	.41	.51	.28
Distraction/Face-to-face	.40	.49	.28
Holding/Rocking	.66	.99	.87
Feeding/Pacifying	.01	.00	.98
Vocalizing	.74	.77	.68
Caretaking	.17	.04	.05

Three State Transition Matrix

To this state:

		State 1	State 2	State 3
From this state:	State 1	.84	.14	.02
	State 2	.02	.96	.02
	State 3	.02	.01	.98

The Six State Model

	State 1	State 2	State 3	State 4	State 5	State 6
Initial Probabilities	.841	.069	.014	.045	.007	.025
Infant Distress Level						
High Intensity	.99	.04	.00	.31	.00	.31
Moderate intensity	.01	.85	.01	.11	.05	.23
Low intensity	.00	.10	.55	.24	.35	.24
None	.00	.01	.44	.34	.60	.22
Maternal Soothing Behaviors						
Touching/Affection	.50	.57	.51	.30	.27	.01
Distraction/Face-to-face	.43	.42	.54	.61	.00	.25
Holding/Rocking	.77	.94	1.00	.72	1.00	.38
Feeding/Pacifying	.01	.00	.00	.89	1.00	.00
Vocalizing	.77	.84	.74	.85	.54	.56
Caretaking	.04	.01	.02	.09	.00	.73

Six State Transition Matrix

To this state:

		State 1	State 2	State 3	State 4	State 5	State 6
From this state:	State 1	.74	.21	.02	.00	.01	.02
	State 2	.06	.67	.23	.01	.01	.01
	State 3	.00	.05	.92	.00	.02	.01
	State 4	.02	.00	.01	.87	.10	.01
	State 5	.00	.00	.01	.00	.99	.01
	State 6	.02	.02	.03	.01	.01	.91

Figure 4.7.   Probability estimates for a three-state and six-state hidden Markov model.

Starting with Loading Matrix B, we see in its first column that State 1 is defined by a high probability of heavy crying (.73) and almost no probability of no crying (.05) or light crying (.05). The most likely soothing strategies used are vocalizing (.74) and holding/rocking (.66), with a slightly lower probability of touching/affection (.41) and distraction/face-to-face contact (.40). Because State 1 has the highest initial probability (.93), most dyads are expected to initially be in this state.

According to Transition Matrix A, the most likely occurrence when in State 1 is to stay in State 1 at the next time point (.84), and the most likely transition is from State 1 to State 2 (.14).

State 2 is composed of infants who are unlikely to be crying heavily (.03) but who could be crying at a medium level (.25), a light level (.43), or not at all (.32). In this state, the probability of holding/rocking increases (.99). Touching/affection (.51) and distraction/face-to-face contact (.49) are slightly more probable; caretaking is a little less probable (.04). The other behaviors occur at essentially the same rates.

From State 2, the probability of remaining in that state at the next time point is .96. A transition from that state is almost as likely to move to State 3 (.02) as to move back to State 1 (.02).

State 3 is composed of infants who tend to cry lightly (.30) or not at all (.49). In terms of the mothers' behaviors, State 3 shows a dramatic increase in feeding/pacifying (.98). Mothers tend to use less touching/affection (.28), less distraction (.28), and somewhat less vocalizing (.68) than in either of the other two states. State 3 appears show infants crying less and being fed or pacified.

Dyads in State 3 tend to stay in State 3 (.98). This could represent the fact that at some point in the sequence the child is fed or pacified and quiets. This usually occurs toward the end of the observation sequence.

Once the model is determined we can use it to generate the sequence of states (one for each observation period) each dyad passes through. These posterior probabilities can be used to describe individual differences among the mother–infant pairs. Their estimation is very similar in concept to the prediction of random effects in a multilevel mixed model. They are predicted assuming a particular distribution and would result in the same model parameter estimates had they been known at the outset. We will hold off showing the sequences until we define a model that represents a better fit for these data.

SELECTING THE MODEL. The three-state model just described was one of many we tried to account for the observed data. To assess the fit of that or any model (i.e., to determine whether the model accounts well for these data), we used the Akaike information criterion (AIC) and the Bayesian information criterion (BIC) provided by the program. The AIC and BIC are loglikelihoods penalized for the number of parameters estimated by the model. Given the penalty they apply, the AIC tends to prefer the more complex model, whereas the BIC would lean toward the more parsimonious model. The model with both a lower AIC and BIC typically represents the best model for a set of data.

For these data set we fit two-, three-, four-, five-, and six-state models to the 6-month mother–infant data. We also fit a four-state model with discrete states to infant distress levels. This model could be considered a confirmatory model. The six-state model turned out to be the best-fitting model for these data. The fit statistics used to make this decision appear in Table 4.1, and the discrete model is shown in the "Four-state fixed" column.

A SIX-STATE HIDDEN MARKOV MODEL FOR THE MOTHER–INFANT DATA. We include the loading and transition matrices for the six-state model in Figure 4.7. The six-state model is characterized by relatively distinct high (State 1) and moderate (State 2) distress states. The soothing behaviors that dominate State 1 are holding/rocking and vocalizing, with somewhat smaller probabilities

Table 4.1. Fit Indices for the 6-Month Inoculation Data

Fit indices	Two-state	Three-state	Four-state	Four-state fixed	Five-state	Six-state
AIC	—	21,264.64	20,201.56	21,836.45	19,725.77	19,310.5
BIC	—	21,505.51	20,552.53	22,104.84	20,200.61	19,922.98
Loglike	—	−10,597.3	−10,049.8	−10,879.2	−9,793.88	−9,566.25
No. parameters	—	61	85	85	111	139
No. free	—	35	51	39	69	89

Note. AIC = Akaike information criterion; BIC = Bayesian information criterion.

of touching/affection and distraction/face-to-face contact. State 2 has a very similar pattern of soothing behaviors, with slightly larger probabilities of holding/ rocking and vocalizing. A simple interpretation would suggest that mothers typically maintain the same behaviors through the more distressed states. The transition matrix indicates that when a dyad moves out of State 1 the change will almost always be to State 2, reinforcing this interpretation.

Two states have a probability of less intense distress: State 3 has somewhat more low-intensity crying, and State 5 has a higher probability of being in the no-distress stage. When moving out of State 3, a dyad is most likely to move back to State 2, with a slightly less probability of moving to State 5. This indicates either that the mother may maintain the same behaviors, resulting in the infant's somewhat increased distress, or the mother may start feeding or pacifying the child, resulting in an increased probability of less distress. Once in State 5 (the feeding/pacifying state), the dyad tends to stay in the state with only a slight probability of movement.

States 4 and 6 have a distribution across all four levels of distress and most likely represent transitional states. State 4, which is marked by increased feeding/pacifying accompanied by vocalizing, holding/rocking, and face-to-face contact, most typically leads to the quiet child in the feeding state. State 6 is indicated by caretaking and vocalizing and can result in transitions to any of the other five states with a transition to States 1, 2, or 3 being slightly more probable.

Taken together, these six states create a general pattern describing the course of the interaction. Given this general trend, we next discuss how to describe individual differences on the basis of this model.

INDIVIDUAL DIFFERENCES USING POSTERIOR PROBABILITIES OF STATE MEMBERSHIP. The model we just described was estimated as a common model for all dyads in the study. To describe individual differences, we assume the states as describing each dyad. Given these states, we allow individual differences by predicting the posterior probability of state membership at each observation within each dyad. This yields the sequence of states through which each dyad passes. This results in the predicted sequence of states for each dyad. Given a sequence, we can compute summary statistics based on the state sequence, the state duration, and the total duration (the proportion of observations spent in each of the states). These summary statistics can be treated as variables that measure individual differences. Given a proper set of covariates, we can account for the variability in these derived measures.

To indicate the variability apparent in these state sequences, we show the sequences for nine of the dyads in the top panel of Figure 4.8. Dyad 85 stays in State 5 throughout the observation period. Dyad 86 begins in State 4, a slightly less probable starting state, which nevertheless has approximately equal probabilities of high intensity and no distress. Because the child has just received the inoculation, it is most likely that the crying here is of high intensity. This stage is marked by relatively high probabilities of face-to-face contact, holding/ rocking, feeding/pacifying, and vocalizing, making it likely that some combination of these soothing strategies is being used. The dyad then moves to State 1, in which crying most likely remains at high intensity with feeding/pacifying no longer a probable behavior. Eventually, the dyad moves to State 5, with distress

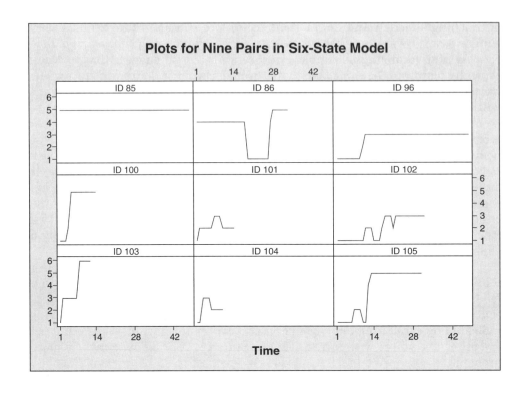

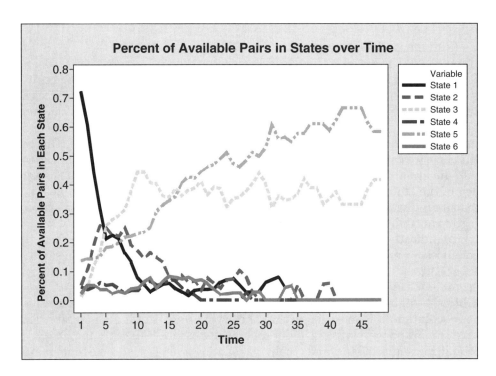

Figure 4.8. Top panel: Posterior plots of state sequences for nine mother–infant pairs. Bottom panel: Posterior plots of the percentage of available pairs in states over time.

intensity lessening with a return to feeding/pacifying and holding/rocking, probably accompanied by vocalizing. The sequence ends after the 32nd observation.

Dyad 96 spends the first 10 observations in State 1, the highest distress state, and then moves to State 3, which is marked by low-intensity to no distress in the presence of holding/rocking with a slightly lower probability of distraction/face-to-face contact and vocalizing. Because State 3 allows both low-intensity and no distress, both levels of distress can occur in that state. Dyad 96 remains in this state for the final 32 observations.

Dyad 102 cycles between States 1 and 2 for the first 16 observations and then cycles between States 2 and 3 before settling into State 3 through the end of the sequence around Observation 32. States 1, 2, and 3 are basically differentiated by the level of distress. In each of these states the probabilities of the soothing behaviors are very similar, with the possible soothing strategies including touching/affection, face-to-face contact, holding/rocking, and vocalizing. For this dyad it is reasonable to assume that the mother is selecting among these strategies as the infant exhibits less and less distress.

Dyad 105 follows a similar pattern by first cycling between States 1 and 2 until finally moving to State 5, which differs from State 3 mainly by replacing distraction/face-to-face contact with feeding/pacifying as a probable strategy.

Dyads 100, 101, 103, and 104 have relatively short observation periods. Dyads 100 and 103 quickly move to a state that includes low-intensity or no distress. For Dyads 101 and 104 some cycling among States 1, 2, and 3 occurs. Each observation period is relatively short.

We can think of each sequence of states as capturing a piece of the story of the interaction defined by state probabilities common to all dyads.

SUMMARIZING INDIVIDUAL DIFFERENCES. To exemplify one way to use the state sequences based on the posterior probabilities, we show in the bottom panel of Figure 4.8 the percentage of available pairs in each state at each occasion. State 1 represents the highest distress state. We can see that by roughly the 12th observation most infants have moved past the highest level of distress. Because the majority of the crying appears in either State 1 or State 2, we see that by approximately the 20th observation the majority of crying is over. Concomitantly, States 3 and 5, the states indicated by holding and rocking either with feeding and pacifying (State 5) or without (State 3), increase with a slightly higher proportion of dyads in State 5, the feeding/pacifying state indicated by a higher probability of no distress. As we can see, States 4 and 6 represent more transient states indicated by a relatively low frequency of occurrence across all observations.

OTHER APPROACHES TO INDIVIDUAL DIFFERENCES. The modeling approach that we have presented represents one approach to the description of individual differences. This approach is based on a common model that is used to define the states. Individual dyads can thus differ only in the sequence of and duration of time spent in these particular states.

A different approach would involve estimating a separate model for each dyad. In this approach, state definitions could and would most likely differ for dyads, making direct comparisons somewhat more difficult. An intermediate approach would involve an attempt to find subgroups for which a common set of state definitions would be adequate. Within each of the subgroups, comparisons of the sequence and duration of states would be possible. Across subgroups, comparisons of the state definitions would represent an interesting way to compare dyads.

To generate these subgroups, we would consider the following type of approach. Starting with the common model, we could use fit criteria such as the contribution to the loglikelihood to determine which dyads are poorly served by the model. After removing those dyads we would reestimate the model for the remaining dyads. State sequences based on posterior probabilities could then be used to describe individual differences within that group. A common model could then be estimated on the basis of the remaining dyads, and the procedure would be repeated until the subgroups have been determined. Within each of the subgroups individual differences would be described in a similar fashion. Between-subgroups differences in the definitions of the states would be the first indicator used to describe individual differences. A group membership variable could then be used to determine whether differences in infant characteristics (e.g., temperament) or mother characteristics (e.g., personality) can account for group differences.

Conclusion

We believe that a hidden Markov modeling approach to the analysis of mother–infant interactions represents an advance over methods that have been used to model such data in the past. The HMM has the advantage of being able to handle multivariate categorical and continuous variables based on time series data collection. The approach provides descriptions of latent states that represent the probabilities of a set of variables occurring. These variables can include characteristics of members of an interacting system resulting in a state definition that includes, for example, characteristics of different family members. The model results in a relatively transparent description of the dynamics of a process by defining the states, the probability of starting in any of the states, and the probability of transitioning from any one state to any other state. On the basis of these results, trajectories can be determined that describe the sequence of states through which each dyad passes during the observation period. One can use this sequence to describe individual differences by allowing the creation of derived variables that can be used to relate to other variables of interest.

The flexibility of the modeling approach for describing individual differences is further enhanced by adding the possibility of estimating different models for different dyads. This can suggest both quantitative and qualitative differences in the behaviors of these interacting dyads.

References

Bakeman, R., & Gottman, J. M. (1997). *Observing interaction: An introduction to sequential analysis* (2nd ed.). New York, NY: Cambridge University Press.
Baker, J. K. (1975). The dragon system: An overview. *IEEE Transactions on Acoustics, Speech, and Signal Processing, 23,* 24–29. doi:10.1109/TASSP.1975.1162650

Baum, L. E., & Petrie, T. (1966). Statistical inference for probabilistic functions of finite state Markov chains. *Annals of Mathematical Statistics, 37,* 1554–1563. doi:10.1214/aoms/1177699147

Baum, L. E., Petrie, T., Soules, G., & Weiss, N. (1970). A maximization technique occurring in the statistical analysis of probabilistic functions of Markov chains. *Annals of Mathematical Statistics, 41,* 164–171. doi:10.1214/aoms/1177697196

Davidov, M., & Grusec, J. E. (2006). Untangling the kinks of parental responsiveness to distress and warmth to child outcomes. *Child Development, 77,* 44–58. doi:10.1111/j.1467-8624.2006.00855.x

Fahrmeir, L., & Tutz, G. (1994). *Multivariate statistical modeling based on generalized linear models.* New York, NY: Springer-Verlag.

Frühwirth-Schnatter, S. (2006). *Finite mixture and Markov switching models.* New York, NY: Springer-Verlag.

Jahromi, L. B., Putnam, S. P., & Stifter, C. A. (2004). Maternal regulation of infant reactivity from 2 to 6 months. *Developmental Psychology, 40,* 477–487. doi:10.1037/0012-1649.40.4.477

Jelinek, F., Bahl, L. R., & Mercer, R. L. (1982). Design of a linguistic statistical decoder for the recognition of continuous speech. *IEEE Transactions on Information Theory, 21,* 250–256.

Leinert, G., von Eye, A., & Rovine, M. (1987). Adjustment of item intercorrelations using symmetry transformations. *EDV in Medizin und Biologie, 18,* 118–124.

Rabiner, L. R. (1989). A tutorial on hidden Markov models and selected applications in speech recognition. *Proceedings of the IEEE, 77,* 257–286.

Roberts, W. L., & Strayer, J. (1987). Parents' responses to the emotional distress of their children: Relations with children's competence. *Developmental Psychology, 23,* 415–422.

Visser, I. (2005). *Depmix: An R-package for fitting mixture models on mixed multivariate data with Markov dependencies.* Unpublished manuscript, Department of Psychology, University of Amsterdam, Amsterdam, The Netherlands.

Visser, I., Raijmakers, M. E. J., & Molenaar, P. C. M. (2002). Fitting hidden Markov models to psychological data. *Science Progress, 10,* 185–199.

Part II

Dynamics of Learning

5

Decomposing the Performance Dynamics of Learning Through Time Scales

Karl M. Newell, Gottfried Mayer-Kress,
S. Lee Hong, and Yeou-Teh Liu

The most common experimental strategy to investigate the processes of learning is to analyze the change in performance outcome on a task or tasks over time. Learning is typically understood in terms of the outcome of the action of a sequence of performance trials on a given task that may occur over a single practice session or over days, weeks, months, or even years of practice (Bryan & Harter, 1897; Crossman, 1959; Ebbinghaus, 1964). This standard analytical approach has led to the study of the dynamics of *learning curves* as the entry (and actually, in many cases, the end point) into revealing the processes of learning and development (Lane, 1987; A. Newell & Rosenbloom, 1981; Snoddy, 1926). It is consistent with the time-honored theoretical notion that learning is reflected in a relatively permanent change in behavior over time (Hilgard & Bower, 1975).

The consequence is that all theories of learning and/or development need to be able to account for the change in performance dynamics over time. The received position on the function of learning is still that of A. Newell and Rosenbloom (1981), who claimed that the *power law* is the universal law of learning. Not until the recent few years of the 21st century has this postulation been challenged from several independent directions (Gallistel, Fairhurst, & Balsam, 2004; Heathcote, Brown, & Mewhort, 2000; K. M. Newell, Liu, & Mayer-Kress, 2001). One of the sources of the challenge reflects a focus of this book, namely, the problem that averaged group functions of learning on many occasions fail to map to the individual pathways of change over time in the performance dynamics.

The approach of mapping a single function to the performance dynamics is grounded in the theoretical postulation of a single process organizing learning and the persistent change in performance over time. The long-standing view is that learning, retention, and transfer are different faces of the same process that is captured in the central construct of *memory strength* (Adams, 1987). The

This work was supported by National Science Foundation Grant 0518845.

performance outcome is taken to reflect the memory strength largely on the basis of the positive influence of the degree of repetition (practice) and the negative influence of the increasing time between practice (or retention) sessions. Indeed, current notions of the power law of learning are still predicated on these assumptions of a single process for learning (Anderson, Fincham, & Douglass, 1999), although by definition a power law has infinite time scales within the range examined. Nevertheless, there is a long history in learning research that has taken the position that the performance dynamics of learning curves are the product of multiple processes that, in addition to memory strength, include constructs such as warm-up, inhibition, noise, and fatigue (Adams, 1961; Hull, 1943; Tucker, 1966).

In this chapter, we build on our dynamical systems theoretical perspective on motor learning and development (K. M. Newell et al., 2001; K. M. Newell, Liu, & Mayer-Kress, 2003, 2005) in presenting a system identification approach to revealing the processes of learning through the determination of the characteristic time scales of performance dynamics. This approach also leads naturally to theoretical and operational distinctions in the analysis of individual and group data—a central focus of this book. Overall, the goal is to reveal the persistent and transitory processes that support the dynamics of the individual pathways of change in learning and development.

Multiple Processes to Performance Dynamics

One of the major challenges in learning research is to interpret the patterns in the performance dynamics, that is, the change in performance outcome over time and the processes that produce them. In the movement domain there are many movement-related variables that could be examined as an index of the change in performance over time, but traditionally the outcome in relation to the action goal has been the focus of investigation. A long-recognized caveat is that learning is an indirect construct in that it is an inference drawn from the change(s) in the performance dynamics. Thus, one directly observes changes in performance, not learning, which is why some have preferred to speak of *performance curves* rather than *learning curves* (Schmidt & Lee, 2005).

Many processes influence performance at any moment in time, together with the sequential product of performance in practice trials. This perspective is well supported by the multiple rates of performance change that are shown in Figure 5.1, which is from Bryan and Harter's (1897) classic early learning study. The figure shows the learning profiles of two participants learning to send and receive Morse code over many weeks of practice. Bryan and Harter recognized the many rates of change in performance dynamics, including the segments of no change over time that are known as *plateaus* in the performance profile. The multiple rates of change in the performance dynamics, such as those shown in Figure 5.1, make inferences about the processes of learning difficult or, at best, less than straightforward.

The data from Bryan and Harter (1897) in Figure 5.1 are from individuals and thus reflect the individual processes of learning, including what some have

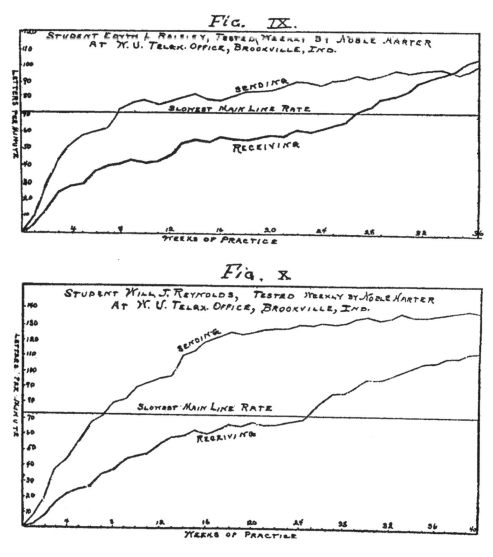

Figure 5.1. Data from two participants learning to receive and send Morse code. From "Studies in the Physiology and Psychology of Telegraphic Language," by W. L. Bryan and N. Harter, 1897, *Psychological Review, 4,* p. 49. In the public domain.

interpreted as randomlike trial-to-trial fluctuations in the performance outcome. The traditional approach to removing this randomlike individual change in the performance dynamics has been to average the data over groups of individuals or trials, usually both. The long-standing idea has been that this averaging of the data deemphasizes the small randomlike changes in the performance dynamics, giving more presence to the apparent persistent memory strength–based changes of learning. However, even with data averaging there is still considerable evidence for multiple processes of learning in the performance dynamics, although the resultant outcome of averaging is usually a smoother learning curve.

A good example of multiple processes in group-averaged data can be found in a study conducted by Adams (1952) on young adults learning the pursuit rotor task. Figure 5.2 shows changes that could be used to support inferences about at least the following processes of learning: the persistent negatively accelerating improvement in performance over time that is typically taken to reflect the persistent changes of learning; the drop-off of performance at the beginning of the next practice session and the rapid recovery from that, known as a *warm-up decrement;* the small drop-off in performance during the final segment of the practice session; and, finally, the randomlike trial-to-trial fluctuations. Thus, at first glance one can interpret the data in Figure 5.2 as reflecting the process of learning, the adaptive processes of warm-up and fatigue (inhibition), and randomlike trial-to-trial processes. Of course, these inferences are based on observation rather than analysis strategies, but the more rapid adaptive processes in the performance dynamics of learning curves can be seen in many studies of motor learning (cf. Schmidt & Lee, 2005).

Thus, there is long-standing evidence for multiple-process contributions to the performance dynamics of learning, but there are still approaches to learning that emphasize only the single process of accumulating memory strength for the performance dynamics. As noted earlier in this chapter, memory strength theories of learning tend to emphasize the number of repetitions of practice trials and the time course between practice sessions. These are fundamental variables of learning, but their significance does not rule out the multidimensional view of the learning process; it just gives a simpler—and, in our view, probably less veridical—framework in which to consider the problem of learning. Finally, it should be recognized that, even if one wants to promote a single construct for a memory strength account of learning, contemporary work in neuroscience has revealed multiple processes of memory consolidation that each have their own time scale of change on the performance dynamics (Kandel, 2006; Shadmehr & Holcomb, 1997; Tse et al., 2007).

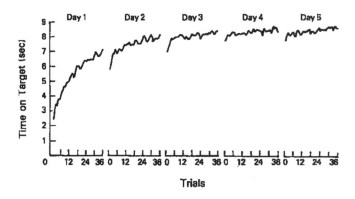

Figure 5.2. Pursuit rotor learning data as a function of days and trials. From "Warm-Up Decrement in Performance on the Pursuit-Rotor," by J. A. Adams, 1952, *American Journal of Psychology, 65,* p. 408. Copyright 1952 by University of Illinois Press. Reprinted with permission.

Time Scales to Decompose Performance Dynamics

The term *time scales* has increasingly been used in recent years in regard to the study of learning and development. This has particularly been the case in approaches to the question of changes in human behavior that are driven by the concepts of connectionist and dynamical systems to behavior and physiology and, more generally, the different levels of analysis of neuroscience. Given the breadth of use of the term *time scales* it is perhaps not surprising that it has sparked different definitions, interpretations, and uses in research.

The most general and common usage of the term *time scales* is to refer to the time or duration of an event, a process to unfold, or an action. In this framework the idea of *shorter* or *longer* time scales refers to the length of time of the event in question. This notion fits nicely with the use of clock time to capture the time scale of an event, as in years, months, weeks, days, hours, minutes, and seconds. These units of time imply the notion of different time scales, whereas the phrase *different time scales* refers to measurement systems with different units to measure the passage of time. However, although the time scale of a day is based on the dynamical process of the circadian rhythm of the rotation of the earth, not all units of time are based on or constrained by dynamical processes. For example, the forms of time known as dynamical, *atomic time* and *coordinate time,* are not based on the standard unit of the day (Haliday, Resnick, & Walker, 2005), but they do relate to properties of dynamical systems.

K. M. Newell et al. (2001) outlined that there are two types of idealized dynamical systems that give rise naturally to the concept of time scales: (a) periodic oscillations (Haken, 1983) and (b) growth/decay at a constant rate (Kaplan & Glass, 1995). In oscillatory systems the intrinsic time scale of the system is the period that is the inverse of frequency that the system requires to complete a full oscillation. In growth/decay systems the intrinsic time scale is the inverse of the growth/decay rate that is also expressed as *doubling* or *half-life* time. In this view of the dynamical systems approach a time scale is not simply the duration of an event but an event that arises from the motions of dynamical processes.

The formal significance of the basic dynamical processes in characterizing a time scale can be expressed as a complex exponential function:

$$x(t) = A e^{(\gamma + i\omega)t}. \qquad (5.1)$$

Here, A is the position at time $t = 0$; the real part of γ of the exponent is the growth/decay rate; and the imaginary part, ω, is the frequency of oscillation. Also, significantly, the reciprocal of the growth or decay rate is the intrinsic or characteristic time scale of the system.

The oscillatory and growth/decay processes just outlined are fundamental to describing behavior close to a *fixed point*—the mathematical concept that is associated with equilibrium regions of the dynamics. Fixed points correspond to the absence of motion in a pendulum at rest. In these systems the motion close to a fixed point can be approximated to be linear. This allows the motion of the trajectory to be characterized by the exponential function of Equation 5.1. Furthermore, the time scale of a growth or decay process to a fixed point is the time for the dynamics to double/half the fixed point.

The principles of dynamical systems allow the processes of learning to be characterized by a superposition of exponential functions that reflect the characteristic time scales of the processes driving the change in performance outcome over time. Furthermore, the multiple time scales of change in task outcome over time are interpreted to originate from the system's trajectory on an evolving attractor landscape (K. M. Newell et al., 2001, 2003, 2005). These time scales can be visualized from the system's trajectory on an attractor landscape, where performance improvements and mastery of the skill can be represented as the eventual stabilization of behavior at the fixed point attractor.

More complicated dynamics of performance outcome can be realized from bifurcations between attractor organizations and transient phenomena. The net result is not that there is a single function of change but rather that a small set of dynamical principles can capture the different functions of change in learning. The general consequence is that the dynamical framework of time scales provides a rational approach to the analysis of learning curves (Thurstone, 1919) in addition to a standard descriptive percentage of variance–driven curve-fitting approach. A dynamical approach tries to understand learning by drawing inferences from the pattern of change in the performance dynamics as opposed to the more traditional view, which focuses on the magnitude of change in performance outcome.

Individual and Averaged Performance Dynamics

It has long been recognized that the function for learning in individual learning curves is typically different than it is in those derived from averaged data (Bahrick, Fitts, & Briggs, 1957; Estes, 1956). A formal position was offered by Tucker (1966), who stated that unless the individual learning curves are linear transformations of each other then the averaged curve would always be nonrepresentative of the data. More recently, Molenaar (2000, 2008) has shown, through ergodic theory, that the standard statistical techniques of interindividual variability are invalid unless a very restricted set of conditions on the intraindividual variability and performance dynamics data are met, which usually they are not.

The net result is that veridical inferences about individual pathways of change in learning and development are not generally possible from the analysis of averaged data. Indeed, in principle, the worst-case scenario could arise of an averaged function for change being of a different class (e.g., a power law) than those of all the individuals in the group (e.g., exponential). Nevertheless, it is still the case that most theoretical and experimental analyses of the functions of learning and development are based on averaged data. It is our position that decomposing the time scales of the respective performance dynamics provides insight into the relation of individual and averaged pathways of change (K. M. Newell et al., 2001, K. M. Newell, Mayer-Kress, & Liu, 2006).

In general, there are two forms of averaging that typically occur in the analysis of learning curves. The most common is that of averaging data across participants, resulting in the inclusion of interindividual variability in the analysis of the performance dynamics. The second form averages individual trial data over blocks or groups of trials. However, in most motor learning studies both forms of averaging are present (as seen in Figure 5.2). These forms of data averaging coalesce to change observations about the time scales of the performance dynamics and can lead to spurious inferences about the functions of learning and development.

As an example, K. M. Newell et al. (2001) showed through simulation that one can approximate a power law from a superposition of exponentials; that is, a family of individual exponential curves with different exponents can be averaged to approximate a power law. Figure 5.3 shows this averaging effect for the superposition of just two exponential functions. Thus, the tendency to find power laws as the function of learning (e.g., A. Newell & Rosenbloom, 1981) could simply be a consequence of the averaging of individual exponential learning. If this were the case, it would be a classic example of the averaging of data to change the resultant class of function of the performance dynamics. This observation becomes particularly important because we have not found in the literature any demonstrations of individual power law motor learning in which the technically appropriate contrast of functions has been made. Furthermore, the problem of averaging data across individual participants is magnified when the functions for learning show transitions and not a continuous monotonic change (Liu, Mayer-Kress, & Newell, 2006).

In motor learning the trials are also usually blocked into averages over groups of trials. This analysis strategy is often used to reduce the trial-to-trial fluctuations, but the consequence is that the time scale of the change of the performance dynamics is compromised. The following extreme case proves the

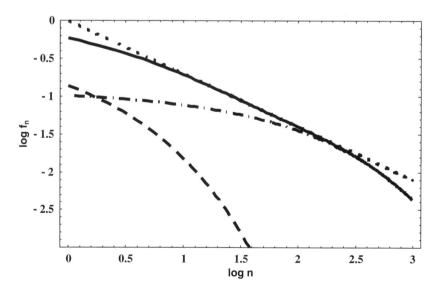

Figure 5.3.   Simulation of a power law function (short dashed line) from two exponential functions (dot-dashed and long-dashed lines). From "Time Scales in Motor Learning and Development," by K. M. Newell, Y.-T. Liu, and G. Mayer-Kress, 2001, *Psychological Review, 108,* p. 68. Copyright 2001 by the American Psychological Association.

point. Consider blocking a set of learning data (individual or group averaged) into only two data points based on the average of the first half of the trials and the average of the second half of the trials: The outcome is a straight line for the function of learning! Liu, Mayer-Kress, and Newell (2003) showed that increasing the number of trials in the trial blocking of data has a systematic effect on the estimate of the time scale of change.

The determination of the function of learning in a century of study has largely been driven by the percentage-of-variance estimates of strictly curve-fitting procedures that are uninfluenced by theory and without consideration of model comparison procedures such as the Akaike Information Criterion (AIC). Model comparison procedures such as the AIC account for the number of parameters of the model and the number of data points included in the fitting process. This methodological consideration is noteworthy because the difference in the percentage of variance accounted for between, for example, an exponential and a power law, is often very small in learning studies (see, e.g., A. Newell & Rosenbloom, 1981). Also, without theory to guide and constrain the curve fitting, as is often the case, the evaluation of the function of learning is on shaky ground. Aside from the need for theory to constrain the curve fitting of the performance dynamics there is an operational need to consider the qualitative properties of the function fitted. Liu et al. (2003) introduced, in an examination of the learning of a limb movement timing task, the proportionality test of the rate of change (a constant for exponentials) and a "fat tail" measure of the change over time as qualitative approaches to test for exponential change.

Thus, averaging learning data typically changes the time scale of the performance dynamics regardless of whether the averaging is done across individuals, trials, or both. It is important to note that most analyses to date of the function of performance dynamics have been of averaged data (cf. Lane, 1987; A. Newell & Rosenbloom, 1981). The net result is that our knowledge of the individual pathways of change in the performance dynamics is very limited and, moreover, may be biased by the consequences of averaging data.

Time Scales and Models of Learning

A central assumption of our dynamical approach to learning is that a mapping can be made between the dynamics of the system state space and learning as reflected in the learning curves of a task outcome variable. The projection is that a small set of dynamical principles can produce a number of functions for learning (exponential, power law, S-shaped, etc.) that have been shown in a variety of learning contexts. Thus, in our view there is not a single function of learning but rather multiple time scales of change that arise from multiple processes that support the emergent performance dynamics and what is known as *motor skill learning* (K. M. Newell et al., 2001).

Motor learning and development are the consequences of the confluence of task, environmental, and organismic constraints to action (K. M. Newell, 1986). Learning theories have traditionally given different emphases to the roles of the organism and the environment in learning, as in the different emphases on nature and nurture, but the role of task constraints in learning and development traditionally has not been considered seriously, in spite of the fact that different kinds of motor tasks tend to lead to different kinds of pathways of change in motor learning.

One useful distinction about motor tasks is that some seem to require a transition in the coordination mode to achieve the task goal, whereas with others the participant has to merely learn to rescale a coordination mode (in terms of space, time, or force) that can already be produced. From this perspective, K. M. Newell (1985) projected that most experimental studies of motor learning, as in the pursuit rotor, single limb positioning and timing tasks, isometric force production, and so on, required primarily the rescaling of a coordination mode that could already be produced. This class of tasks seems to map well to the consideration of learning as that of fixed-point dynamics where there are no changes in the attractor landscape. In contrast, there are motor tasks that require the learning of a new coordination mode—as in, for example, the fundamental movement sequence of infancy, learning to juggle, and ride a bicycle—whereby the learner is at first unable to perform the task and, after some practice, masters a task-relevant coordination pattern. As a consequence, the practice-induced transitions in the coordination mode can be represented as changes in the attractor landscape. Changes in the attractor landscape are also more likely to occur as the duration of learning the task over the life span increases and if it maps to particular more rapid and extensive periods of developmental change (K. M. Newell et al., 2001).

Thus, in our view the different kinds of change with learning reflect different changes in the attractor dynamics but nevertheless are all part of a coherent dynamical approach to learning that is based on a few core principles (K. M. Newell et al., 2001, 2003, 2005). Our modeling approach has been to begin with the study of tasks that are widely used in experimental psychology. This class of tasks can be viewed as the scaling of an already-learned coordination mode in that they yield performance dynamics that are reflected by gradual improvements toward the individual's point of best performance. Such performance dynamics are particularly suited to be modeled by a superposition of exponentials that correspond to particular growth and decay processes. In contrast, there are skills that require the learner to acquire and stabilize a never-before-produced coordination mode, and the dynamics of learning this class of tasks require the consideration of bifurcations in the attractor dynamics (Liu et al., 2006) that would be observed as an abrupt jump in performance. The learning patterns of such skills (e.g., riding a bicycle) would not lend themselves to a superposition of exponential functions and can be represented only by more complex models.

Two-Time-Scale Model of Motor Learning

One of the most prevalent trends in the practice data of learning studies is for there to be a warm-up decrement at the beginning of the subsequent practice session; that is, after a period during which no practice takes place—for example, a day or a week—there is a decrement in performance on the initial performance trial of the new practice session and a relatively rapid performance improvement over the subsequent early trials to reachieve performance that is at the level of the previous practice session. This decrement in performance is known as a *warm-up decrement* and is generally interpreted as a separate process from that of the relatively permanent process of change (Adams, 1961). This more rapid change in performance has also been interpreted as part of the single persistent change of learning and the memory strength losses over time without practice, which occur as the result of forgetting that takes place between practice sessions (Anderson et al., 1999).

The two-time-scale model characterizes the observed performance improvements as an exponential approach toward a fixed point that occurs along two characteristic time scales, one associated with slow but persistent change (learning) and the other one with a fast but transient improvement (warm-up adaptation). Both processes are in effect active during a practice session; however, some of the fast time scale gains are relinquished during the rest period. Between the practice sessions the adaptation dynamics reverses their sign, thereby degrading the performance level, whereas the slow time scale learning dynamics continue to progress toward the goal state, albeit at a different rate. One can then extrapolate the time taken to complete the trials using the exponents of the model, transitioning from trials as the unit of time to clock time of hours, minutes, and seconds.

We modeled the performance dynamics as the superposition of two exponential functions with different characteristic exponents associated with each of the above-mentioned processes:

$$V_j(n) = V_{inf} + a_s e^{-\gamma_s n} + a_j e^{-\gamma_j(n-n_{j-1})}. \qquad (5.2)$$

The characteristic time scale model in Equation 5.2 can be used on individual or group-averaged learning data. The model captures a performance variable, $V_j(n)$, that converges to an asymptotic target value, V_{inf}, as time n—measured in units of trial numbers—increases. The slow time scale (s) is taken across all the data, whereas the fast time scale (j) is taken on the trials from each day. Example fits of the two-time-scale model to two individual learners practicing a computerized star tracing task for 50 trials per day over 5 days are shown in the upper panels of Figure 5.4 (Stratton, Liu, Hong, Mayer-Kress, & Newell, 2007).

This model has a slow ($-\gamma_s$) exponent and a fast ($-\gamma_j$) exponent that describe the time scales of change in performance between and within practice days. The sequence of practice days is denoted by the subscript j; thus, the slow time scale progresses as a function of the overall trial number, n, whereas the fast time scale is a function of the trials within each day. The trial numbers for the fast time scale are reset at the beginning of each day, when the first trial of each day is always equal to 1. This is achieved by setting the performance changes within a practice day as the exponential function $n - n_{j-1}$, where n_j represents the last trial of each day. As a result, if a practice day has 20 trials, $n_j = 20$ when $j = 1$, and $n_j = 40$ when $j = 2$, and so on. Thus, if it is the first trial of the second practice day, $n - n_{j-1} = 21 - 20 = 1$. When the two-time-scale model is fitted to the data different values are obtained for a_j when $j = 1$ and for all $j > 1$. The value of γ_j is constant for all values of j. Having a different parameter for a_j for the first day allows for a better approximation of the rapid performance gains

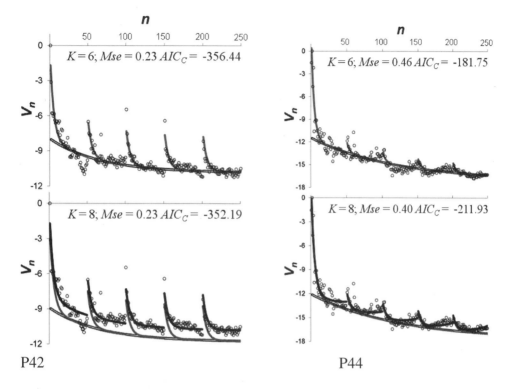

P42   P44

Figure 5.4.   Data from two participants (Ps) learning to draw through a maze with two- and three-time-scale model fits. Data are from Stratton et al. (2007). AIC = Akaike Information Criterion.

that are seen during early practice, albeit along the same time scale of change (constant γ_j).

K. M. Newell, Mayer-Kress, Hong and Liu (2009) contrasted the fit of the two-time-scale model with several other model equations on the data of four motor learning studies that included both group and individual trial analyses. The models compared were those that the authors saw as the primary published candidate models for motor learning in addition to variants of the characteristic time scale model. The eight models compared were (a) exponential, (b) power law, (c) Anderson et al.'s (1999) power law model (AFD), (d) two-power law, (e) five-parameter two-time scale, (f) six-parameter two-time scale, (g) five-parameter two-time scale (with adaptation off during practice), and (h) six-parameter two-time scale (with adaptation off during practice). Here we emphasize the contrast between the two-time-scale model and the AFD model that has the following form:

$$\text{AFD model:} V_n = A - B * \sum_{i=1}^{n} t_{ij}^{-d}, \qquad (5.3)$$

where $t_{ij} = n - i + jH$, t_{ij} is a representation of the time that has passed since the ith performance of the task on the jth practice day, where n represents the number of evenly spaced trials performed since the beginning of the experiment. H represents a multiplier that approximates the number of practice trials equivalent to the passing of a day when no trials were performed on that day. In the AFD model the parameter A denotes the best performance level. The parameter B provides the difference in the level of cognitive complexity if compared across tasks. Larger values of B are indicative of a less cognitively complex task because the rate of the memory strength gain is enhanced by this multiplier.

For two data sets the AFD was a slightly better fit than the two-time-scale model, and for the other two data sets the reverse outcome was obtained. Of key interest was that the two-time-scale model tended to fit the data better than the AFD model on the individual-trial analyses. It is relevant that this trend can be predicted from the observation noted earlier whereby averaging can introduce artificial time scales to the data. Thus, our preliminary analysis shows that the two-time-scale model holds up well in contrast to traditional functions of learning, even on averaged data. The analysis that is fully presented in K. M. Newell et al.'s article (2009) shows that the two-time-scale model is a viable alternative to consider in the study of learning, but it has a theoretical basis that is very different from those of established models.

The AFD model views performance decrements between practice sessions as degradation in memory. The two-time-scale model, however, views these as the loss of transient gains that need to be readapted during the early portions of each practice session, a warm-up process. On the slower time scale performance improvements continue as the persistent aspects of change are not lost and continue to be stabilized. A second theoretical difference pertains to the units of time used by the models. Whereas the AFD holds that practice is a function of "psychological" time, the exponents in our two-time-scale model can be converted from trials to actual wall clock time. Thus, one can estimate the loss of performance between practice sessions by simply reversing the sign of the fast-time-scale exponent and using the number of hours that have passed between practice sessions to estimate its decay. We were able to do this using Snoddy's (1926) data as presented in K. M. Newell et al.'s (2009) article.

Empirically speaking, the AFD model would predict that practicing once a week would result in a much slower accumulation of memory strength than practice once a day, that is, longer rest periods between practice sessions result in slower learning and delayed performance gains. However, the two-time-scale model would hold that the actual trajectory of persistent learning gains would remain unaltered by the amount of time between practice sessions. Rather, the rate of performance gains (fast-time-scale exponent) during practice and the length of time between sessions would determine the magnitude of between-session performance losses. Unlike the AFD, these losses would then be rapidly regained at the beginning of the following practice session, allowing for performance to rejoin the trajectory of the slow time scale by the end of the practice session. These distinct differences in predictions that each of the models provide clearly highlight the need for experiments that directly test the different predictions of the two-time-scale and AFD models, moving their comparisons beyond goodness of fit.

Three-Time-Scale Model of Motor Learning

Human learning is not necessarily the product of practice and rest alone because there are other processes that could influence an individual's performance dynamics. An important feature of our approach to the decomposition of characteristic time scales in the performance dynamics is that the basic two-time-scale equation of superimposed exponentials can be extended to accommodate additional adaptive processes associated with learning. To provide an example, we add here a growth process for fatigue/inhibition that is building up through the practice trials of each session (Hull, 1943) and that in some instances leads to a performance decrement in the later trials of a practice session. This adaptive process has a negative effect on the performance dynamics and, therefore this process is taken into account as a reversal of performance gains along a third time scale (γ_f):

$$V_f(n) = V_{inf} + a_s e^{-\gamma_s n} + a_j e^{-\gamma_j(n-nj-1)} + a_f e^{\gamma_f(n-nj-1)}. \qquad (5.4)$$

Keeping in mind that the task variable requires a minimization of the outcome score, the fatigue exponential is a growth process, hence the positive exponent of γ_f that represents a movement away from better performance. When fitted to the data different values are obtained for a_j when $j = 1$ and for all js > 1, similar to the two-time-scale model. Parameter values obtained for a_f, γ_f, and γ_j were constant across all values of j.

Figure 5.4 depicts the fit with the two- and three- (bottom panels) time-scale models and shows that the additional process of fatigue/inhibition is present in only one of the participants. This observation is supported by the mean square error and AIC comparisons. Although the addition of the third time scale reduces the mean square error for the fit of the data from Participant 44, the mean square error remained unchanged for the fit of Participant 42. Thus, the additional two parameters for the third time scale resulted in a poorer AIC score for the fit of Participant 42, showing that the added parameters were superfluous. This is an example of how learning dynamics can clearly differ from one individual to another. Visual inspection of the data from Participant 42 indicates that this participant continued to improve toward the later trials of the practice session. Participant 44, on the other hand, clearly showed signs of fatigue, as evidenced by the decline in performance during the trials near the end of the session. What we have here is an agreement between the inferences made on the basis of the dynamical approach and a qualitative visual inspection of the performance data. These individual differences—in particular, process contributions to the performance dynamics—would have been lost in the analysis of averaged learning curves. The time scale approach provides a framework to explore individual differences in performance gains during practice, allowing inferences about different processes of adaptation and learning in the performance dynamics.

Further Model Development and Limitations

The characteristic time scale model of superimposing exponentials can in principle be extended to include a large number of adaptive processes beyond those presented here. There may well be some practical limits, however, to the number of exponentials that can be meaningfully superimposed, in particular as a function of the degree of trial-to-trial fluctuations. Of course, in principle an infinite set of distinct time scales would lead to a power law, but this theoretical possibility is unlikely to be strictly met by the data. Several theoretical aspects to the basic characteristic time model need to be tested and developed further, and we now consider some of these.

First, we assume here that the time scale for the adaptive change of warm-up is the same for each practice session. This assumption simplifies the model, appears to fit the data well, and is a useful conservative approach to the modeling strategy. Nevertheless, more detailed study of the initial conditions of a practice session is in order. For example, in Figure 5.2 it appears that, on average, more skilled performers require fewer trials to warm up, even if the rate of change of the adaptive process is preserved over practice. On the other hand, observation suggests that highly skilled performers in a range of physical activities have extensive warm-up routines that probably exceed those of relative beginners in terms of time duration and number of repetitions.

Second, the examinations to date that we have made of the decay process of fatigue and inhibition have shown more between-participant variability than that of the warm-up process. This may be due in part to the particular practice schedule used in each of the data sets we have examined. Thus, a more massed, and longer, duration of practice in a session would be expected to reveal a stronger role for the influence of the decaying adaptive process on the performance dynamics. The time scale decomposition strategy might also help distinguish distinct roles for fatigue and inhibition, which we have used loosely here as a collective negative process to performance. Moreover, the composition strategy would be useful when relooking at massed and distributed practice effects on learning and the general and traditional distinction between learning and performance.

Third, our characteristic time scale model has each process in the respective equation continually evolving in time. There are theoretical reasons for this assumption, and support was obtained from our initial tests contrasting this assumption against the same time scale model with the adaptive process turned off when the persistent learning process is on (K. M. Newell et al., 2009). Nevertheless, there has been little systematic study of the different ways to represent the time scale of change in performance dynamics, and the current model, among others, could be further investigated in this regard.

Fourth, the modeling approach presented here to performance dynamics and learning does not take into account the role of random stochastic processes. Nevertheless, it is possible to generalize the characteristic time scale model approach to include stochastic processes. Some beginning developments along these lines were presented by Liu, Mayer-Kress, and Newell (1999).

Finally, we reiterate that this model of adaption and learning is limited to performance change that can be modeled as fixed-point dynamics. This assumption fits well with data from many of the scaling tasks that have been used to study motor learning. Our modeling to date has emphasized three critical aspects: (a) the persistence of learning and the more transient adaptive processes of (b) warm-up and (c) fatigue. Although the modeling here is conducted in terms of trials, we have shown that the time scale of change holds up just as well in real clock time (K. M. Newell et al., 2009) without the need to invoke the more abstract notion of psychological time (Anderson et al., 1999). A broader set of dynamics is required to model the influence of the confluence of organismic, environmental, and task constraints to learning and performance over the life span that give rise to transient processes and bifurcations (Liu et al., 2006; K. M. Newell et al., 2001).

References

Adams, J. A. (1952). Warm-up decrement in performance on the pursuit-rotor. *American Journal of Psychology, 65,* 404–414. doi:10.2307/1418761

Adams, J. A. (1961). The second facet of forgetting: A review of warm-up decrement. *Psychological Bulletin, 58,* 257–273. doi:10.1037/h0044798

Adams, J. A. (1987). Historical review and appraisal of research on learning, retention, and transfer of human motor skills. *Psychological Bulletin, 101,* 41–74. doi:10.1037/0033-2909.101.1.41

Anderson, J. R., Fincham, J. M., & Douglass, S. (1999). Practice and retention: A unifying analysis. *Journal of Experimental Psychology: Learning, Memory, and Cognition, 25,* 1120–1136. doi:10.1037/0278-7393.25.5.1120

Bahrick, H. P., Fitts, P. M., & Briggs, G. E. (1957). Learning curves—Facts or artifacts? *Psychological Bulletin, 54,* 256–268. doi:10.1037/h0040313

Bryan, W. L., & Harter, N. (1897). Studies in the physiology and psychology of telegraphic language. *Psychological Review, 4,* 27–53. doi:10.1037/h0073806

Crossman, E. R. F. W. (1959). A theory of the acquisition of speed-skill. *Ergonomics, 2,* 153–166. doi:10.1080/00140135908930419

Ebbinghaus, H. (1964). *Memory: A contribution to experimental psychology.* New York, NY: Dover.

Estes, W. K. (1956). The problem of inference from curves based upon group data. *Psychological Bulletin, 53,* 134–140. doi:10.1037/h0045156

Gallistel, C. R., Fairhurst, S., & Balsam, P. (2004). The learning curve: Implications of a quantitative analysis. *Proceedings of the National Academy of Sciences USA, 101,* 13124–13131. doi:10.1073/pnas.0404965101

Haken, H. (1983). *Synergetics: An introduction* (3rd ed.). Berlin, Germany: Springer-Verlag.

Haliday, D., Resnick, R., & Walker, J. (2005). *Fundamentals of physics* (6th ed.). New York, NY: Wiley.

Heathcote, A., Brown, S., & Mewhort, D. J. K. (2000). The power law repealed: The case for an exponential law of practice. *Psychonomic Bulletin & Review, 7,* 185–207. Hilgard, E. R., & Bower, G. H. (1975). *Theories of learning.* Englewood Cliffs, NJ: Prentice Hall.

Hull, C. L. (1943). *Principles of behaviour: An introduction to behavior theory.* New York, NY: Appleton-Century-Crofts.

Kandel, E. R. (2006). *In search of memory: The emergence of a new science of the mind.* New York, NY: Norton.

Kaplan, D., & Glass, L. (1995). *Understanding nonlinear dynamics.* New York, NY: Springer-Verlag.

Lane, N. E. (1987). *Skill acquisition rates and patterns: Issues and training implications.* New York, NY: Springer-Verlag.

Liu, Y.-T., Mayer-Kress, G., & Newell, K. M. (1999). A piecewise linear map model for the sequential trial strategy of discrete timing tasks. *Acta Psychologica, 103,* 207–228. doi:10.1016/S0001-6918(99)00037-2

Liu, Y.-T., Mayer-Kress, G., & Newell, K. M. (2003). Beyond curve fitting to inferences about learning. *Journal of Motor Behavior, 35,* 197–207.

Liu, Y.-T., Mayer-Kress, G., & Newell, K. M. (2006). Qualitative and quantitative change in the dynamics of motor learning. *Journal of Experimental Psychology: Human Perception and Performance, 32,* 380–393. doi:10.1037/0096-1523.32.2.380

Molenaar, P. C. M. (2000). A manifesto on psychology as idiographic science: Bringing the person back into scientific psychology, this time forever. *Measurement: Interdisciplinary Research & Perspective, 2,* 201–218.

Molenaar, P. C. M. (2008). On the implications of the classical ergodic theorems: Analysis of developmental processes has to focus on intra-individual variation. *Developmental Psychobiology, 50,* 60–69. doi:10.1002/dev.20262

Newell, A., & Rosenbloom, P. S. (1981). Mechanisms of skill acquisition and the law of practice. In J. R. Anderson (Ed.), *Cognitive skills and their acquisition* (pp. 1–55). Hillsdale, NJ: Erlbaum.

Newell, K. M. (1985). Coordination, control and skill. In D. Goodman, I. Franks, & R. Wilberg (Eds.), *Differing perspectives in motor learning, memory and control* (pp. 295–317). Amsterdam, The Netherlands: North-Holland.

Newell, K. M. (1986). Constraints on the development of coordination. In M. G. Wade & H. T. A. Whiting (Eds.), *Motor skill acquisition in children: Aspects of coordination and control* (pp. 341–360). Amsterdam, The Netherlands: Martinus Nijhof.

Newell, K. M., Liu, Y.-T., & Mayer-Kress, G. (2001). Time scales in motor learning and development. *Psychological Review, 108,* 57–82. doi:10.1037/0033-295X.108.1.57

Newell, K. M., Liu, Y.-T., & Mayer-Kress, G. (2003). A dynamical systems interpretation of epigenetic landscapes for infant motor development. *Infant Behavior and Development, 26,* 449–472. doi:10.1016/j.infbeh.2003.08.003

Newell, K. M., Liu, Y.-T., & Mayer-Kress, G. (2005). Learning in the brain–computer interface: Insights about degrees of freedom and degeneracy in a landscape model of motor learning. *Cognitive Processing, 6,* 37–47. doi:10.1007/s10339-004-0047-6

Newell, K. M., Mayer-Kress, G., Hong, S. L., & Liu, Y.-T. (2009). Adaptation and learning: Characteristic time scales of performance dynamics. *Human Movement Science, 28,* 655–687. doi:10.1016/j.humov.2009.07.001

Newell, K. M., Mayer-Kress, G., & Liu, Y.-T. (2006). Human learning: Power laws or multiple characteristic time scales? *Tutorials in Quantitative Methods in Psychology, 2,* 66–76.

Schmidt, R. A., & Lee, T. D. (2005). *Motor control and learning: A behavioral emphasis* (4th ed.). Champaign, IL: Human Kinetics.

Shadmehr, R., & Holcomb, H. H. (1997, August 8). Neural correlates of motor memory consolidation. *Science, 277,* 821–825. doi:10.1126/science.277.5327.821

Snoddy, G. S. (1926). Learning and stability. *Journal of Applied Psychology, 10,* 1–36. doi:10.1037/h0075814

Stratton, S. M., Liu, Y.-T., Hong, S. L., Mayer-Kress, G., & Newell, K. M. (2007). Snoddy revisited: Time scales of motor learning. *Journal of Motor Behavior, 39,* 503–515. doi:10.3200/JMBR.39.6.503-516

Thurstone, L. L. (1919). The learning curve equation. *Psychological Monographs, 26*(Whole No. 114), 1–51.

Tse, D., Langston, R. F., Kakeyama, M., Bethus, I., Spooner, P. A., Wood, E. R., et al. (2007, April 6). Schemas and memory consolidation. *Science, 316,* 76–82. doi:10.1126/science.1135935

Tucker, L. (1966). Learning theory and multivariate experiment: Illustration by determination of generalized learning curves. In R. B. Cattell (Ed.), *Handbook of multivariate experimental psychology* (pp. 476–501). Chicago, IL: Rand McNally.

6

A State Space Approach to Representing Discontinuous Shifts in Change Processes

Sy-Miin Chow and Guillaume Filteau

Outlier detection has been an important topic in all areas of statistical analysis. Within the context of time series analysis, researchers have distinguished between two kinds of outliers: (a) *additive outliers* and (b) *innovative outliers*. Additive outliers are those that affect only the measurement characteristics of a set of data at one single time point. In contrast, innovative outliers affect the dynamic characteristics of the data over an extended period of time (Fox, 1972; Tsay, 1988). Traditionally used to represent the effects of an external intervention (e.g., the introduction of a new political or economic policy, a crash in the stock market that marks the onset of a prolonged recession, enrollment in a drug rehabilitation program), the impact of an innovative outlier may be momentary or, in certain cases, irreversible.

Although the role of additive outliers has been discussed extensively in the psychometric literature, the need to consider innovative outliers in repeated measurement data has rarely been discussed. The scarcity of research on innovative outliers in mainstream modeling work is unfortunate, because innovative outliers can provide key insights into critical developmental and sociobehavioral changes; specifically, innovative outliers can help identify the point(s) at which individuals show uncharacteristic shifts in dynamics. One such example was advanced by Piaget (1960) in his theory of stagewise cognitive development, which posits that critical developmental changes unfold in stages, as opposed to continuously over time. Such critical changes are accompanied by flags such as sudden level shifts and increase in response variability, all of which can be regarded as "innovative outliers" that mark an individual's transition to a new developmental stage.

Methodologically speaking, some of the prevalent approaches for representing discrete changes in dynamics include regime-switching models (Kim & Nelson, 1999); Hidden Markov models (Elliott, Aggoun, & Moore, 1995); latent transition analysis (Collins & Wugalter, 1992); nonlinear dynamical systems

We thank Jason Allaire for allowing us to use his data for the empirical illustration and Michael Marsiske for his comments on earlier versions of this chapter.

models with bifurcation (Van der Maas & Molenaar, 1992);[1] and approaches grounded within popular time series models, such as autoregressive models (Tsay, 1989). In this chapter, we consider a data-driven approach for evaluating signs of discontinuous shifts in dynamics in the exploratory phases of model development. In particular, we propose incorporating individualized discrete shifts in dynamics into a group-based model by extending de Jong and Penzer's (1998) approach for detecting outliers in single-subject state space models (SSMs) to group-based SSMs. Compared with approaches that place explicit emphasis on discrete changes, such as the hidden Markov models, our approach has the flexibility to incorporate both continuous and discontinuous change patterns within a single model. This approach may thus be especially suited to instances in which some but not all individuals in a sample show discontinuous shifts in dynamics over time.

This chapter is organized as follows. We first introduce the state space modeling framework, a general modeling framework on which our simulation examples are based. We then discuss the distinctions between additive and the innovative outliers through a series of simulation examples; specifically, we draw on several published modeling examples in the social and behavioral sciences to demonstrate when and how innovative outliers might be useful in the modeling of human dynamics. We then present a methodological approach for detecting and incorporating outliers into group-based SSMs based on a multiple-subject extension of the approach proposed by de Jong and Penzer (1998). We also discuss, within the context of our modeling examples, further elaborations on how social and behavioral researchers might use variations of the proposed technique to study discrete shifts in dynamics.

State Space Modeling Framework

The state space modeling framework provides a general way of representing the relationships among a set of dynamic latent variables and their associated observed data. Broadly speaking, an SSM encompasses a dynamic model and a measurement model; specifically, we consider multiple-subject or group-based SSMs, wherein modeling parameters are held invariant across persons and time. This SSM specification is expressed as follows:

$$\eta_{i,t+1} = \alpha + B\eta_{it} + H\varepsilon_{it}, \eta_{i1} \sim N(a,P), t=1,\ldots,T; i=1,\ldots,N, \qquad (6.1)$$

$$y_{it} = \tau + \Lambda\eta_{it} + G\varepsilon_{it}, \varepsilon_{it} \sim \text{NID}(0,I), \qquad (6.2)$$

where $\text{NID}(\mu, \Sigma)$ indicates an independent sequence of normally distributed random vectors with mean μ and covariance matrix Σ, η_{it} is a $w \times 1$ vector of latent variables (also called *state variables*) for person i at time t, apprehended through a $p \times 1$ vector of manifest variables, y_{it}; α is a $w \times 1$ vector of constants, B is a $w \times w$ transition matrix depicting the transition of the system from time

---

[1]*Bifurcation* refers to qualitative changes in the dynamics of a system with continuous changes in the parameter(s) of a model.

t to $t + 1$, Λ is a $p \times w$ matrix of factor loadings, τ is a $p \times 1$ vector of constants in the measurement model. Also, ε_{it} is a $u \times 1$ vector of disturbances appearing in both the dynamic and measurement functions, whereas H and G are $w \times u$ and $p \times u$ matrices such that HH' and GG' yield Ψ and Θ, the process noise and measurement noise covariance matrices, respectively. Other SSM specifications may allow some of the elements in α, τ, B, Λ, H, and G to vary across time and persons.

The state space formulation provides a general platform for representing a wide range of linear Gaussian dynamic models, including autoregressive moving average models, dynamic factor analysis models, and growth curve models (see, e.g., Durbin & Koopman, 2001; Harvey, 2001). Once a model has been expressed in state space form, the Kalman filter (KF) and the related Kalman smoothers can be used to estimate η_{it} (viz., an individual's true scores or factor scores) at time t. Specifically, the KF can be used to derive conditional state estimates based on manifest observations up to time t (denoted herein as $\eta_{it}|t$). In one Kalman smoother procedure, the *fixed interval smoother* (FIS), the aim is to derive conditional state estimates using all available data. These smoothed state estimates are denoted herein as $\eta_{it|T}$.

For parameter estimation purposes, a loglikelihood function, referred to herein as the multiple-subject *prediction error decomposition function* (PED; Caines & Rissanen, 1974; Schweppe, 1965), can be constructed using by-products from the KF. This PED function can then be optimized with respect to the modeling parameters to yield maximum likelihood estimates of the parameters in α, τ, B, Λ, H, and G. Detailed descriptions of the KF, the FIS, and the PED can be found elsewhere (Durbin & Koopman, 2001; Harvey, 2001). A brief summary is included in Appendix 6.1.

Detecting Structural Changes

Following the seminal work of Fox (1972), many researchers have come to classify outliers as additive outliers versus innovative outliers (Tsay, 1988). The former are used to describe data points that show unusual characteristics at one particular time point only. Innovative outliers, in contrast, reflect unusual shocks—or abrupt perturbations—to the dynamic functions. This kind of shocks can lead to sustained changes (i.e., structural changes) in the dynamics of a system.

De Jong and Penzer (1998) presented a general framework for incorporating additive and innovative outliers into single-subject SSMs. Extending this approach to group-based SSMs, Equations 6.1 and 6.2 now constitute the null SSM of no shocks. In our proposed alternative model individualized shocks are incorporated into the group-based dynamic and measurement functions as

$$\eta_{i,t+1} = W_{it}\delta_{it} + \alpha + B\eta_{it} + H\varepsilon_{it}, \quad (6.3)$$

$$y_{it} = X_{it}\delta_{it} + \tau + \Lambda\eta_{it} + G\varepsilon_{it}, \quad (6.4)$$

where at a particular shock point for person i—say, $t = j_i$—W_{ij} and X_{ij} are person-specific indicator matrices with elements set to either 0 or unity. They serve to indicate the person-specific state and measurement components that are shocked, respectively. Additive outliers are specified using X_{ij}, whereas innovative outliers are specified using W_{ij}. At other time points, W_{it} and X_{it} are null matrices and the model depicted in Equations 6.3 and 6.4 reduces to the null SSM as shown in Equations 6.1 and 6.2. At $t = j_i$, δ_{ij} is a $q_{ij} \times 1$ vector carrying the magnitudes of the shocks. Multiple shock points can also be incorporated, if needed, but in our formulation the precise location of the shock point(s) generally varies across persons.

The impact of additive and innovative outliers can be better understood by examining the *shock signature* yielded from the model depicted in Equations 6.3 and 6.4. The shock signature, denoted in Equation 6.5 as $D_{it}(j)$, is a $T \times q_{ij}$ matrix of coefficients that describes the impact of each shock on the manifest observations at different time points. For a system that is shocked once at $t = j_i$, $D_{it}(j)$ can be obtained for person i by iterating Equations 6.3 and 6.4, which yields the following (see also Equation 11 in de Jong & Penzer, 1998):

$$D_{it}(j) = \begin{cases} 0, & t = 1, \ldots, j-1, \\ X_{ij}, & t = j, \\ \Lambda_{it} B^{t-(j+1)} W_{ij}, & t = j+1, \ldots, T, \end{cases} \quad (6.5)$$

where B^k denotes k repeated matrix multiplications of B, with $B^0 = I$. Subject and time indices are added to Λ to reflect our empirical model. Equation 6.5 indicates that an additive outlier affects only selected measurement components of individual i at $t = j_i$ through the selection matrix, X_{ij}. In contrast, the impact of an innovative outlier is propagated over time through the transition matrix, B, and its effects on the observed measurements are scaled by the factor loading matrix, Λ_{it}. The term $D_{it}(j)\delta_{ij}$ thus reflects how the shocks change the model-implied means of an individual's data at different time points. The precise forms of the shock signatures vary depending on the specific null SSM in which such shocks are imposed.

Following de Jong and Penzer's (1998) approach, initial exploration for the location of shock points is guided by evaluating two chi-square statistics, $\rho^{*2}_{state,it}$ and $\rho^{*2}_{meas,it}$, which have w and p degrees of freedom, respectively. Given the model parameters under the null hypothesis of no shocks, these statistics reflect the maximum shocks to the dynamic and measurement components of the model at time t, respectively. Following that, the magnitude of δ_{ij} and its associated covariance matrix are estimated by means by a generalized least squares procedure, and the need to retain these shock points is assessed by means of the Wald test (see Appendix 6.2 for actual implementation details). After incorporating the statistically significant individualized shock points, parameters for the final group-based SSM with shocks are then reestimated using the multiple-subject PED function, and new conditional state estimates are derived using the KF or FIS as usual.

To summarize, our proposed approach combines de Jong and Penzer's (1998) approach for detecting outliers within single-subject SSMs with procedures for fitting group-based SSMs. Embedding outlier detection procedures within the state space framework has several notable advantages. First, an SSM, which comprises a measurement and a dynamic model, provides a natural platform for distinguishing additive (measurement) outliers from innovative (dynamic) outliers. Second, standard state space estimation procedures such as the KF and FIS give rise to by-products that can be readily used to construct diagnostic tests for detecting outliers. Third, and most important, the flexibility of the state space formulation enables researchers to represent a broad array of continuous and discontinuous shifts in dynamics by incorporating innovative outliers into the dynamic model of a SSM. Doing so within a group-based SSM further allows researchers to strike a balance between deriving a group-based change trajectory on the one hand and evaluating evidence for individual-specific structural changes on the other hand.

Simulation Examples

Longitudinal Mediation Model

One way to clarify the causal pathway that links an independent variable (or exogenous variable) to an outcome variable is by means of *mediation analysis,* in which, a third variable, called the *mediator,* is hypothesized to mediate the effect of an independent variable on an outcome variable. Mediation typically is investigated with variations of a model expressed as follows:

$$m = ax + \zeta_m$$
$$y = bm + cx + \zeta_y,$$

where x is the independent variable; m is the mediator; y is the outcome variable; $a, b,$ and c are regression coefficients, and ζ_m and ζ_m are disturbances. If c is not statistically different from 0 after m has been added to the model as a regressor, then m is said to be a mediator of the relationship between x and y.

Cole and Maxwell (2003) proposed a longitudinal framework for representing mediation effect by taking into consideration the time-dependent relationships between variables. We consider one particular longitudinal mediation model they presented. In state space form, this model can be expressed using a measurement model written as

$$\begin{bmatrix} x_{1it} \\ m_{1it} \\ y_{1it} \end{bmatrix} = \begin{bmatrix} x_{it} \\ m_{it} \\ y_{it} \end{bmatrix}, \qquad (6.6)$$

where $x_{1it}, m_{1it},$ and y_{1it} are manifest observations used to identify the true scores of the independent variable (x_{it}), the mediator (m_{it}), and the dependent variable (y_{it}). The corresponding dynamic model is expressed as

$$\begin{bmatrix} x_{i,t+1} \\ m_{i,t+1} \\ y_{i,t+1} \end{bmatrix} = \begin{bmatrix} \phi_x & 0 & 0 \\ \phi_{x \to m} & \phi_m & 0 \\ 0 & \phi_{m \to y} & \phi_y \end{bmatrix} \begin{bmatrix} x_{it} \\ m_{it} \\ y_{it} \end{bmatrix} + \begin{bmatrix} \zeta_{x,t} \\ \zeta_{m,t} \\ \zeta_{y,t} \end{bmatrix}. \qquad (6.7)$$

The fact that it takes time for variables to have effects is embodied in the very structure of the model: Variables at a specific time t do not instantly influence each other. Instead, variables at time t have effects on variables at time $t + 1$ through the paths $\varphi_{x \to m}$ and $\varphi_{m \to y}$. In this specific mediation model, x_{it} is hypothesized to have a unidirectional influence on $m_{i, t+1}$. By the same token, the influence of m_{it} on $y_{i, t+1}$ is also hypothesized to be unidirectional. In addition, all three variables are hypothesized to show autoregressive dynamics overtime with autoregressive weights φ_x, φ_m, and φ_y. Thus, this version of longitudinal mediation model is essentially a restricted version of a vector autoregressive model of lag 1 (VAR[1] model) with selected cross-regression weights set to 0.

We simulated data using this longitudinal mediation model with parameter vector $\theta = [\varphi_x, \varphi_m, \varphi_y, \varphi_{x \to m}, \varphi_{m \to y}, \sigma^2_{\zeta x}, \sigma^2_{\zeta m}, \sigma^2_{\zeta y}] = [.9, .7$ or $-.7, .7, .4, .4, .03, .03, .03]$. For illustrative purposes, we applied a single shock to x_{it} at $j_i = 5$. Because x is located at the very start of the causal chain, shocking x_t generates changes that extend to the entire system. Such effects are distinct from the more "localized" impact obtained from shocking m_{it} or y_{it}.

We generated the shock signature associated with Equations 6.6 and 6.7 for $t = 1, \ldots, 40$, with a single shock to x at $t = 5$. In this case, the shock signature at each time point, $D_{it}(5)$, is a 3×1 vector of shock coefficients, and these weights are plotted in Figures 6.1A and 6.1B. The three coefficients in $D_{it}(j)$ portray how the model-implied means for the observed indicators, x_{1t}, m_{1t}, and y_{1t}, are altered at each time point as a consequence of the shock to x at $t = 5$.

Applying a single shock to person i's x score at $j_i = 5$ leads to a transient surge in the level of x at time $t + 1$ (i.e., $t = 6$) that eventually dissipates over time (see Figures 6.1A and 6.1B and Figures 6.2A and 6.2D). The shock, in turn, leads to a lagged influence on m and, consequently, y; that is, it takes one additional time point for the shock to transmit to m (at $t = 7$) and yet another time point (at $t = 8$) to transmit to y. The effect of the shock on y (i.e., the outcome or end point of the causal chain) is also determined jointly by the dynamics of x and m. For instance, when φ_m is equal to $-.7$ such that the mediator, m, is fluctuating at a high frequency, the shock is also propagated over time in y in a damped oscillatory fashion. Thus, shocking x leads to a ripple effect that propagates to y through m after a certain delay.

We use a modeling example presented by Chow, Hamagami, and Nesselroade (2007) to give a more concrete example of what such shocks may represent in an empirical mediation setting. In this study, a multiple-group VAR(1) was used to represent age differences in the linkages among fluctuations in cognitive performance, positive emotion, and negative emotion. Results from model fitting indicated that older adults manifested significant unidirectional coupling from negative emotion to cognitive performance. Unlike older adults, younger adults manifested significant unidirectional coupling from negative emotion to positive emotion and from cognitive performance to both positive and negative emotions. In other words, among younger adults, cognitive performance may be viewed as the independent variable, x; positive emotion may be viewed as the outcome variable, y; and negative emotion may be viewed

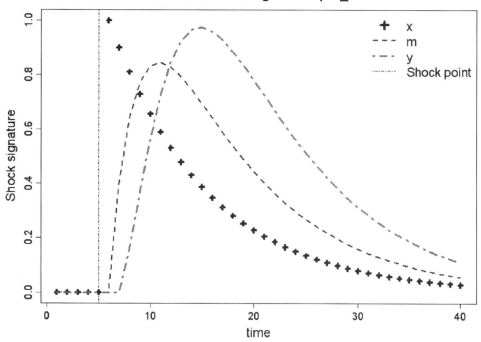

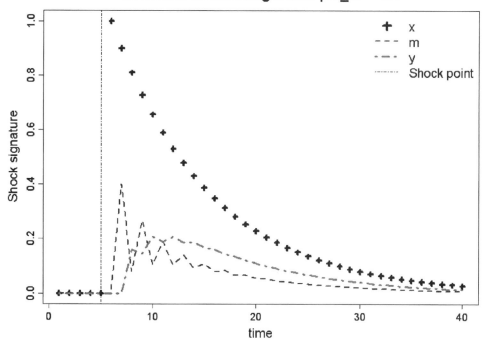

Figure 6.1. Panel A: the shock signature entailed from applying a single shock to x at $t = 5$ with $\varphi_m = .7$. Panel B: the shock signature entailed from applying a single shock to x at $t = 5$ with $\varphi_m = -.7$.

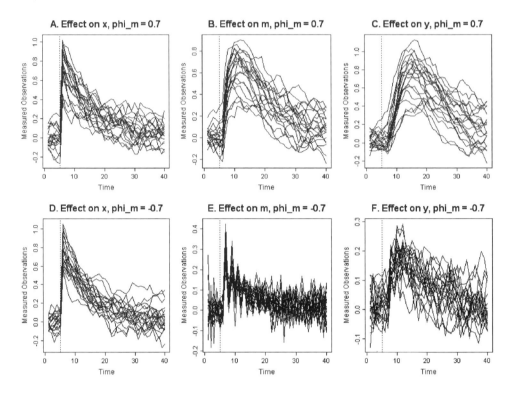

Figure 6.2.   Panel A: the consequences of shocking x in the longitudinal mediational model. Panels A, B, and C: effects of shocking x on x, m, and y, respectively, with $\varphi_m = .7$; Panels D, E, and F: effects of shocking x on x, m, and y, respectively, with $\varphi_m = -.7$.

as a partial mediator, m, of the relationship between cognitive performance and positive emotion. The mediating relationship is a partial one because cognitive performance still has a direct lagged effect on positive emotion.

In Chow et al.'s (2007) study the participants were subjected to ongoing "cognitive shocks" because the difficulty level of the cognitive task on which they were working was systematically altered throughout the experiment to induce fluctuations in the participants' cognitive performance and emotions. The shock induced by a sudden decrease in the difficulty level of the cognitive task, for instance, may lead to a surge in a participant's cognitive score and, subsequently, a decrease in his or her negative emotion and a boost in positive emotion. However, the impact of such cognitive performance changes on the individual's positive emotion depends in part on the dynamics of his or her negative emotion. If the individual is able to maintain high continuity in his or her low negative emotion state, the boost in positive emotion induced by the increase in cognitive score would also persist for a longer period. If the individual tends to show rapid ebbs and flows in negative emotion, the corresponding boost in positive emotion would also fluctuate rapidly through its linkage to negative emotion.

Dynamic Harmonic Regression Model

In the study of cyclic dynamics, a time series for person i is often expressed as a linear combination of sinusoids or cycles in the form of

$$y_{it} = \sum_{k=1}^{M} C_{kit} + e_{it}, \qquad (6.8)$$

$$C_{kit} = R_k \cos(w_k t + \varphi_k), \qquad (6.9)$$

where y_{it} is the manifest observation from person i at time t, $(t = 0, \ldots, T)$, e_{it} is the measurement error at time t, C_{kit} corresponds to the kth cycle $(k = 1, \ldots, M)$, R_k is the amplitude associated with the kth cycle, $\omega_k = 2\pi/\lambda_k$ is the frequency associated with the kth cycle in radian units, where λ_k is cycle k's period of oscillation (in units of t). In Equation 6.9, φ_k is the phase of cycle k, or the discrepancy between the position of the cycle at time 0 and the first peak of the cycle, expressed in radian units. For instance, if $\varphi_k = \pi$, this means that the kth cycle's first peak is offset from the ordinate by half a cycle and that it is going to reach its first peak in half a cycle.

The nonlinear model in Equation 6.9 can be reexpressed as a linear regression equation composed of a series of cosine and sine terms as follows:

$$C_{kit} = a_k \cos(\omega_k t) + b_k \sin(\omega_k t), \qquad (6.10)$$

where the amplitude R_k is a function of the coefficients a_k and b_k, written as

$$R_k = \sqrt{a_k^2 + b_k^2}, \qquad (6.11)$$

and the phase φ_k can be computed as

$$\phi_k = \tan^{-1}\left(\frac{-b_k}{a_k}\right). \qquad (6.12)$$

When all the frequency values (i.e., ω_k, $k = 1, \ldots, M$) are known, rewriting Equation 6.9 into the form in Equation 6.10 allows Equation 6.8 to be fitted as a multiple regression model, in which case $\cos(\omega_k t)$ and $\sin(\omega_k t)$ are included as regressors.

Young, Pedregal, and Tych (1999) proposed a time-varying cyclic model in which the amplitude and phase associated with a cycle are allowed to change dynamically over time. This model is referred to as the *dynamic harmonic regression model*. In this model each set of coefficients defines a cycle that varies in amplitude and phase over time, recovered for each occasion using Equations 6.11 and 6.12, respectively. Given one cycle ($M = 1$) of frequency

ω_1, for example, the measurement part of the state space model is written as follows:

$$y_{it} = \Lambda_t \eta_{it} + e_{it}$$

$$= \left[\cos(\omega_1 t)\sin(\omega_1 t)\right]\begin{bmatrix} a_{1it} \\ b_{1it} \end{bmatrix} + e_{it}, \mathrm{Var}(e_{it}) = \sigma_e^2. \qquad (6.13)$$

The coefficients a_{kit} and b_{kit} can be used to derive the cycle's amplitude and phase offset at time t using Equations 6.11 and 6.12. Notice also in Equation 6.13 that the coefficients a_{1it} and b_{1it} appear in the vector of state/latent variables. As a result, each person's coefficients for each time point (i.e., a_{1it} and b_{1it}) can be estimated by means of the KF, the FIS, or other related smoothers as latent variable scores. The cosine and sine terms, by contrast, now appear as part of the factor loading matrix, Λ_t. Equation 6.13 can thus be viewed as a factor analysis model with nonlinear constraints on the factor loading matrix whose "factors" are time-varying coefficients that reflect possible changes in a cycle's amplitude and phase. Because Λ_t contains time-varying cosine and sine coefficients, this specific model deviates slightly from the group-based state space framework outlined in Equations 6.1 and 6.2. However, we still consider this model to be a group-based SSM because all values in Λ_t are fixed at the same known values for all individuals in the sample.

A dynamic model has to be specified next to represent the changes in a_{kit} and b_{kit} and their associated variances, σ_{ak}^2 and σ_{bk}^2, over time. Suppose that we are interested in extracting one single cycle and that this cycle shows invariant characteristics over person and time. This can be accomplished by constraining the dynamic model as follows:

$$\begin{bmatrix} a_{1i,t+1} \\ b_{1i,t+1} \end{bmatrix} = \begin{bmatrix} 1 & 0 \\ 0 & 1 \end{bmatrix}\begin{bmatrix} a_{1it} \\ b_{1it} \end{bmatrix}. \qquad (6.14)$$

In addition, because this dynamic model posits that each individual's amplitude and phase are invariant over time, between-individual differences in amplitude and phase can be appropriately incorporated into the initial condition specification and subsequently estimated as part of other time-invariant modeling parameters. For instance, we may specify the initial condition as follows:

$$\left[a_{i,1|1}, b_{i,1|1}\right]' \sim N\left(\left[\mu_a, \mu_b\right]', \mathrm{diag}\left[\sigma_{a10}^2, \sigma_{b10}^2\right]\right), \qquad (6.15)$$

where μ_a and μ_b are the average cosine and sine coefficients in the sample, respectively. The variances σ_{a10}^2 and σ_{b10}^2 capture the between-individual differences in initial cosine and sine coefficients which, by the time-invariant nature of these coefficients, also reflect between-individual differences in cosine and sine coefficients over all time points. These variance terms can either be constrained to be uncorrelated with one another or equal to one another for iden-tification purposes. Here, we impose both constraints.

Applying shocks to the otherwise time-invariant cosine and sine coeffi-cients would lead to sudden amplitude and phase shifts in the individuals' cyclic dynamics. Instances of sudden phase shifts have been reported in the study of movement and coordination dynamics. The Haken, Kelso, and Bunz (1985) model of interlimb coordination and its subsequent extensions, for instance, have been used to explain the empirical phenomenon of a sudden shift in the oscillatory motions of two index fingers from in phase to out of phase with continuous changes in the driving frequency of the two fingers.

The Haken, Kelso and Bunz (1985) model is a confirmatory model that is subjected to explicit constraints on how the phase shifts are tied to changes in another control variable: oscillation frequencies of the fingers. Here, we con-sider an exploratory case without such theoretical constraints; specifically, we generated simulated individual trajectories using this model over 30 time points and applied a single shock to each individual's cosine coefficient at $t = 10$. We set the parameter vector to be $\theta = [\mu_a, \mu_b, \sigma^2_{a10}, \sigma^2_{b10}, \sigma^2_e], = [.5, .5, 1, 1, .0001]'$. The resultant trajectories are plotted in Figures 6.3A and 6.B. In Figure 6.3A we consider a special case in which the shock at $t = 1$ led to a phase shift but no amplitude change. In Figure 6.3B we generated individual trajectories that were subjected to both positive and negative shocks. The shocks led to abrupt

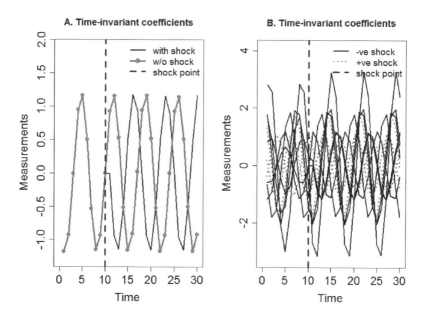

Figure 6.3. The effects of applying shocks to the latent variables in the dynamic har-monic regression model with time-invariant cosine and sine coefficients. Panel A: the trajectories of a randomly selected individual with and without shock at $t = 10$. Panel B: the trajectories of a sample of 10 individuals with shocks to their cosine coefficients at $t = 10$. −ve = negative; +ve = positive.

increases (with positive shocks) and decreases (with negative shocks) in amplitudes, as well as corresponding changes in phases.

Cyclic models have been an integral part of many other contemporaries theories in psychology beyond the area of movement and motor development. Affect researchers, for instance, have used the analogy of a thermostat to describe the ways in which individuals regulate their emotions or actions toward a set point (e.g., Carver & Scheier, 1982; Chow, Ram, Boker, Fujita, & Clore, 2005; Larsen, 2000); that is, such actions are posited to unfold in a damped oscillatory fashion. We can represent such changes by combining the sinusoidal model with a dynamic model in which the cosine and sine coefficients are specified as an autoregressive process of order 1,termed an *AR(1) process*. Furthermore, we impose the constraints that no process noise is present and that the autoregression parameter, φ_1, is positive but less than 1. The resultant model is expressed as follows:

$$\begin{bmatrix} a_{i,t+1} \\ b_{i,t+1} \end{bmatrix} = \begin{bmatrix} \phi_1 & 0 \\ 0 & \phi_1 \end{bmatrix} \begin{bmatrix} a_{it} \\ b_{it} \end{bmatrix}, \quad 0 < \phi_1 < 1, \qquad (6.16)$$

where φ_1 is the lag-1 autoregressive weight. The same measurement model as that depicted in Equation 6.13 is used. Individual differences in cosine and sine coefficients can be incorporated using the same specification as in Equation 6.15.

Simulated trajectories based on this model and the parameter vector $\theta = [\varphi_1, \mu_a, \mu_b, \sigma^2_{a10}, \sigma^2_{b10}, \sigma^2_e]' = [.85, .5, .5, 1, 1, .0001]'$ are plotted in Figures 6.4A and 6.4B. The autoregressive specification in Equation 6.16 essentially dictates the initial individual differences in cosine and sine coefficients to eventually dissipate to 0 in the absence of other external perturbations. This dissipation process is perturbed at $t = 10$, thereby causing some cycles to dissipate faster (in the case of negative shocks) or slower (with positive shocks) compared with their original pathways.

Univariate Latent Difference Score Model

McArdle and Hamagami (2001) formulated a difference equation as a structural equation model to capture the sigmoid-shaped growth curves typically seen in cognitive developmental data. They termed this model the *dual-change score model* (DCSM) because two components—a slope and an autoregressive component—collectively define a difference equation that dictates the dynamics of the system. This specific model can be expressed in state space form as follows:

$$\begin{bmatrix} \mu_{i,t+1} \\ \mu_{si,t+1} \end{bmatrix} = \begin{bmatrix} 1+\beta & 1 \\ 0 & 1 \end{bmatrix} \begin{bmatrix} \mu_{it} \\ \mu_{sit} \end{bmatrix}, \qquad (6.17)$$

where μ_{it} is the true score of person i at time t and μ_{sit} is the local slope of person i at time t. The latter is constrained to be invariant over time to establish its equivalence to the constant slope in McArdle and Hamagami's (2001) for-

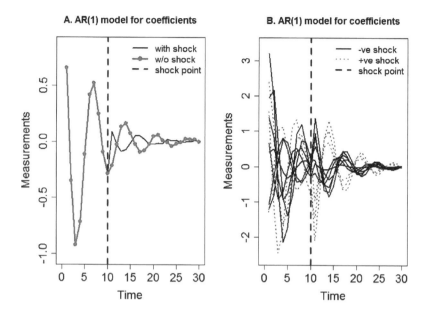

Figure 6.4. The effects of applying shocks to the latent variables in the dynamic harmonic regression model with cosine and sine coefficients that conform to an autoregressive (AR[1]) model. Panel A: the trajectories of a randomly selected individual with and without shock at $t = 10$. Panel B: the trajectories of a sample of 10 individuals with shocks to their cosine coefficients at $t = 10$. −ve = negative; +ve = positive.

mulation. Under this constraint, μ_{sit} reduces to a constant term that determines person i's average magnitude of change in μ per unit of time. The parameter β is a person-invariant self-feedback parameter that governs the magnitude of change proportionate to the previous level of μ at $t − 1$. If $\beta < 0$, this parameter drives the system to self-regulate toward an asymptote, determined jointly by μ_{sit} and β. The latent variables, μ_{it} and μ_{sit}, are the two components that define the dual-change representation in the original DCSM. Both latent processes in the dynamic model in Equation 6.17 are constrained to be deterministic (i.e., no process noise components are present in the equation).

At the measurement level, if a single indicator, y_{it}, is used to identify person i's true score, μ_{it}, the corresponding measurement level is expressed as follows:

$$y_{it} = \begin{bmatrix} 1 & 0 \end{bmatrix} \begin{bmatrix} \mu_{it} \\ \mu_{sit} \end{bmatrix} + e_{it}, \qquad (6.18)$$

where e_{it} is the measurement error and $E(e_{it}^2) = \sigma_e^2$.

To capture between-person differences in learning dynamics, McArdle and Hamagami (2001) expressed μ_{i1}, the intercept term of person i at Time 1, as a function of a group average, μ_0, and an individualized deviation from this group average, $\zeta_{\mu i}$. Likewise, the constant slope for person i, μ_{si}, is also expressed as a function of a group average, μ_s, and an individualized deviation from this group average, $\zeta_{\mu si}$. The same specification can be adapted within the state space framework by specifying the initial condition as follows:

$$\mu_{i1|1} = \begin{bmatrix} \mu_0 \\ \mu_s \end{bmatrix} \text{ for all } i \text{ and} \qquad (6.19)$$

$$P_{i1|1} = \begin{bmatrix} \sigma^2_{\mu_0} & \sigma_{\mu_0,\mu_s} \\ \sigma_{\mu_0,\mu_s} & \sigma^2_{\mu_s} \end{bmatrix} \text{ for all } i, \qquad (6.20)$$

where μ_0 represents the group's average initial level at time $t = 1$ and μ_s represents the group's average slope across all time points, $\sigma^2_{\mu_0}$ captures the between-person variance in initial level, $\sigma^2_{\mu_s}$ represents the between-person variance in average slope, and σ_{μ_0,μ_s} represents the covariance between the two. The initial condition parameters can be estimated using the PED with other time- and person-invariant parameters.[2]

The results obtained from shocking the two latent variables in the DCSM are summarized in Figures 6.5A through 6.5C. Applying a single shock to the level component, μ_{it}, leads to a transient level shift that slowly dissipates over time, after which the system's dynamics are governed by the null SSM again (see Figures 6.5A and 6.5C). Shocking the slope component, μ_{sit}, in contrast, leads to increases in manifest scores (if δ_{ij} is positive for all individuals, as in this simulation) that eventually level off to a second asymptote (see Figures 6.5B and 6.5C). The sudden growth spurts unfold more gradually and subtly than the abrupt level shifts yielded from shocking μ_{it}. These changes are summarized in the corresponding shock signature in Figure 6.5C.

Chow, Hamaker, and Allaire (2009) used the DCSM with shocks to represent cognitive learning dynamics among a group of older adults. Using this model, Chow and colleagues found that several older participants showed signs of sudden shifts in their levels of cognitive performance, and shifts in their learning slopes that marked the onset of a learning spurt or, alternatively, the abrupt transition to a performance plateau. Substantial individual differences also existed in the locations of the shock points. Thus, incorporating innovative outliers into the original DCSM results in an alternative, multistage model of learning.

The notion of discrete shifts in cognitive dynamics discussed by Chow et al. (2009) has other familiar counterparts in the developmental literature. For instance, researchers have long conjectured that multiple cognitive growth and decline phases exist throughout the life span. As an example, accelerated

---

[2] Other approaches for initializing the KF have been discussed elsewhere (e.g., de Jong, 1989; Harvey, 2001). A practical alternative for setting initial conditions in group-based SSMs using interindividual differences information at $t = 1$ can be found in Oud, Jansen, van Leeuwe, Aarnoutse, and Voeten (1999).

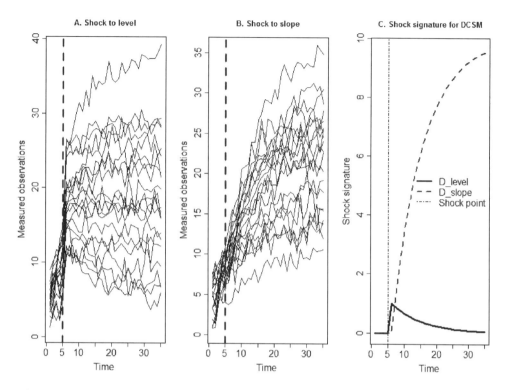

Figure 6.5. Effects of applying shocks the latent variables in the dual-change score model (DCSM). Panel A: the manifest trajectories of 20 individuals with a single shock to the local level, μ_{it} at $t = 10$. Panel B: the trajectories of 20 individuals with a single shock to the local slope, μ_{sit} at $t = 10$. Panel C: the shock signature entailed from shocking the two latent variables in the DCSM.

growth in fluid intelligence is expected throughout childhood and adolescence, whereas stability and decline have been found to characterize middle adulthood and older adulthood, respectively (Cattell, 1971; Horn & Cattell, 1966). Methods such as the double exponential model (McArdle, Ferrer-Caja, Hamagami, & Woodcock, 2002) and multiphase mixed-effects models (Cudeck & Klebe, 2002) have been used to empirically identify the ages—or change points—at which individuals transition to different developmental phases. The outlier-based procedure presented in this chapter offers an exploratory approach to identifying unusual deviations that may be indicative of such critical developmental changes.

Empirical Illustration

The empirical illustration we consider in this section was adapted from the example discussed by Chow et al. (2009). The data were collected from 38 community-dwelling older adults recruited from local senior centers and community organizations (for details, see Allaire & Marsiske, 2005). Participants in the study completed an extensive daily assessment protocol daily for 60 consecutive days. In this chapter, we use the participants' daily scores on a letter series task as the dependent variable of interest in our modeling example. The letter series task (Thurstone, 1962) is a measure for assessing inductive reasoning, namely, an individual's ability to deduce novel relationships in overlearned material. This test consisted of 30 items that asked participants to identify the letter that would come next in a series of letters (e.g., a b a d c b c d ?). The number of correctly answered items was summed to produce an overall score, which was then used for model-fitting purposes.

By combining a DCSM and a regression model with a time-varying regression coefficient, Chow et al. (2009) found that several older participants showed signs of sudden shifts in their letter series scores that concurred with sudden changes in the role of perceived control, a time-varying covariate used to predict individuals' day-to-day fluctuations in letter series performance in the study. Many participants also manifested shifts in their learning slopes that marked the onset of a learning spurt or, alternatively, the abrupt transition to a performance plateau.

Although level shifts in manner of a step function were observed among a few participants, such level shifts did not always coincide with concurrent shifts in the participants' levels of perceived control. In this chapter, we adapted the model considered by Chow et al. (2009) to allow for simple level shifts; specifically, we modified McArdle and Hamagami's (2001) DCSM as follows:

$$
\begin{bmatrix} \mu_{i,t+1} \\ \mu_{si,t+1} \\ \mu_{0i,t+1} \end{bmatrix} = \begin{bmatrix} 1+\beta & 1 & 0 \\ 0 & 1 & 0 \\ 0 & 0 & 1 \end{bmatrix} \begin{bmatrix} \mu_{it} \\ \mu_{sit} \\ \mu_{0it} \end{bmatrix}, \qquad (6.21)
$$

where an individual's intercept or initial performance level was formulated as a separate latent variable, μ_{0it}. In contrast to the transient level shift obtained by shocking μ_{it} in the formulation in our simulation example (see Equation 6.17 and Figures 6.5A–6.5C), shocking this specific latent variable allows for an irreversible level shift.

At the measurement level, we used a single indicator (viz., each person's daily letter series score), y_{it}, to identify person i's true score, μ_{it}, as follows:

$$
y_{it} = \begin{bmatrix} 1 & 0 & 1 \end{bmatrix} \begin{bmatrix} \mu_{it} \\ \mu_{sit} \\ \mu_{0it} \end{bmatrix} + e_{it}, \qquad (6.22)
$$

where e_{it} is the measurement error and $E(e_{it}^2) = \sigma_e^2$.

We specified the initial condition to be

$$
\mu_{i1|1} = \begin{bmatrix} 0 \\ \mu_s \\ \mu_0 \end{bmatrix} \text{ for all } i \text{ and} \qquad (6.23)
$$

$$
P_{i1|1} = \begin{bmatrix} 0 & 0 & 0 \\ 0 & \sigma_{\mu s}^2 & \sigma_{\mu 0,\mu s} \\ 0 & \sigma_{\mu 0,\mu s} & \sigma_{\mu 0}^2 \end{bmatrix} \text{ for all } i. \qquad (6.24)
$$

The parameter vector $\theta = [\beta, \mu_0, \mu_s, \sigma_{\mu 0}^2, \sigma_{\mu 3}^2, \sigma_{\mu 0, \mu s}\ \sigma_e^2]'$ was estimated by means of the PED.

Inspection of chi-square diagnostic measures indicated that substantial deviations were observed in the individuals' learning trajectories. A total of 35 out of 38 participants showed signs of innovative outliers in their data at the .05 significance level, whereas only 9 individuals manifested significant deviations in the form of additive outliers. Focusing on examining innovative outliers, we incorporated up to two statistically significant shock points for each individual to allow for shocks to the individual's intercept (μ_{it}) and slope (μ_s). Results from fitting the null DCSM and the DCSM with these additional shock points are summarized in Table 6.1.

The negative $\hat{\beta}$ estimates obtained from fitting the null DCSM and DCSM with shocks indicated that the individuals' letter series performance self-regulated toward their respective asymptotes instead of growing without boundary. Substantial interindividual differences also existed in the participants' initial levels and slopes. Particularly worth noting is that, after including the individualized shock points, the measurement error variance (σ_e^2) and between-individual variance in intercept ($\sigma_{\mu 0}^2$) were both markedly reduced. The standard error estimate associated with $\hat{\sigma}_{\mu 0}^2$ was also greatly reduced in the full model with shocks. Note also that greater between-individual variance in slope ($\sigma_{\mu s}^2$) was observed in the full model. This was likely the case because the full model could better distinguish individuals' varying learning slopes during different learning phases, thus allowing more of the variability in letter series performance to be absorbed into between-person differences in learning slope.

Post hoc inspection of the participants' model-implied trajectories suggested some commonalities in the participants' change patterns. We grouped the participants into three exploratory clusters based on commonalities in their learning trajectories; specifically, the first group included participants who manifested positive shocks to their slopes that led to the subsequent attainment of a second, higher asymptote (see Figure 6.6A). The

Table 6.1. Parameter Estimates From Fitting the Group-Based Dual-Change Score Model With and Without Shocks

Parameter	Estimates in null model (*SE*)	Estimates in model with shocks (*SE*)
μ_0	10.51 (0.68)	9.48 (0.31)
μ_s	0.54 (0.03)	0.61 (0.08)
β	−0.04 (0.002)	−0.05 (0.001)
$\sigma_{\mu 0}^2$	16.59 (3.78)	3.31 (0.35)
$\sigma_{\mu s}^2$	0.03 (0.008)	0.24 (0.08)
$\sigma_{\mu 0, \mu s}$	−0.08 (0.12)	−0.09 (0.09)
σ^2	3.02 (0.09)	1.62 (0.03)

Note.   All parameter estimates except for $\sigma_{\mu 0, \mu s}$ are statistically different from zero at the .05 level.

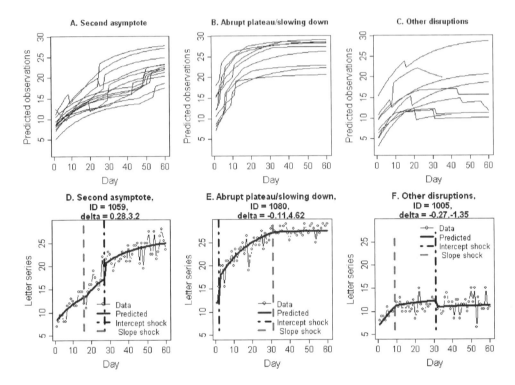

Figure 6.6. Predicted measurements generated for three groups of individuals identified through post hoc inspection of their model-implied trajectories. Panel A: a group of participants who manifested positive shocks in their slopes and the attainment of a second, higher asymptote. Panel B: a group of individuals who showed pronounced learning spurts followed by abrupt performance plateaus. Panel C: a group of individuals who showed signs of disruptions in their performance trajectories. Panels D, E, and F: plots of the actual data, the predicted measurements based on the model with shocks, and shock points for Participants 1059, 1080, and 1005.

second group included the "fast learners," who showed pronounced learning spurts that transitioned abruptly to sudden performance plateaus (see Figure 6.6B). Individuals who showed transient or more lasting signs of disruptions in their performance trajectories were included in the third group (see Figure 6.6C).

Compared with the results Chow et al. (2009) reported, more individuals were found to show simple level shifts of varying magnitudes, as opposed to level shifts that were linked to concurrent shifts in perceived control. To highlight how the individual shock points help capture idiographic change patterns, we plotted the trajectories of three randomly selected individuals from the three clusters (see Figures 6.6D–6.6F). In Participant 1059 there was a transition to a steeper learning slope on the 16th day that eventually led to a higher second asymptote. In contrast, Participant 1080 exhibited an early level shift and a very steep learning curve, which came to an abrupt plateau with a shock on the 31st day. The level shift on the 27th day further accelerated this process. Unlike Participants

1059 and 1080, Participant 1005 showed notable disruptions in his or her performance trajectory by first manifesting a negative slope change followed by another drop in performance level (i.e., through a negative shock to the intercept on the 31st day).

Closing Remarks

In this chapter, we generalized the outlier detection procedure proposed by de Jong and Penzer (1998) to a multiple-subject setting to better tailor to the kind of multiple-subject-moderate-T data sets typically available in the social and behavioral sciences. We also presented several theoretical and empirical examples of how innovative outliers can be used to capture critical shifts in the study of intraindividual change. For instance, we found that a group-based null DCSM, though providing a reasonable representation at the group level, did not capture some of the idiosyncratic change patterns in the participants' cognitive performance.

Innovative outliers in state space models collectively provide an alternative way of representing different forms of unusual deviations in individuals' change processes. Embedding individualized outliers within a group-based model further allows researchers to consider possible idiographic features within a nomothetic framework. In our view, this is one of the many possible ways of reconciling idiographic and nomothetic representations of change within a single modeling framework. We do, however, believe that idiographic and nomothetic approaches each have their own respective merits. The "compromises" put forth in this chapter in no way negate the need for developing methods that can effectively capture these changes, either separately or in conjunction with one another.

Appendix 6.1: The Kalman Filter, Fixed Interval Smoother, and Prediction Error Decomposition Function

Suppose the data set $Y_{it} = [Y_{1it}, Y_{2it}, \ldots, Y_{pit}]'$ from person i is available for estimation purposes, where Y_{kit} is itself a $t \times 1$ time series for manifest variable k. Once a model has been expressed in state space form, the Kalman filter (KF; Harvey, 2001) can be used to derive conditional state estimates based on manifest observations up to time t and the associated covariance matrix (i.e., $\eta_{it|t} = E[\eta_{it}|Y_{it}]$ and $P_{it|t} = \text{Cov}[\eta_{it}|Y_{it}]$) as follows:

$$\eta_{it|t} = \eta_{it|t-1} + P_{it|t-1}\Lambda'F_{it}^{-1}v_{it}, \quad (6A.1)$$

$$P_{it|t} = P_{it|t-1} - P_{it|t-1}\Lambda'F_{it}^{-1}\Lambda P_{it|t-1}, \quad (6A.2)$$

$$v_{it} = y_{it} - \tau - \Lambda\eta_{it|t-1}, \quad (6A.3)$$

$$F_{it} = \Lambda P_{it|t-1}\Lambda' + GG', \quad (6A.4)$$

$$M_{it} = BP_{it|t-1}\Lambda' + HG', \qquad (6A.5)$$

$$\eta_{i,t+1|t} = B\eta_{it|t-1} + K_{it}v_{it}, \qquad (6A.6)$$

$$P_{i,t+1|t} = BP_{it|t-1}B' + HH' - K_{it}M'_{it}, \qquad (6A.7)$$

where $K_{it} = M_{it}F_{it}^{-1}$ is the Kalman gain matrix, $\eta_{i,t+1|t} = E(\eta_{i,t+1}|Y_{it})$ and $P_{i,t+1|t} = \text{Cov}(\eta_{i,t+1}|Y_{it})$ are the conditional one-step-ahead state estimates and the associated covariance matrix.

The fixed interval smoother is one possible Kalman smoother, whose function is to derive conditional state estimates using all available data, namely, $E[\eta_{it}|Y_{iT}] = \eta_{it|T}$ and the associated covariance matrix, $P_{it|T}$. One version of the fixed interval smoother (de Jong, 1989; Kohn & Ansley, 1989) can be implemented by performing a backward recursion for $t = T, \ldots, 1$ as

$$\eta_{it|T} = \eta_{it|t-1} + P_{it|t-1}r_{i,t-1}, \qquad (6A.8)$$

$$P_{it|T} = P_{it|t-1} - P_{it|t-1}N_{i,t-1}P_{it|t-1}, \qquad (6A.9)$$

$$u_{it} = F_{it}^{-1}v_{it} - K'_{it}r_{it}, \qquad (6A.10)$$

$$r_{i,t-1} = \Lambda'u_{it} + B'r_{it}, \qquad (6A.11)$$

$$N_{i,t-1} = \Lambda'F_{it}^{-1}\Lambda + L'_{it}N_{it}L_{it}, \qquad (6A.12)$$

where $L_{it} = B - K_{it}\Lambda$. The recursion is initiated by setting $r_{iT} = 0$ and $N_{iT} = 0$. The element u_{it} is a scaled smoothed disturbance and, together with r_{it} and N_{it}, these elements play an important role in helping to detect structural changes (De Jong & Penzer, 1998).

As the KF is cycling through the estimation across T time points and N persons, several by-products from the KF can be substituted into a multiple-subject formulation of the prediction error decomposition function (Caines & Rissanen, 1974; Harvey, 2001; Schweppe, 1965) to yield maximum likelihood estimates of all pertinent modeling parameters in Λ, τ, B, α, Ψ, and Θ. The loglikelihood function can be written as a function of the individual innovation vector, v_it, and its associated covariance matrix, F_{it}, defined earlier, yielding

$$\log f(\theta) = \frac{1}{2}\sum_{i=1}^{N}\sum_{t=1}^{T} -p_{it}\log(2\pi) - \log|F_{it}| - v'_{it}F_{it}^{-1}v_{it}, \qquad (6A.13)$$

where p_{it} is the number of complete manifest variables at time t for person i. Other modified recursions to improve the numerical stability of the optimization process have also been proposed elsewhere (Ansley & Kohn, 1985; de Jong, 1989).

Appendix 6.2: Deriving Shock Estimates via Generalized Least Squares

The generalized least squares estimate of δ_{ij} is given by (de Jong & Penzer, 1998)

$$\hat{\delta}_{ij} = S_{ij}^{-1} s_{ij} \qquad (6A.14)$$

and

$$\text{Cov}\left(\hat{\delta}_{ij}\right) = S_{ij}^{-1} \qquad (6A.15)$$

where

$$s_{ij} = X'_{ij} u_{ij} + W'_{ij} r_{ij}, \qquad (6A.16)$$

$$S_{ij} = X'_{ij} F_{ij}^{-1} X_{ij} + Q'_{ij} N_{ij} Q_{ij}, \qquad (6A.17)$$

$$Q_{ij} = W_{ij} - K_{ij} X_{ij}. \qquad (6A.18)$$

A t statistic using r_{it} and N_{it} from the fixed interval smoother as

$$t_{l,it} = r_{l,it} / \sqrt{N_{ll,it}}, \qquad (6A.19)$$

where $r_{l,it}$ indicates the lth element of person i's vector r at time t and $N_{ll,it}$ is the lth diagonal element of the matrix N_{it}. With w state variables, $(T-1)w$ t tests can be performed to evaluate the statistical significance at each t with $T - w$ degrees of freedom.

For general diagnostic purposes, some of the by-products from running the Kalman filter and the fixed interval smoother can be used to construct an initial test of whether there are data points with unusual measurement or dynamic characteristics. In particular, $\rho^{*2}_{state,it} = r'_{it} N_{it}^{-1} r_{it}$ and $\rho^{*2}_{meas,it} = v'_{it} F_{it}^{-1} v_{it}$, given the model parameters under the null hypothesis of no shocks, reflect the maximum shocks to the dynamic and measurement components of the model at time t, respectively, and they are chi-square distributed with w and p degrees of freedom, respectively (de Jong & Penzer, 1998).

References

Allaire, J. C., & Marsiske, M. (2005). Intraindividual variability may not always indicate vulnerability in elders' cognitive performance. *Psychology and Aging, 20,* 390–401.

Ansley, C. F., & Kohn, R. (1985). Estimation, filtering and smoothing in state space models with incompletely specified initial conditions. *Annals of Statistics, 13,* 1286–1316.

Caines, P. E., & Rissanen, J. (1974). Maximum likelihood estimation of parameters. IEEE Transactions on Information Theory, 20, 102–104. doi:10.1109/TIT.1974.1055155

Carver, C. S., & Scheier, M. F. (1982). Control theory: A useful conceptual framework for personality-social, clinical, and health psychology. *Psychological Bulletin, 92,* 111–135. doi:10.1037/0033-2909.92.1.111

Cattell, R. B. (1971). *Abilities: Their structure, growth, and action.* Boston, MA: Houghton Mifflin.

Chow, S.-M., Hamagami, F., & Nesselroade, J. R. (2007). Age differences in dynamical cognition–emotion linkages. *Psychology and Aging, 22,* 765–780. doi:10.1037/0882-7974.22.4.765

Chow, S.-M., Hamaker, E., & Allaire, J. C. (2009). Using innovative outliers to detect discrete shifts in dynamics in group-based state-space models. *Multivariate Behavioral Research, 44,* 465–496.

Chow, S.-M., Ram, N., Boker, S. M., Fujita, F., & Clore, G. (2005). Emotion as thermostat: Representing emotion regulation using a damped oscillator model. *Emotion, 5,* 208–225. doi:10.1037/1528-3542.5.2.208

Cole, D. A., & Maxwell, S. E. (2003). Testing mediational models with longitudinal data: Questions and tips in the use of structural equation modeling. *Journal of Abnormal Psychology, 112,* 558–577. doi:10.1037/0021-843X.112.4.558

Collins, L. M., & Wugalter, S. E. (1992). Latent class models for stage-sequential dynamic latent variables. *Multivariate Behavioral Research, 28,* 131–157.

Cudeck, R., & Klebe, K. J. (2002). Multiphase mixed-effects models for repeated measures data. *Psychological Methods, 7,* 41–46.

de Jong, P. (1989). Smoothing and interpolation with the state-space model. *Journal of the American Statistical Association, 84,* 1085–1088. doi:10.2307/2290087

de Jong, P., & Penzer, J. (1998). Diagnosing shocks in time series. *Journal of the American Statistical Association, 93,* 796–806. doi:10.2307/2670129

Durbin, J., & Koopman, S. J. (2001). *Time series analysis by state-space methods.* New York, NY: Oxford University Press.

Elliott, R. J., Aggoun, L., & Moore, J. (1995). *Hidden Markov models: Estimation and control.* New York, NY: Springer.

Fox, A. J. (1972). Outliers in time series. *Journal of the Royal Statistical Society Series B, 34,* 350–363.

Haken, H., Kelso, J. A. S., & Bunz, H. (1985). A theoretical model of phase transitions in human hand movements. *Biological Cybernetics, 51,* 347–356. doi:10.1007/BF00336922

Harvey, A. C. (2001). *Forecasting, structural time series models and the Kalman filter.* Cambridge, England: Cambridge University Press.

Horn, J. L., & Cattell, R. B. (1966). Refinement and test of the theory of fluid and crystallized general intelligences. *Journal of Educational Psychology, 57,* 253–270.

Kim, C.-J., & Nelson, C. R. (1999). *State-space models with regime switching: Classical and Gibbs-sampling approaches with applications.* Cambridge, MA: MIT Press.

Kohn, R., & Ansley, C. F. (1989). A fast algorithm for signal extraction, influence and cross-validation. *Biometrika, 76,* 65–79.

Larsen, R. J. (2000). Toward a science of mood regulation. *Psychological Inquiry, 11,* 129–141. doi:10.1207/S15327965PLI1103_01

McArdle, J. J., Ferrer-Caja, E., Hamagami, F., & Woodcock, R. W. (2002). Comparative longitudinal structural analyses of the growth and decline of multiple intellectual abilities over the life span. *Developmental Psychology, 38,* 115–142.

McArdle, J. J., & Hamagami, F. (2001). Latent difference score structural models for linear dynamic analysis with incomplete longitudinal data. In L. Collins & A. Sayer (Eds.), *New methods for the analysis of change* (pp. 139–175). Washington, DC: American Psychological Association. doi:10.1037/10409-005

Oud, J. H. L., Jansen, R. A. R. G., van Leeuwe, J. F. L., Aarnoutse, C. A. J., & Voeten, M. J. M. (1999). Monitoring pupil development by means of the Kalman filter and smoother based upon SEM state space modeling. *Learning and Individual Differences, 11,* 121–136. doi:10.1016/S1041-6080(00)80001-1

Piaget, J. (1960). The general problems of the psychobiological development of the child. In J. M. Tanner & B. Inhelder (Eds.), *Discussions on child development* (Vol. 4, pp. 3–28). London, England: Tavistock.

Schweppe, F. (1965). Evaluation of likelihood functions for Gaussian signals. *IEEE Transactions on Information Theory, 11,* 61–70. doi:10.1109/TIT.1965.1053737

Thurstone, L. L. (1962). *Primary mental abilities.* Chicago, IL: Science Research Associates.

Tsay, R. S. (1989). Testing and modeling threshold autoregressive processes. *Journal of the American Statistical Association, 84,* 231–240.

van der Maas, H. L. J., & Molenaar, P. C. M. (1992). Stagewise cognitive development: An application of catastrophe theory. *Psychological Review, 99,* 395–417. doi:10.1037/0033-295X.99.3.395

Young, P. C., Pedregal, D. J., & Tych, W. (1999). Dynamic harmonic regression. *Journal of Forecasting, 18,* 369–394. doi:10.1002/(SICI)1099-131X(199911)18:6{369::AID-FOR748}3.0.CO;2-K

7

A Framework for Discrete Change

Ingmar Visser, Brenda R. J. Jansen, and Maarten Speekenbrink

Discrete change frequently occurs in learning and development: in learning concepts and discrimination learning; in performance on Piagetian tasks, such as the conservation-of-liquid task and the balance scale task; and in conditioning. This chapter is concerned with detecting and characterizing such discrete changes in (individual) time series data. We present a framework of dependent mixture models (DMMs) that can be used to test whether discrete learning events are present and, if they are, to test at which point in time those changes are taking place. We first review some examples from the developmental psychology literature in which discrete change is typically found, and then we turn to describing the model more formally.

Piagetian developmental theory assumes stepwise changes in the rules that children apply in all kinds of tasks, such as in conservation learning and in the balance scale task (Siegler & Alibali, 2005). Van der Maas and Molenaar (1992) developed a catastrophe model to describe stepwise changes predicted to occur by Piagetian theory; it is important to note that they derived precise statistical criteria for testing whether two discretely different stages exist. They applied the catastrophe model to development on the conservation-of-liquid task (Inhelder & Piaget, 1958), in which children have to judge relative volumes of liquid in glasses of different heights and widths. Young children tend to ignore the width dimension and hence always choose the glass with the highest level of liquid (Inhelder & Piaget, 1958). It is assumed that there is a sudden transition, or a discrete change—to a new rule, for example, a rule in which the children also take the width of the glasses into account when judging the volume of liquids.

Jansen and Van der Maas (2001) applied the catastrophe model to development of reasoning on the balance scale task (Siegler, 1981), in which participants have to judge which side of a balance goes down when the number of weights and their distances to the fulcrum are varied over trials. Younger children tend to ignore the distance dimension in this task and instead focus solely

Ingmar Visser was supported by European Commission Framework 6 Grant, Project 516542. Maarten Speekenbrink was supported by the Economic and Social Research Council Centre for Economic Learning and Social Evolution. We thank Hilde Huizenga, Brenda Jansen, and Anna van Duijvenvoorde for the Iowa Gambling Task data and David Lagnado for the Weather Prediction Task data.

on the number of weights on each side of the fulcrum. This strategy for solving balance scale items is called *Rule 1* (Siegler, 1981). Older children include the distance dimension in determining their response to balance scale problems; however, they do so only when the weight dimension does not differ between the sides of the balance, that is, when the number of weights is equal on both sides of the balance scale. This strategy is called *Rule 2* (Siegler, 1981).

Jansen and Van der Maas (2001) found evidence for stagewise transitions, or *discrete change* in our model, between Rule 1 and Rule 2 by testing criteria that were derived from the catastrophe model; specifically, they found bimodal test scores and inaccessibility. The latter means that there are no in-between rules: Children apply either Rule 1 or Rule 2; there is no in-between option. Jansen and Van der Maas also found evidence for *hysteresis,* that is, the phenomenon that switching between rules is asymmetric. Children can switch from Rule 1 to Rule 2 and back, but this occurs at different values of a continuously changing independent variable. In particular, if the distance dimension in the balance scale problem is made increasingly more salient by increasing the distance difference between weights on either side of the balance scale, then children may switch from Rule 1 to Rule 2. If subsequently the distance difference is decreased again, children may switch back to using Rule 1. Hysteresis is the phenomenon that this switchback occurs at a different value of the control variable, in this case the distance difference.

Evidence also has been found for discrete changes in response behavior in animal learning and conditioning. For example, Gallistel, Fairhurst, and Balsam (2004) found evidence for sudden onset of learning: At the start of their learning experiment, pigeons did not learn anything, and performance was stable; after a number of trials, learning kicked in, and there were large increases in performance. Gallistel et al. focused on modeling the distribution of onset times, that is, the trials on which learning suddenly takes off. A similar interest in process onset times can be found in addiction research. For example, Sher, Gotham, and Watson (2004) studied the age at which children start using alcohol and how this relates to eventual outcomes in terms of (severity of) addiction.

Sudden transitions in learning are also observed in simple discrimination learning paradigms in which participants learn to discriminate a number of stimuli on the basis of a single dimension, such as form or color. Raijmakers, Dolan, and Molenaar (2001) found evidence for two different rules applied by children when faced with such a learning task. Schmittmann, Visser, and Raijmakers (2006) reanalyzed Raijmakers et al.'s data using hidden Markov models (HMMs) to show that both rules are characterized by discrete changes during the learning process.

In aforementioned applications, the data consist mostly of a few repeated measurements administered to large groups of participants. The focus in this chapter instead is on data that consist of many repeated measurements, or time series, observed in only a few participants or even just a single participant. For example, Visser, Raijmakers, and Van der Maas (2009) analyzed data from a single participant in an experimental task that manipulated the trade-off between speed and accuracy. The data consisted of three time series, each with approximately 150 repeated measurements of both reaction time and accuracy. In the following paragraphs we provide examples of analyzing time series from single participants from two experiments: one from the Iowa Gambling Task (IGT) and one from the Weather Prediction Task (WPT). The purpose of these tasks is to show that participants develop different rules over time in responding to the stimuli and that the transition from one rule to the next is a discrete event. Before presenting these illustrations, we provide a brief formal definition of DMMs and an overview of the depmixS4 package that was developed to specify and fit such models.

Dependent Mixture Models

In this section we describe a class of models that are especially suitable for describing and testing discrete change in (individual) time series data. The DMM is similar to, but slightly different from, two other types of models that are in use for modeling discrete change: (a) HMMs and (b) latent Markov models.

Markov models have been used for a long time in the social sciences, for example, in analyzing language learning (Miller, 1952; Miller & Chomsky, 1963) and in analyzing paired associate learning (Wickens, 1982). Langeheine and Van de Pol (1990) discussed latent Markov models and their use in sociology and political science (see also McCutcheon, 1987). Latent Markov models have been used to study the development of math skills (Collins & Wugalter, 1992) and in medical applications (Reboussin, Reboussin, Liang, & Anthony, 1998). Kaplan (2008) provided an overview of such models, also called *stage-sequential models,* and their application in developmental psychology.

HMMs tend to be used in the analysis of long (univariate, individual) time series; for example, they are the model of choice in speech recognition applications (Rabiner, 1989). In biology, HMMs are used to analyze DNA sequences (Krogh, 1998), and in econometric science, to analyze changes in stock market prices and commodities (Kim, 1994).

The DMM that we propose here spans the range from latent Markov models for a few repeated measurements with many participants to HMMs for individual time series. In addition, the DMM includes multivariate responses and covariates. The DMM for a time series O_t consists of the following three elements:

1. S is a collection of discrete states, forming the state space.
2. $S_t = AS_{t-1} + \xi_t$, with A a transition matrix.
3. $O_t = B(S_t) + \zeta_t$, with B an observation density.

Here ξ_t and ζ_t are independent error processes (Elliott, Aggoun, & Moore, 1995).

The state space S captures the different states that the learning or developmental process under consideration can be in. In the balance scale example mentioned earlier, children apply one of two possible rules in responding to the items. The states are characterized by their corresponding observation densities. Using a particular rule in the balance scale task leads to correct answers on some items and incorrect answers on others. A different rule may lead to correct answers on some items and to guessing behavior on others. As another example, in analyzing categorization learning data, in which participants learn to categorize a set of objects, a typical initial state is that participants are guessing because at the start of the task they have no knowledge of which features are important in categorization. Hence, the states in the state space represent knowledge states of the participants, such that different knowledge states lead to different observed behaviors or responses.

Transition matrix A describes the transitions between states over repeated measurements. This matrix summarizes the probabilities of transitioning from one state to another, which represents learning or development. The transition model contains the Markov assumption

$$Pr(S_t|S_{t-1},\ldots S_1) = Pr(S_t|S_{t-1}), \qquad (7.1)$$

where Pr is the probability. The Markov assumption means that the current state (at time t) depends only on the previous state S_{t-1}, and not on earlier states.

The observation densities B form the measurement part of the model; these describe the distributions of the observations conditional on the current state S_t. For example, in the balance scale example the observation distributions are binomials because the items are scored as correct or incorrect. When the responses are continuous, B can be a normal distribution, which may, for example, be applicable in modeling response times instead of response accuracies. Hence, these distributions characterize the state, and in our examples these characterize the rule that a participant is using at a given measurement occasion.

DepmixS4

The depmixS4 package (Visser & Speekenbrink, 2008), which is used to analyze data in the illustrations that follow, implements a general framework for defining and fitting dependent mixture models in the R programming language (R Development Core Team, 2008). This includes standard Markov models, latent Markov models and HMMs, and latent class and finite mixture distribution models. The models can be fitted on mixed multivariate data with error distributions from the generalized linear model framework, such as Gaussian, binomial, multinomial logistic, and so on.

The depmixS4 package was motivated by the fact that Markovian models are used commonly in the social sciences but no comprehensive package was available for fitting such models in R. Common programs for Markovian models include Panmark (Van de Pol, Langeheine, & Jong, 1996) and, for latent class models, Latent Gold (Vermunt & Magidson, 2003). Those programs lack a number of features that were needed in our research. In particular, depmixS4 was designed to meet the following goals:

- to fit transition models with covariates, that is, such that the transition probabilities depend on a time-dependent covariate;
- to include covariates in the prior or initial state probabilities of models;

- to allow for easy extensibility—in particular, to be able to add new response distributions, both univariate and multivariate, and similarly to allow for the addition of other transition models (e.g., models for observations in continuous time); and
- to fit models on arbitrary length individual time series.

Although depmixS4 is designed to deal with longitudinal or time series data for, say, $T > 100$, it can also handle the limit case with $T = 1$ in analyzing cross-sectional data. In those cases there are no time dependencies between observed data, and the model reduces to a finite mixture model (McLachlan & Peel, 2000) or a latent class model (McCutcheon, 1987). Although there are other specialized (R) packages to deal with mixture data, these do not allow the inclusion of covariates on the prior probabilities of class membership.

To allow easy extensibility, depmixS4 is built using S4 classes (object-oriented classes in R; Chambers, 1998). A depmix model consists of the following:

- a model for the initial or prior probabilities, possibly depending on covariates;
- a list of transition models, with one model for each row of the transition matrix, possibly depending on covariates; and
- a list of response models for each of the states of the model; this is a list of lists in the case of multivariate responses.

We briefly address each of these in the sections that follow.

Transition and Prior Probabilities Models

By default, each row of the transition matrix and the vector of initial state probabilities is modeled as a baseline-category multinomial logistic model (see Agresti, 2002, chap. 4). This means that covariates can be used as predictors in these models. In particular, the model for each multinomial is

$$p_i = \exp(\alpha_i + \beta_i'\mathbf{x})/[1 + \Sigma_j \exp(\alpha_j + \beta_j'\mathbf{x})], \qquad (7.2)$$

where p_i is the probability (e.g., the probability of the ith initial state); the α_i are the category intercepts; the β_i are the category regression coefficients; $\mathbf{x}$ is a vector of covariates or predictors; and the sum runs from 1 to $J - 1$, where J is the number of states. In this example, J serves as the baseline-category, meaning that α_J and β_J are zero.

Response Models

Response models in depmixS4 interface with the *glm* functions (R Development Core Team, 2008) available in R and with the *nnet*-package (Venables & Ripley, 2002) for the multinomial logistic models. This interface consists in the use of the same formulae to specify *glm*s as in the *glm* package; moreover, the fitting of these distributions for each state relies on the fitting functions available in that package. Normally distributed data can hence be modeled with direct effects included as well. For example, normal data are modeled as follows:

$$O_t | S_t = \mu + \beta'\mathbf{x} + \varepsilon_t, \quad (7.3)$$

where μ is the (state-dependent) mean, $\mathbf{x}$ is a vector of covariates or predictors, β is the vector of (state-dependent) regression coefficients, and ε_t is a normally distributed error term with (state-dependent) standard deviation σ. To illustrate, when the response O_t is a reaction time, these can be modeled as having different means between different states of the model. For an example of this see Visser et al. (2009), in which a two-state model was used to model the speed–accuracy trade-off. In this model the two states have different means of the reaction times: Guess responses are associated with fast reaction times, whereas accurate responses are associated with much longer reaction times. Furthermore, in this example B may represent trial number to allow for training effects in the data; one may assume that participants' performance becomes better because of training on a particular task, which would lead to an overall decrease in response times, while at the same time there are still two different modes of responding, one fast and one slow.

Multinomial responses are modeled by the same multinomial baseline-category logistic model as is used for the transition probabilities and the initial state probabilities. Other response functions from the generalized linear model family that can be used include binomial logistic regression, Poisson regression, gamma, and inverse Gaussian. There is also support for the multivariate normal distribution.

Parameter Estimation

Parameters are estimated in depmixS4 using the EM algorithm or through the use of a general Newton–Raphson optimizer. EM is used by default in unconstrained models, but otherwise direct optimization is done using RDONLP2 (Spellucci, 2002; Tamura, 2007), because it handles general linear (in)equality constraints and, optionally, nonlinear constraints. Both the forward algorithm (Baum & Petrie, 1966; Rabiner, 1989) and the version by Lystig and Hughes (2002) are implemented in depmixS4; the latter is implemented to allow easy computation of the gradients of the parameters.

Illustrations

We now provide two illustrations of models used to analyze single-participant time series data from two common experimental paradigms. In both of these participants learn different rules through trial and error. The main goal of these illustrations is to establish the possibility of analyzing single-participant data using the depmixS4 framework.

Iowa Gambling Task

The IGT is an experimental paradigm designed to mimic real-life decision-making situations (Bechara, Damasio, Damasio, & Anderson, 1994), in the way that it factors uncertainty, reward, and punishment (Dunn, Dalgleish, & Lawrence, 2006). The task requires the individual to select cards from four decks. Each deck is characterized by a certain amount of gain (delivered on each draw), frequency of loss, and amount of loss. Two decks (A and B) yield consistently not only high rewards but also high probabilistic penalties and are both (equally) disadvantageous in the long run. The other two decks (C and D) yield consistently smaller rewards but low probabilistic penalties and are both (equally) advantageous in the long run. It is assumed that the ventromedial prefrontal cortex is active in the IGT because patients with ventromedial prefrontal cortex lesions show impaired task performance. Their preference for the decks with immediate high rewards indicates "myopia for the future" (Bechara et al., 1994).

Crone and Van der Molen (2004) designed a developmentally appropriate analogue of the IGT, the Hungry Donkey Task (HDT), with a similar win–loss schedule, although the absolute amounts were reduced by a factor of 25. The HDT is a prosocial game that invites the player to help a hungry donkey collect as many apples as possible, by opening one of four doors. Again, Doors A and B are characterized by a high constant gain (10 apples), whereas Doors C and D deliver a low constant gain (2 apples) at each trial. At Doors A and C a loss of 10 apples (Door A) or 2 apples (Door C) is delivered in 50% of the trials. For Doors B and D the frequency of loss is only 10%. The median losses of Doors B and D are 50 and 10, respectively. Crone and Van der Molen administered the HDT to children from four age groups (6- to 9-, 10- to 12-, 13- to 15-, and 18- to 25-year-olds) and concluded that children have difficulty taking future consequences into account.

A reanalysis of this data set (Huizenga, Crone, & Jansen, 2007) indicated that participants might solve the task by sequentially considering the three dimensions (constant gain, frequency of loss, and amount of loss) to choose a door. Most of the youngest children seem to focus on frequency of loss, resulting in equal preference for Doors B and D. It is assumed that frequency of loss is the dominant dimension in this task. Older participants seem to use a two-dimensional rule whereby they first focus on the frequency of loss and then consider amount of loss, resulting in a preference for Door D. A third, very small subgroup seems to use an integrative rule whereby participants combine all three dimensions in the appropriate way. Participants using the integrative rule pick cards from Doors C and D, which are both equally advantageous in the long run, although Door D shows a higher volatility.

Huizenga et al. (2007) used the last 60 trials in a series of 200, as is typically done in analyzing this task. Doing so silently assumes that behavior has stabilized after 140 trials of learning; this may not be the case, and it is highly likely that there are individual differences in this learning process. Hence, here we analyze IGT learning data from a single participant with the aim of establishing two things: (a) at which trial learning stops (i.e., at which trial behavior has stabilized) and (b) what rules participants use during and at the end of learning. Models with an increasing number (from two through five) of latent states were fitted to the time series of a single participant. The responses were fitted with multinomial logistic models for the four possible choices that participants make in this task. There were no covariates on any of the parameters. The only constraint imposed on the models' parameters was that there were designated begin and end states. This means that the initial state probabilities were fixed to 1 for the first state and to 0 for the remaining states. For the transition matrix this means that the final state was an absorbing one: the probability of transitioning out of the final state was set to 0. This was done to ensure that there would be a final state in which participants end that provides the possibility of immediately seeing participants' behavior at the end of the task. Models were selected using the Akaike Information Criterion (AIC; Akaike, 1973). The data were best described by a four-state model; the parameters of this model are listed in Table 7.1. As can be seen from the transition matrix parameters, the final state is absorbing. States 2 and 3 are also fairly stable with high diagonal probabilities of .89 and .95, respectively.

The states have clear interpretations. States 3 and 4 are both dominated by C responses, and State 4 has a low probability of B responses. States 1 and 2 are dominated by C and D responses and A and B responses, respectively. To get a clearer interpretation of these states it is necessary to consider when they are visited during the learning process. The Viterbi algorithm (Rabiner, 1989) provides us with the posterior state sequence, that is, the sequence of states in which the participant is at each trial. This sequence is depicted in Figure 7.1.

At the start of training there are many switches between States 1 and 2, indicating that behavior comprises mostly random choices among all four categories, albeit with a slight preference for Doors B and D over Doors A and C. This preference indicates a focus on the frequency of loss associated with each of the doors because B and D both have low frequency of loss. After this, there is a period of stable State 2 behavior associated with A and B choices. After that there is stable State 3 behavior, consisting only of C responses, a short transitional period, and then State 4 behavior, consisting of 94% Door C choices and some Door B choices, that is, almost optimal behavior. The choice proportions and the model predicted choice proportions are depicted in Figure 7.2. Although there is quite some variability in the data, the model predicted choice proportions are generally close to the data. Note that in Figure 7.2 the proportions are averaged over blocks of 10 trials.

The initial preference for B and D choices confirms the theory expressed by Huizenga et al. (2007) that frequency of loss is the dominant dimension in the IGT. The final states, with mostly C choices, represent one of the optimal rules,

Table 7.1. Estimates for Response Probabilities (ps) and Transition Probabilities in the Iowa Gambling Task Model

State (S)	$p(A)$	$p(B)$	$p(C)$	$p(D)$	To S1	To S2	To S3	To S4
S1	0	.06	.31	.63	.64	.33	.00	.03
S2	.33	.67	0	0	.10	.89	.01	.00
S3	0	0	1	0	.05	.00	.95	.00
S4	0	.06	.94	0	.00	.00	.00	1.00

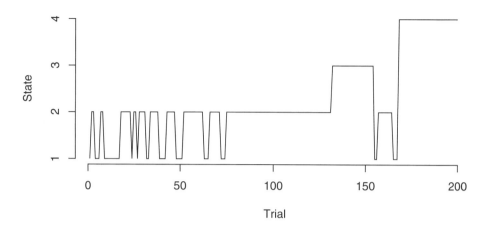

Figure 7.1. Posterior state sequence for the four-state model of the Iowa Gambling Task data.

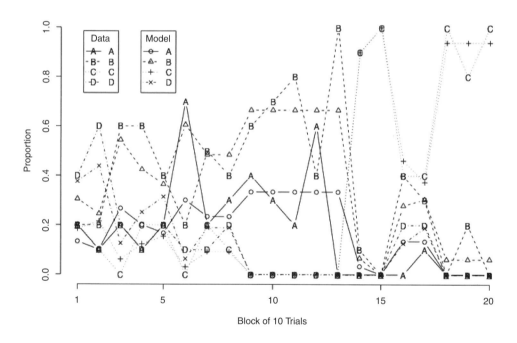

Figure 7.2. Data- and model-predicted proportions of door choices in the Iowa Gambling Task. Depicted are the proportions of door choices in blocks of 10 consecutive trials for each of the doors: A, B, C, and D. The data are depicted by lines with letters in them. The corresponding proportions that are derived from the four-state model are represented by the other lines with circles, triangles, "+"s, and "x"s.

which consist of both C and D responses. Note that C and D responses generate equal profits in the long run.

Weather Prediction Task

The WPT (Knowlton, Squire, & Gluck, 1994) is a probabilistic categorization task in which participants learn to predict (or categorize) the state of the weather (sun or rain) on the basis of four "tarot" cards (cards with abstract geometrical patterns). On a given trial, one, two, or three cues are present. There are a total of 14 possible cue patterns, and each cue pattern is associated with a particular probability distribution over the states of the weather. To perform well on the task, participants must predict the weather in accordance with these conditional probabilities.

There are different accounts of probabilistic category learning (see, e.g., Ashby & Maddox, 2005, for an overview). According to instance or exemplar learning theories, participants learn by storing each encountered cue–outcome pair. When presented with a probe cue pattern, the participant makes a response by retrieving these exemplars from memory and weighting them according to their similarity to the probe cue pattern. In contrast, according to associative learning theories, participants learn by gradually associating the individual cues (or cue patterns in configural learning) to the outcomes. Finally, in rule learning participants learn to extract rules by which to categorize the different cue patterns. Gluck, Shohamy, and Myers (2002) proposed a number of such rules. The rules differ in the way the cues are combined into a response. The main difference concerns whether responses are based on the presence or absence of a single cue or whether information from multiple cues is integrated. Gluck et al. (2002) formulated all rules in a deterministic and optimal manner (e.g., the multicue rule corresponded to giving the optimal response to each cue pattern). Meeter, Myers, Shohamy, Hopkins, and Gluck (2006) allowed for probabilistic responding (a small probability of responding nonoptimally) as well as switches between rules during learning. However, both rules and response probabilities remained predefined. Alternative nonrule-based analyses of the WPT (Lagnado, Newell, Kahan, & Shanks, 2006; Speekenbrink & Shanks, 2008) have estimated response distributions through logistic regression, allowing the regression coefficients to change smoothly over time.

Here, we combine the regression and rule-based approaches, and analyze the behavior of a single individual performing the WPT for 200 trials. We are particularly interested in evidence for rule switching and whether a DMM can recover rules in accordance with Gluck et al. (2002). We chose to analyze the average participant (the participant with performance closest to the group average) in a large unpublished data set. We let each state be characterized by a generalized linear model with a binomial distributed response and logistic link function (i.e., a logistic regression model; see Equation 7.2). The regression coefficients of a model relating the cues to the state of the weather are given in the "Validity" column in Table 7.2. Note that identical coefficients for the model relating the cues to responses would indicate probability matching. A maximizing strategy is indicated by more extreme regression coefficients.

Table 7.2. Parameter Estimates and Fit Measures of Models
for the Weather Prediction Task Data

Parameter	Validity[a]	One state (S1)	Two state S1	Two state S2	Two state (constrained) S1	Two state (constrained) S2
Intercept	0	−0.69	−2.73	0.88	−1.24	0
Cue 1	2.10	1.69	2.12	1.60	1.65	1.97
Cue 2	0.58	1.12	0.97	1.63	0	1.92
Cue 3	−0.58	−0.49	0.91	−2.03	0	−1.58
Cue 4	−2.10	−1.32	0.69	−3.16	0	−2.67
AIC		204.47	187.50		185.24	

Note. Parameter estimates are the logistic regression coefficients of a model to predict the (conditional) probability of "sun" responses. Parameter values can range on the whole real line; positive (negative) values indicate a higher likelihood of sun (rain). AIC = Akaike Information Criterion.
[a]The objective parameters for the task environment (obtained from fitting a model to the true conditional probabilities of the state of the weather).

As we fitted a DMM to the data of a single participant we placed some constraints on the model to decrease the number of free parameters and improve estimation. Specifically, we constrained the state transitions to be in a left–right format (states can proceed only to the immediately adjacent state, never back, and must start in the initial state). We fitted models with one, two, or three states to the data. The AIC values of these models showed that the two-state model outperformed the one- and three-state models.

Investigation of the parameter estimates (see Table 7.2) showed that the regression coefficient for the first cue was of much larger magnitude than that of the other cues. Because of this, the first state seems representative of single cue rule. Alternatively, because all regression coefficients are positive, it could indicate a counting heuristic, whereby the propensity of "sun" responses increases when more cues are present (regardless of which cues they are). However, in that case we would expect the regression coefficients to be of roughly identical magnitude. The second state represents a multicue rule, because all cues had regression coefficients of reasonable magnitude in the direction of the objective cue validities.

To reduce the degrees of freedom and improve parameter estimates, we implemented constraints to force State 1 into a single-cue rule (fixing the coefficients of the remaining three cues to 0) and State 2 into a multicue rule (forcing the intercept to 0). These restrictions resulted in a better AIC value: 185.24 ($df = 7$). It is interesting that the single-cue rule was somewhat different than that described by Gluck et al. (2002). Parameter estimates indicated relatively more consistent predictions of "rain" in the absence of Cue 1 (Pr(sun) = .22) and more inconsistent predictions of "sun" in the presence of Cue 1 (Pr(sun) = .60). The cue weights of the multicue rule were in the direction of the optimal weights. The Viterbi state sequence indicated that the participant used the single-cue rule for the first 60 trials and then switched to the multicue rule.

Discussion

Discrete change is hypothesized to occur in many domains in experimental psychology, especially in learning and developmental tasks. Piagetian theory predicts that discrete changes will occur in a number of developmental tasks (Inhelder & Piaget, 1958). There is a growing body of evidence showing that discrete change does indeed occur during development and learning (Jansen & Van der Maas, 2001; Raijmakers et al., 2001; Schmittmann et al., 2006; Van der Maas & Molenaar, 1992). Discrete rules have recently been hypothesized to play an important role in learning tasks such as the IGT (Huizenga et al., 2007) and the WPT (Gluck et al., 2002). Until now, such data were always analyzed on a group basis, that is, by pooling the data of many participants together. Given that it is extremely likely that there are individual differences between participants, such pooling of data may not be warranted and may lead to suboptimal results (Gallistel et al., 2004; Molenaar, 2005).

In this study, we showed the feasibility of analyzing single-participant data in two common experimental tasks, thereby avoiding the pitfalls of pooling data from individuals that may differ in important respects. The illustrations show that single-participant data comprising only 200 trials can be analyzed and lead to nontrivial models with multiple states. This opens up possibilities for analyzing data from other experimental tasks on an individual basis.

In addition to analyzing single-participant data, the depmixS4 package that we have presented here offers the possibility of further combining models of single-participant data into larger models and testing whether, for example, some rules are identical between (groups of) participants. Performing such analyses and aggregating models afterward on the basis of commonalities and differences between participants avoids unwarranted assumptions about homogeneity between participants. A similar approach using continuous latent variable models (i.e., factor models) was used by Hamaker, Dolan, and Molenaar (2007) to integrate within- and between-person variability in the domain of personality research.

Our illustration with the IGT data led to a four-state model. The states of the model corresponded very well with earlier analyses by Huizenga et al. (2007), showing a number of discrete rules. Even within a single participant a number of different rules were observed during the acquisition process; learning started with behavior close to guessing, which is best interpreted as exploring behavior, and was followed by two states with close to optimal performance. In addition to confirming the existence of discrete rules, the use of DMM analyses provides us with information of the dynamics of knowledge acquisition in this task.

Analyzing the WPT data on an individual level allowed us to precisely estimate idiographic rules and their progression during learning. Moreover, using DMMs one can combine an individual- and a group-level analysis, increasing reliability of the individual analyses while allowing for substantial individual differences. Previous analyses (e.g., Meeter et al., 2006) have used predefined individual rules, based on participants' self-reports in Gluck et al. (2002). It is interesting that Gluck et al. noted that these self-reports often did not correspond to the rules evident in participants' responses. It is well known that people may find it difficult to verbalize the way in which they integrate multiple sources of information. This problem is even more severe in the study of young children. Because of this, estimating rules directly from participants' responses results in a more valid assessment of their response rules and provides a direct test of the validity of the rule set Gluck et al. identified.

In sum, DMMs have been shown to be feasible models of individual time series. Moreover, depmixS4 can be used to build models of groups of participants combined and allows for testing to determine whether pooling individual participants' data is warranted. Because of the use of S4 classes, the depmixS4 package is highly flexible and easily extensible. Future options are to include other measurement models, such as the factor model or models with autoregressive coefficients. Also, extensions of the transition model are easily implemented; for example, the addition of support for continuous time measurement in contrast to equally spaced measurement occasions as were used in the illustrations we have presented in this chapter. DMMs, hence, have great potential in enlarging our insights into important issues in learning and development, in particular in modeling and testing the occurrence of discrete change.

References

Agresti, A. (2002). *Categorical data analysis* (2nd ed.). Hoboken, NJ: Wiley Interscience.

Akaike, H. (1973). Information theory and an extension of the maximum likelihood principle. In B. N. Petrov & F. Csaki (Eds.), *Second International Symposium on Information Theory* (pp. 267–281). Budapest, Hungary: Academiai Kiado.

Ashby, F. G., & Maddox, W. T. (2005). Human category learning. *Annual Review of Psychology, 56,* 149–178. doi:10.1146/annurev.psych.56.091103.070217

Baum, L. E., & Petrie, T. (1966). Statistical inference for probabilistic functions of finite state Markov chains. *Annals of Mathematical Statistics, 37,* 1554–1563. doi:10.1214/aoms/1177699147

Bechara, A., Damasio, A. R., Damasio, H., & Anderson, S. (1994). Insensitivity to future consequences following damage to human prefrontal cortex. *Cognition, 50*(1–3), 7–15. doi:10.1016/0010-0277(94)90018-3

Chambers, J. M. (1998). *Programming with data: A guide to the S language.* New York, NY: Springer-Verlag.

Collins, L. M., & Wugalter, S. E. (1992). Latent class models for stage-sequential dynamic latent variables. *Multivariate Behavioral Research, 27,* 131–157. doi:10.1207/s15327906mbr2701_8

Crone, E. A., & Van der Molen, M. W. (2004). Developmental changes in real life decision making: Performance on a gambling task previously shown to depend on the ventromedial prefrontal cortex. *Developmental Neuropsychology, 25,* 251–279. doi:10.1207/s15326942dn2503_2

Dunn, B. D., Dalgleish, T., & Lawrence, A. D. (2006). The somatic marker hypothesis: A critical evaluation. *Neuroscience & Biobehavioral Reviews, 30,* 239–271. doi:10.1016/j.neubiorev.2005.07.001

Elliott, R. J., Aggoun, L., & Moore, J. B. (1995). *Hidden Markov models: Estimation and control.* New York, NY: Springer-Verlag.

Gallistel, C. R., Fairhurst, S., & Balsam, P. (2004). The learning curve: Implications of a quantitative analysis. *Proceedings of the National Academy of Sciences USA, 101,* 13124–13131. doi:10.1073/pnas.0404965101

Gluck, M. A., Shohamy, D., & Myers, C. (2002). How do people solve the weather prediction task?: Individual variability in strategies for probabilistic category learning. *Learning & Memory, 9,* 408–418. doi:10.1101/lm.45202

Hamaker, E. L., Dolan, C. V., & Molenaar, P. C. M. (2007). The integrated trait–state model. *Journal of Research in Personality, 41,* 295–315. doi:10.1016/j.jrp.2006.04.003

Huizenga, H. M., Crone, E. A., & Jansen, B. R. J. (2007). Decision-making in healthy children, adolescents and adults explained by the use of increasingly complex proportional reasoning rules. *Developmental Science, 10,* 814–825. doi:10.1111/j.1467-7687.2007.00621.x

Inhelder, B., & Piaget, J. (1958). *The growth of logical thinking from childhood to adolescence.* New York, NY: Basic Books.

Jansen, B. R. J., & Van der Maas, H. L. J. (2001). Evidence for the phase transition from Rule I to Rule II On the balance scale task. *Developmental Review, 21,* 450–494. doi:10.1006/drev.2001.0530

Kaplan, D. (2008). An overview of Markov chain methods for the study of stage-sequential developmental processes. *Developmental Psychology, 44,* 457–467. doi:10.1037/0012-1649.44.2.457

Kim, C.-J. (1994). Dynamic linear models with Markov-switching. *Journal of Econometrics, 60,* 1–22. doi:10.1016/0304-4076(94)90036-1

Knowlton, B. J., Squire, L. R., & Gluck, M. A. (1994). Probabilistic classification learning in amnesia. *Learning & Memory, 1,* 106–120.

Krogh, A. (1998). An introduction to hidden Markov models for biological sequences. In S. L. Salzberg, D. B. Searls, & S. Kasif (Eds.), *Computational methods in molecular biology* (pp. 45–63). Amsterdam, the Netherlands: Elsevier.

Lagnado, D. A., Newell, B. R., Kahan, S., & Shanks, D. R. (2006). Insight and strategy in multiple cue learning. *Journal of Experimental Psychology: General, 135,* 162–183. doi:10.1037/0096-3445.135.2.162

Langeheine, R., & Van de Pol, F. (1990). A unifying framework for Markov modeling in discrete space and discrete time. *Sociological Methods & Research, 18,* 416–441. doi:10.1177/0049124190018004002

Lystig, T. C., & Hughes, J. P. (2002). Exact computation of the observed information matrix for hidden Markov models. *Journal of Computational and Graphical Statistics, 11,* 678–689.

McCutcheon, A. L. (1987). *Latent class analysis.* Beverly Hills, CA: Sage.

McLachlan, G. J., & Peel, D. (2000). *Finite mixture models.* New York, NY: Wiley-Interscience.

Meeter, M., Myers, C. E., Shohamy, D., Hopkins, R. O., & Gluck, M. A. (2006). Strategies in probabilistic categorization: Results from a new way of analyzing performance. *Learning & Memory, 13,* 230–239. doi:10.1101/lm.43006

Miller, G. A. (1952). Finite Markov processes in psychology. *Psychometrika, 17,* 149–167. doi:10.1007/BF02288779

Miller, G. A., & Chomsky, N. (1963). Finitary models of language users. In R. Luce, R. R. Bush, & E. Galanter (Eds.), *Handbook of mathematical psychology* (pp. 419–491). New York, NY: Wiley.

Molenaar, P. (2005). A manifesto on psychology as ideographic science: Bringing the person back into scientific psychology, this time forever. *Measurement: Interdisciplinary Research & Perspective, 2,* 201–218.

Rabiner, L. R. (1989). A tutorial on hidden Markov models and selected applications in speech recognition. *Proceedings of the IEEE, 77,* 257–286. doi:10.1109/5.18626

Raijmakers, M. E. J., Dolan, C. V., & Molenaar, P. C. M. (2001). Finite mixture distribution models of simple discrimination learning. *Memory & Cognition, 29,* 659–677.

R Development Core Team. (2008). *R: A language and environment for statistical computing.* Retrieved from http://cran.r-project.org/doc/manuals/refman.pdf

Reboussin, B. A., Reboussin, D. M., Liang, K.-Y., & Anthony, J. C. (1998). Latent transition modeling of progression of health-risk behavior. *Multivariate Behavioral Research, 33,* 457–478. doi:10.1207/s15327906mbr3304_2

Schmittmann, V. D., Visser, I., & Raijmakers, M. E. J. (2006). Multiple learning modes in the development of rule-based category-learning task performance. *Neuropsychologia, 44,* 2079–2091. doi:10.1016/j.neuropsychologia.2005.12.011

Sher, K. J., Gotham, H. J., & Watson, A. L. (2004). Trajectories of dynamic predictors of disorder: their meanings and implications. *Development and Psychopathology, 16,* 825–856. doi:10.1017/S0954579404040039

Siegler, R. S. (1981). Developmental sequences within and between concepts. *Monographs of the Society for Research in Child Development, 46*(2), 1–84. doi:10.2307/1165995

Siegler, R. S., & Alibali, M. W. (2005). *Children's thinking.* Upper Saddle River, NJ: Prentice Hall.

Speekenbrink, M., & Shanks, D. R. (2008). Through the looking glass: A dynamic lens model approach to learning in MCPL tasks. In N. Chater & M. Oaksford (Eds.), *The probabilistic mind: Prospects for rational models of cognition* (pp. 409–430). Oxford, England: Oxford University Press.

Spellucci, P. (2002). *DONLP2.* Retrieved from ftp://ftp.mathematik.tu-darmstadt.de/pub/department/software/opti/DONLP2/

Tamura, R. (2007). *RDONLP2: An R extension library to use Peter Spelluci's DONLP2 from R* (R package version 0.3-1). Retrieved from http://arumat.net/Rdonlp2/

Van de Pol, F., Langeheine, R., & Jong, W. D. (1996). *Panmark 3: Panel analysis using Markov chains. A latent class analysis program.* Voorburg, The Netherlands: Statistics Netherlands.

van der Maas, H. L. J., & Molenaar, P. (1992). Stagewise cognitive development: An application of catastrophe theory. *Psychological Review, 99,* 395–417. doi:10.1037/0033-295X.99.3.395

Venables, W. N., & Ripley, B. D. (2002). *Modern applied statistics with S* (4th ed.). New York, NY: Springer-Verlag.

Vermunt, J. K., & Magidson, J. (2003). Latent Gold 3.0 [Computer software]. Belmont, MA: Statistical Innovations.

Visser, I., Raijmakers, M. E. J., & Van der Maas, H. L. J. (2009). Hidden Markov models for individual time series. In J. Valsiner, P. C. M. Molenaar, M. C. D. P. Lyra, & N. Chaudhary (Eds.), *Dynamic process methodology in the social and developmental sciences* (pp. 269–290). New York, NY: Springer.

Visser, I., & Speekenbrink, M. (2008). *DepmixS4: S4 Classes for hidden Markov models* (R package version 0.2-0). Available from the Comprehensive R Archive Network, http://cran.r-project.org/

Wickens, T. D. (1982). *Models for behavior: Stochastic processes in psychology.* San Francisco, CA: Freeman.

8

State Space Methods for Item Response Modeling of Multisubject Time Series

Peter van Rijn, Conor V. Dolan,
and Peter C. M. Molenaar

Item response theory (IRT) is an important area of research in psychometrics. It provides a theoretical framework for the construction, application, and evaluation of tests in psychological and educational measurement. Within contemporary IRT, probabilistic models are used to describe the relations between observable item responses and unobservable psychological traits or abilities (Hambleton & Swaminathan, 1985). A primary purpose of IRT, and of test theory in general, is to describe the differences in item responses and test scores between individuals because most applications are more suited for describing groups than individuals (Lord & Novick, 1968, p. 32). The purpose of this chapter is to describe IRT models that are based on differences in item responses within individuals to whom the same test has been repeatedly administered over time, that is, to describe dynamic IRT models. For the analysis of this type of measurements, the *state space framework* is used (Durbin & Koopman, 2001). The state space methodology is capable of handling both standard and dynamic IRT models. In addition, variation between and within individuals can be analyzed simultaneously.

Most IRT models are developed to account for the variation in item responses that arises when items are administered to different individuals. The argument for the development of such models is to explain the differences between, rather than within, individuals. One can argue that, at least on a theoretical level, this focus is one sided and that it is of interest to develop IRT models that account for the variation within individuals. For a thorough argument in favor of developing models for describing variation within individuals, see Molenaar (2004) and the subsequent discussion. One of the arguments for pursuing the development of such models is that a model that provides an informative account of interindividual differences is not necessarily valid at the level of intraindividual differences, as has been observed in repeated measures obtained from a single individual (Borsboom, Mellenbergh, & van Heerden, 2003; Kelderman & Molenaar, 2007). Although the ultimate goal of a standard application of IRT is to make inferences about a person's position on one or more latent dimensions of interindividual differences, such inferences are not necessarily correct at the intraindividual level. More specifically, the constitution of the latent space of interindividual traits or abilities that one intends to measure may be either incomplete or overly complete at the intraindividual level; that is, while ignoring a latent dimension contributing to an individual's development on the one hand, too much importance might be attached to certain factors that can be relevant for only some individuals on the other hand. In addition, a person's latent position can change over time, and individual differences can exist in such changes.

The preceding argument can be related to a discussion of two commonly used interpretations of probability in IRT (see Fischer & Molenaar, 1995; Holland, 1990). In describing the two views, a single administration of a single specific test is considered. The first view is the so-called *random-sampling view,* according to which the only source of variation is the random sampling of individuals. According to this view, individuals conceivably possess fixed yet unknown response patterns. By sampling individuals at random from a population with a certain latent position, variation in response patterns is likely to occur. The probability of a response pattern can then be viewed as the proportion of individuals from that population who would show that pattern under repeated random sampling. The second, more popular view is the *stochastic-subject view,* according to which each individual possesses a certain latent position and probability is defined by the proportion of response patterns obtained by hypothesized repeated and independent administrations of the same test under the exact same circumstances.

This latter view is adopted when defining IRT models from variation within individuals over time, except that the administrations are not independent, and circumstances are subject to change. In defining a dynamic IRT model in this sense, an individual can at the first instance be considered as fixed, but within this individual a stochastic process unfolds such that variation in response patterns is likely to arise from different administrations of the same test. Because of their sequential nature, these administrations cannot be considered to be independent. This sequential dependence then should be accounted for in the model. Thus, we are dealing with a time series, and methods to model the dependencies and changes in time series explicitly are widely available (see, e.g., Hamilton, 1994; Lütkepohl, 2005).

An important topic that arises when one is interested in models for intraindividual variation is *stationarity.* A second topic that is important when one is concerned with more than one individual is *ergodicity.* Stationarity concerns the lack of time dependence of the distribution of a single time series (Hamilton, 1994), and ergodicity concerns the distributional properties of an ensemble of time series. The notion of ergodicity, to which we adhere, can be formulated as follows: If the model is stationary and the same for each individual, then the collection of individuals is considered ergodic. This means that individuals are interchangeable and that an analysis of a collection of individuals at a single time point provides the same results as an analysis of a randomly selected single individual on a collection of time points. Generalizations can then be conducted either way. Consider the following example: If a model with a univariate latent process can be used to explain the response patterns obtained by repeated administrations of the same test to a single individual, and the model parameters and the distribution of this process do not change over time, then the condition of stationarity is met. If the same model and univariate latent process hold for the collection of individuals, then the condition of ergodicity is said to be met.

In comparing the two types of variation within IRT, two implications of the ergodic notion are pertinent. First, the number of latent dimensions that best describe the item responses might differ between individuals. If this is the case, ergodicity does not hold, and each individual or cluster of individuals needs to be analyzed separately. Second, even if the latent processes of two persons are stationary and of the same dimension, the specific time dependencies can be different. For example, an autoregressive and a white noise process can both be stationary and univariate. If this combined model proves to be best fitting for the data of two individuals, can the interpretation of the two latent processes be equated? In terms of the psychological content of the processes, there is no definitive answer. These issues complicate matters substantially in comparing individual differences in variation over time.

Many models for dynamic testing and measuring change have been described (e.g., Embretson, 1991; Fischer, 1989), some of which are of special interest here. Within the framework of IRT, Kempf (1977) dropped the assumption of local independence. He derived sufficient statistics for the person parameters by conditioning on the sum score of previous responses. Verhelst and Glas (1993) circumvented dropping the assumption of local independence by deftly manipulating the concept of incomplete designs. They developed a dynamic Rasch model (RM) and a marginal maximum likelihood (MML) estimation procedure. In this chapter, we describe a dynamic model for responses to repeatedly administered items in which latent variables are replaced by latent processes. An extended version of the Kalman filter and smoother (KFS), which is based on the posterior distribution of so-called "states" of a state space model, is used to estimate the parameters (Fahrmeir, 1992; Fahrmeir & Wagenpfeil, 1997).

The outline of this chapter is as follows. First, we discuss the RM and the partial credit model (PCM), and then we describe commonly used parameter estimation methods and the assessment of model fit. Next, we introduce the dynamic versions of the RM and PCMs. We then describe how to specify both standard and dynamic IRT models as a state space model, and we discuss the estimation by means of Kalman filtering and smoothing. We illustrate the methods with two example data sets, one standard IRT analysis and one dynamic IRT analysis. We conclude the chapter with an overarching discussion.

Standard Item Response Theory

Models

In a basic IRT setting a unidimensional latent variable, θ, is assumed to be related to the probability of the responses y on a test of n items by a monotonically increasing function. This function is referred to as the *item response function.* The latent variable θ refers to some unobserved psychological trait of an individual—for example, math ability—that the items are supposed to measure, and it describes the differences between individuals. The characteristics of an item can be described by one or more parameters. Rasch (1960/1980) developed such a model for dichotomous item responses, that is, when the elements of y can each be scored as either 0 or 1. In this model the probability that a person with a certain θ responds to item i with threshold parameters β_i with 1 is determined by the logistic function as follows:

$$p(y_i = 1|\theta) = p_i(\theta) = \frac{\exp(\theta - \beta_i)}{1 + \exp(\theta - \beta_i)}, \qquad i = 1, \ldots, n. \qquad (8.1)$$

If a person's θ exceeds the item's threshold β_i, the response 1 is more likely, and if β_i exceeds θ, the response 0 is more likely. This model has been used extensively in educational settings in which dichotomous item responses can often be scored as incorrect (0) or correct (1). The parameter β_i has therefore acquired the interpretation as item difficulty. The model in Equation 8.1 has come to be known as the *Rasch model,* although it is also referred to as the *one-parameter logistic model* (Hambleton & Swaminathan, 1985). The RM possesses the property of *specific objectivity,* which states that the comparison of items is dependent only on the difference in difficulty (β), and in turn the comparison of persons is dependent only on the difference in ability (θ). For two different items and two different persons, specific objectivity is obtained by simplifying the following log odds ratios:

$$\log\left(\frac{\frac{p_1(\theta)}{1 - p_1(\theta)}}{\frac{p_2(\theta)}{1 - p_2(\theta)}}\right) = \beta_2 - \beta_1 \qquad \text{and} \qquad \log\left(\frac{\frac{p_i(\theta_1)}{1 - p_i(\theta_1)}}{\frac{p_i(\theta_2)}{1 - p_i(\theta_2)}}\right) = \theta_1 - \theta_2. \qquad (8.2)$$

The RM for dichotomous items can be extended to allow for more differences between items than the difficulty alone. For instance, differences in steepness of the item response functions can be represented in the model by the inclusion of a discrimination parameter. It can also be extended to allow for guessing if ability items with a closed response format are concerned. These extensions were developed by Birnbaum (1968) for the logistic model. Rasch and others extended the models to allow for items with more than two responses, that is, for polytomous items (Andersen, 1995; Samejima, 1969). Because these extensions allow not only for polytomously scored ability items but also for the use of Likert scale formats, IRT models have found their way outside the realm of ability testing. Apart from educational settings, applications can nowadays be found in clinical psychology, personality testing, and attitude measurement (see Embretson & Reise, 2000; van der Linden & Hambleton, 1997).

One polytomous extension of the dichotomous RM is the *rating scale model* discussed by Andrich (1978). Masters (1982) obtained a somewhat more general extension for items with ordered categories scored from $k = 0, \ldots, q$. This model is known as the *partial credit model,* and it is used here. Without loss of generality, it is assumed throughout that all items have an equal number of categories, that is, $q + 1$. Then, the conditional probability that a person with a certain θ responds to item i with threshold parameters $\beta_i = (\beta_{i1}, \ldots, \beta_{iq})$ with response k is determined by the logistic function as follows:

$$p(y_i = k|\theta) = p_{ik}(\theta) = \frac{\exp \sum_{v=0}^{k}(\theta - \beta_{iv})}{\sum_{c=0}^{q} \exp \sum_{v=0}^{c}(\theta - \beta_{iv})}, \qquad k = 0, 1, \ldots, q, \qquad (8.3)$$

$$i = 1, \ldots, n,$$

where $\sum_{v=0}^{0}(\theta - \beta_{iv}) \equiv 0$. The preceding function is referred to as the kth item category response function. The following representation can be used as well:

$$p_{ik}(\theta) = \frac{\exp\left(k\theta - \sum_{v=0}^{k}\beta_{iv}\right)}{1 + \sum_{c=1}^{q} \exp\left(c\theta - \sum_{v=1}^{c}\beta_{iv}\right)}, \qquad (8.4)$$

in which case we define $\beta_{i0} \equiv 0$. For $k = 1, \ldots, q$ it holds that, given that a person responded to item i in category k or $k - 1$, the probability of response k is governed by the RM, that is,

$$p(y_i = k|y_i = k \text{ or } k - 1, \theta) = \frac{\exp(\theta - \beta_{ik})}{1 + \exp(\theta - \beta_{ik})}. \qquad (8.5)$$

The item category parameters $\beta_{i1}, \ldots, \beta_{iq}$ are interpreted as threshold locations on the θ scale (see Masters & Wright, 1997). If θ exceeds β_{ik}, then category k becomes more probable than category $k - 1$. If it does not, then category $k - 1$ is more probable than category k. The location on the θ scale at which $\theta = \beta_{ik}$ indicates that the adjacent item category response functions intersect. Note that the item category parameters do not need to be ordered as is the case in other polytomous item response models, such as the *graded response model* developed by Samejima (1969). The RM and its extensions, such as the PCM, are exponential family models and therefore have certain favorable properties, such as sufficient statistics for their parameters.

Estimation

In the estimation of item parameters the person parameters θ and item parameters β are referred to as *incidental* and *structural parameters,* respectively (Fischer & Molenaar, 1995; Neyman & Scott, 1948). This is because the number of person parameters increases as the sample size N increases, whereas the number of item parameters does not. With the increase in sample size, the item parameter estimates improve in terms of accuracy and precision, whereas the person parameters do not. Reiterating that the final object of any psychological or educational test is to make inferences about persons, the sometimes-used term *nuisance parameter* for θ is meaningful only in the phase of item parameter estimation. In fact, van der Linden and Hambleton (1997, p. 5) instead referred to the person parameters as *structural parameters* and to the item parameters as *nuisance parameters*. Needless to say, if test length is increased, person parameter estimates improve, and item parameter estimates do not. Item and person parameters are usually estimated separately, and thus item parameter estimation methods are distinguished from person parameter estimation methods. In the following paragraphs we discuss some commonly used methods.

In general, both item and person parameter estimation methods are based on the loglikelihood function of the observed responses, possibly in combination with some appropriate prior distribution of the item and person parameters. Given a set of n dichotomous items administered to N persons, the loglikelihood function of $\theta = (\theta_1, \ldots, \theta_N)$ and $\beta = (\beta_1, \ldots, \beta_n)$ for the RM can be written as

$$\log L(y;\theta,\beta) = \sum_{j=1}^{N} \sum_{i=1}^{n} y_{ij} \log[p_i(\theta_j)] + (1 - y_{ij})\log[1 - p_i(\theta_j)]$$

$$= \sum_{j=1}^{N} \sum_{i=1}^{n} y_{ij}(\theta_j - \beta_i) - \log[1 + \exp(\theta_j - \beta_i)]. \quad (8.6)$$

For polytomous items the loglikelihood function is obtained as follows. Let the polytomous response y_{ij} be replaced by a dummy vector of length q, of which each element y_{ijk}, $k = 1, \ldots, q$ is scored 1 if category k is observed and 0 otherwise. Then, the loglikelihood function for polytomous PCM items can be given by

$$\log L(y;\theta,\beta) = \sum_{j=1}^{N} \sum_{i=1}^{n} \left(\sum_{k=1}^{q} y_{ijk} \log[p_{ik}(\theta_j)] + \left(1 - \sum_{k=1}^{q} y_{ijk}\right) \log\left[1 - \sum_{k=1}^{q} p_{ik}(\theta_j)\right] \right). \quad (8.7)$$

The three most commonly used item parameter estimation methods for the RM and the PCM are *joint maximum likelihood* (JML), *conditional maximum likelihood* (CML), and *MML estimation* (see Fischer & Molenaar, 1995; and Andersen, 1995). JML estimation is an iterative procedure in which both item and person parameters are estimated. First, starting values for the item parameters are considered as fixed, and the person parameters are estimated by maximizing the loglikelihood function. In turn, the obtained person parameter estimates are considered as fixed, and the item parameters are estimated again by maximizing the loglikelihood. This procedure is repeated until the estimates of both sets of parameters have converged. The JML procedure cannot be applied when either persons or items obtain minimum or maximum scores, because the loglikelihood has no finite maximum in that case. For polytomous PCM items JML estimation also poses problems when categories have zero frequencies, so-called *null categories* (see Wilson & Masters, 1993). Bertoli-Barsotti (2005) stated necessary and sufficient conditions for existence and uniqueness of JML item parameter estimates for the PCM for this case.

CML estimation is a procedure that makes use of the fact that the RM and its extensions are exponential family models, in which case a person's sum score is a sufficient statistic for θ. By conditioning on this sufficient statistic, θ can be removed from the likelihood, and the item parameters are estimated by maximizing the thus-obtained conditional likelihood (Andersen, 1972). Again, estimation problems arise in cases of minimum or maximum item scores and null categories.

In the MML estimation procedure the likelihood is multiplied by a probability density function for θ that is assumed over persons. The normal density is an obvious choice, yet other distributions can be used as well (see Thissen, 1982). The MML procedure generally starts out by integrating θ out of the product of the likelihood and the assumed density, and the thus-obtained marginal likelihood is maximized to find item parameter estimates. Because the integration cannot be performed exactly, one usually resorts to some kind of numerical approximation, such as Gauss–Hermite quadratures. An advantage of this procedure is that item parameter estimates can be found for extreme item scores as well as null categories.

A comparison of the three methods reveals there is no obvious advantage, although some comparisons can be made (see also Holland, 1990). The CML and MML procedures are known to produce consistent estimates, whereas the JML procedure does not necessarily do so. CML estimation has attractive asymptotic features and does not need to make assumptions about the distribution of θ. On the other hand, some information can be lost in CML estimation (see Holland, 1990; and Eggen, 2000). On the whole, MML estimation is most widely applicable, whereas CML estimation possesses the most attractive properties when applicable. However, note that the advantages of MML are largely due to additional assumptions, which are not necessary to apply the JML and CML estimation procedures.

Except for the JML procedure, item parameters are generally estimated first. Then these estimates are considered fixed, and θ is estimated by some appropriate procedure. Note that CML estimation is also applicable to the estimation of person parameters for RMs, although this is unusual and computationally cumbersome. Commonly used methods for the estimation of θ with fixed item parameters are maximum likelihood, weighted maximum likelihood, or a Bayesian estimation procedure such as Bayesian modal (BM) estimation (see also Hoijtink & Boomsma, 1995). In maximum likelihood estimation θ, the loglikelihoods in Equations 8.6 and 8.7 are simply maximized while keeping item parameters fixed. Again, no estimates are available for extreme response patterns. Warm (1989) developed *weighted maximum likelihood,* an alternative procedure that overcomes this problem and in which the likelihood is multiplied by a weight function involving the test information function and then maximized with respect to θ. In BM estimation the likelihood function is multiplied by a distribution function for θ and the mode of the resulting posterior is used as an estimate for θ. If a standard normal distribution is used, the log posterior can be written as (Hambleton & Swaminathan, 1985, p. 94)

$$f(\theta|y) \propto \log L(y;\theta,\beta) - \frac{1}{2}\sum_{j=1}^{N} \theta_j^2. \qquad (8.8)$$

Tsutakawa and Johnson (1990) discussed a person parameter estimation procedure that accounted for the uncertainty in the item parameter estimates.

Evaluation

In general, a thorough evaluation of the fit of an IRT model consists of several stages, and many aspects of the model and estimation procedure can be tested. Glas and Verhelst (1995) distinguished three aspects of evaluating model fit: (a) the assumptions and properties of the selected model and estimation procedure, (b) the type of statistic, and (c) the mathematical refinement of the method. One can select appropriate fit measures on the basis of which aspects are deemed important for a particular application of IRT.

The basic assumptions, such as the (uni)dimensionality of the model and local independence, are checked first. For RMs combined with CML estimation the sufficiency of the sum score can be tested. If MML is used, fit measures testing the appropriateness of the assumed distribution for θ can be used. In addition, properties pertaining to specific models can be investigated. If the RM holds, there exist no differences in discrimination between the items and, in ability testing, the probability of guessing the correct answer is minimal. Such properties can, for instance, be tested with likelihood ratio tests. Furthermore, the fit of certain elements of the model can be studied separately. For example, the fit of a specific item can be investigated, and person fit statistics can be constructed to detect aberrant response behavior.

Because a full discussion of model fit procedures is beyond the scope of this chapter, we discuss only procedures to evaluate overall fit and to inspect item and person fit that we use in our subsequently presented analyses. Measures of overall goodness of fit are often based on differences between observed and expected response patterns. Usually, some approximation to the chi-square distribution is calculated from the n-dimensional contingency table and the model used. However, such contingency tables rapidly become very large as the number of items and categories increases; that is, the table rapidly becomes sparse, and the chi-square approximations are valid only if the sample size is very large, which in turn increases the power of the test. In addition, the implications of rejecting the null hypothesis depend on the model and estimation procedure.

Within the realm of MML, for each possible response pattern an expected frequency can be calculated on the basis of the marginal probabilities. These expected frequencies can be obtained with the following marginal probability of a given response vector $\mathbf{y}$:

$$p_{\mathrm{MML}}(y) = \int_{-\infty}^{\infty} \left(\prod_{i=1}^{n} \prod_{k=1}^{q} p_{ik}(\theta)^{y_{ik}} \left(1 - \sum_{k=1}^{q} p_{ik}(\theta) \right)^{1 - \sum_{k=1}^{q} y_{ik}} \right) f(\theta) d\theta, \quad (8.9)$$

where the integral can be approximated numerically by, say, Gauss–Hermite quadrature. A simple chi-square approximation, such as the Pearson chi-square or the likelihood-ratio statistic G^2, is easily computed by

$$X^2 = N \sum_y \frac{(p_{\text{OBS}}(y) - p_{\text{MML}}(y))^2}{p_{\text{MML}}(y)},$$

$$G^2 = 2N \sum_y p_{\text{OBS}}(y) \log\left(\frac{p_{\text{OBS}}(y)}{p_{\text{MML}}(y)}\right), \qquad (8.10)$$

where $p_{\text{OBS}}(y)$ is the observed proportion of response pattern **y** and the summation occurs over all possible response patterns, that is, over all cells in the n-dimensional contingency table. Note that the observed proportion is required to be larger than zero in order to compute G^2.

Masters and Wright (1997) discussed infit and outfit measures for inspecting item and person fit. For each response, a standardized residual can be calculated from the observed and expected response by

$$z_{ij} = \frac{y_{ij} - E(y_{ij}|\theta)}{\sqrt{\text{Var}(y_{ij}|\theta)}}, \qquad (8.11)$$

where $E(y_{ij}|\theta)$ and $\text{Var}(y_{ij}|\theta)$ are the expected response and variance given by

$$E(y_{ij}|\theta) = \sum_{k=p}^{q} k p_{ik}(\theta_j), \qquad \text{Var}(y_{ij}|\theta) = \sum_{k=0}^{q} (k - E(y_{ij}|\theta))^2 p_{ik}(\theta_j). \qquad (8.12)$$

Note that the probability $p_{ik}(\theta_j)$ can be calculated in different ways depending on which estimation procedure was used to estimate the item and person parameters. Item and person fit indices can be obtained by

$$u_i = \sum_{j=1}^{N} z_{ij}^2 \qquad \text{and} \qquad u_j = \sum_{i=1}^{n} z_{ij}^2, \qquad (8.13)$$

respectively. The asymptotic distribution of the preceding measures is unknown, and no rules of thumb are available for the interpretation of their values, yet it is safe to say that items and persons with relatively large residuals require close inspection if overall fit measures such as the chi-square and G^2 indicate a bad fit.

Dynamic Item Response Theory

Models

The dynamic item response models used here are straightforward extensions of the RM and the PCM. The relations and parameters, however, are interpreted at the level of a single individual. We are assuming throughout that time unfolds in equidistant discrete steps, that item parameters are constant over time, and that θ is unidimensional. These assumptions are not strictly necessary, but they simplify considerably the presentation and illustration of the models and methods. The dichotomous or polytomous n-variate time series y_t is observed from $t = 1, 2, \ldots, T$. We do not distinguish between a time series and a realization thereof. The conditional probability of response $y_{it} = 1$ of a person with a certain θ_t to dichotomous item i at time t is defined by

$$p\left(y_{it} = 1 \middle| y_{t-1}^{*}, \theta_t, \beta_i\right) = p_i(\theta_t) = \frac{\exp(\theta_t - \beta_i)}{1 + \exp(\theta_t - \beta_i)}, \qquad (8.14)$$

where $y_t - 1$ denotes the complete history of responses of a person, that is, $(y_t - 1, \ldots, y_1)$, and θ_t is a latent process. The preceding dynamic RM can be extended in the same manner as the RM to allow for polytomous time series. This dynamic PCM is then determined by the conditional probability that a person with a certain θ_t at time t responds to item i with threshold parameters $\beta_i = (\beta_{i1}, \ldots, \beta_{iq})$ with response k as follows:

$$p\left(y_{it} = k \middle| y_{t-1}^{*}, \theta_t, \beta_i\right) = p_{ik}(\theta_t) = \frac{\exp\left(k\theta_t - \sum_{v=0}^{k} \beta_{iv}\right)}{1 + \sum_{c=1}^{q} \exp\left(c\theta_t - \sum_{v=1}^{c} \beta_{iv}\right)}, \qquad (8.15)$$

where $\beta_{i0} \equiv 0$. We discuss the specification of the latent person process and further assumptions in the next section.

State Space Representation

In general, a *state space model* concerns the relations between an observed time series and an unobserved time series (for an overview, see Sage & Melsa, 1971; or Durbin & Koopman, 2001). The relation between the observed time series y_t and a series of unobserved states α_t is specified in an observation model. In addition, a transition model describes the evolution of the unobserved states over time. The observation and transition model together form what is referred to as the state space model. The state space modeling framework is comparable to the framework of structural equation modeling (SEM) often used in behavioral research (MacCallum & Ashby, 1986). Whereas the state space framework generally pertains to within-system variation—for example, the tracking of the position, direction, and speed of an airplane—the SEM framework usually concerns between-systems variation, that is, individual differences on some psychological variables of interest. The simplest of state space models is that in which all variables are normally distributed and all relationships are linear. The generality of state space modeling lies in the fact that the same estimation methods can be applied to a very wide range of time series models. For the normal linear case, dynamic regression models, structural time series models, and autoregressive moving average models can all be analyzed within this framework after being represented in state space form. This is analogous to the procedure in SEM in which a variety of regression and factor models can be estimated after being put in SEM form.

The specific state space model considered here concerns non-normally distributed variables and nonlinear relationships. Now, the observation models for the dynamic RM and dynamic PCM have already been given in Equations 8.14 and 8.15, respectively. The approach to the modeling of dichotomous and polytomous time series presented here resembles Fahrmeir and Tutz's (2001,

Chapter 1) discussion of dynamic generalized linear models for categorical time series. The relations between the observed and latent time series are specified by the construction of a linear predictor, η_t. To this end, an $(n \times q) \times m$ design matrix Z_t with known elements and the m-dimensional series of unobserved states α_t are related to the mean of the observed time series by

$$\mu_t = h(\eta_t) = h(Z_t \alpha_t), \qquad (8.16)$$

where the function $h(.)$ is referred to as the *response function*. The covariance matrix of the observed time series is denoted by Σ_t. The design matrix Z_t can consist of fixed values, covariates, and past values of y_t. For the evolution of α_t the following linear transition equation is used:

$$\alpha_t = F_t \alpha_{t-1} + R_t \xi_t, \qquad \xi_t \sim N(0, Q_t), \qquad (8.17)$$

where F_t is an $m \times m$ transition matrix, R_t is an $m \times p$ selection matrix, and ξ_t is a p-dimensional white noise sequence with associated covariance matrix Q_t. The state vector α_t can consist of time-varying and time-constant elements, which are selected by R_t. The initial state α_0 is normally distributed with mean a_0 and covariance matrix Q_0. In our present situation the state vector can consist of multiple person processes, person means, and item parameters. We discuss examples of specifying IRT models in state space form in the next section.

In addition to the observation and transition equation, the following assumptions are made. Let y_{t-1}^* and α_t^* denote the complete histories of the observed and unobserved time series, that is, $y_{t-1}^* = (y_{t-1}, \ldots, y_1)$ and $\alpha_t^* = (\alpha_t, \ldots, \alpha_0)$. Then, it is assumed that y_t is independent of α_{t-1}^*, that is,

$$p\left(y_t \middle| y_{t-1}^*, \alpha_t^*\right) = p\left(y_t \middle| y_{t-1}^*, \alpha_t\right). \qquad (8.18)$$

In addition, it is assumed that the state process α_t is first-order Markovian, that is,

$$p\left(\alpha_t \middle| \alpha_{t-1}^*, y_{t-1}^*\right) = p(\alpha_t | \alpha_{t-1}). \qquad (8.19)$$

The final assumption resembles the assumption of local independence in IRT and is given by

$$p\left(y_t \middle| y_{t-1}^*, \alpha_t\right) = \prod_{i=1}^{n} p\left(y_{it} \middle| y_{t-1}^*, \alpha_t\right). \qquad (8.20)$$

Examples of Model Specification

To illustrate the generality of the state space modeling framework we now provide two examples of how the discussed IRT models can be specified in state space form.

The first example is the specification of the RM, for which we use a data set to estimate its parameters with state space methods and compare it with the estimation methods commonly used in IRT. We consider an RM for five items and for persons who have been tested on only one occasion. Although it is an atypical application of the state space framework, this model can be specified in state space form as follows. The observation equation has already been given by Equation 8.1. The transition equation consists of an independent normally distributed process; however, it describes not the variation over time but the variation between persons. In the specification, the index t can now be replaced by j to emphasize that persons instead of time points are being considered. Note that by specifying the transition equation in this manner a distribution for θ is assumed, which is generally not necessary in an RM. However, if MML estimation is used a (standard) normal distribution is usually assumed in the estimation of item parameters. The design matrix specifies the relation between the person parameters θ and the item parameters β, which are stacked in the state vector α_j. For the model under consideration, this results in

$$Z = \begin{bmatrix} 1 & 1 & -1 & 0 & 0 & 0 & 0 \\ 1 & 1 & 0 & -1 & 0 & 0 & 0 \\ 1 & 1 & 0 & 0 & -1 & 0 & 0 \\ 1 & 1 & 0 & 0 & 0 & -1 & 0 \\ 1 & 1 & 0 & 0 & 0 & 0 & -1 \end{bmatrix} \quad \text{and} \quad \alpha_j = \begin{bmatrix} \theta_j \\ \mu_\theta \\ \beta_1 \\ \beta_2 \\ \beta_3 \\ \beta_4 \\ \beta_5 \end{bmatrix}. \quad (8.21)$$

For identification purposes, the mean μ_θ is fixed at 0, and all corresponding elements of the model vectors and matrices can be deleted. The response function $h(.)$ is the logistic, that is, $\dfrac{\exp(.)}{1+\exp(.)}$. One can easily verify that by inserting the preceding specification into Equation 8.16, the relation of Equation 8.1 is obtained. Note that the vector containing the n item probabilities $p(\theta_j)$ is equal to $h(Z\alpha_j)$. We can then denote the covariance matrix by making use of the assumption of local independence as follows:

$$\Sigma_j = \begin{bmatrix} p_1(\theta_j)q_1(\theta_j) & & & & \\ 0 & p_2(\theta_j)q_2(\theta_j) & & & \\ 0 & 0 & p_3(\theta_j)q_3(\theta_j) & & \\ 0 & 0 & 0 & p_4(\theta_j)q_4(\theta_j) & \\ 0 & 0 & 0 & 0 & p_5(\theta_j)q_5(\theta_j) \end{bmatrix}, \quad (8.22)$$

where $q_i(\theta_j) = 1 - p_i(\theta_j)$, $i = 1, \ldots, 5$. Keeping in mind that μ_θ is fixed, the transition, selection, and error covariance matrices for this model are specified by

$$F = \begin{bmatrix} 0 & 0 & 0 & 0 & 0 & 0 \\ 0 & 1 & 0 & 0 & 0 & 0 \\ 0 & 0 & 1 & 0 & 0 & 0 \\ 0 & 0 & 0 & 1 & 0 & 0 \\ 0 & 0 & 0 & 0 & 1 & 0 \\ 0 & 0 & 0 & 0 & 0 & 1 \end{bmatrix}, \quad R = \begin{bmatrix} 1 \\ 0 \\ 0 \\ 0 \\ 0 \\ 0 \end{bmatrix}, \quad \text{and} \quad Q = \sigma_\theta^2. \quad (8.23)$$

The initial state and covariance a_0 and Q_0 can be disregarded in this situation because it is assumed that the observations are independent. The model can be extended in a straightforward manner, for instance, to analyze multiple groups and inspect group differences and uniform differential item functioning.

As a second example, consider the time series obtained from the scores of three persons measured from $t = 1, \ldots, T$ on two items, each with three categories following a PCM. The observed time series vector $\mathbf{y}_t$ consists of the stacked dummy coded response vectors of each person and is of length $N \times n \times q = 3 \times 2 \times 2 = 12$. Assume that the first person follows a zero mean independent normally distributed process, the second latent process is a zero mean first-order autoregression, and the third latent process obeys a zero mean first-order random walk. Then, the design matrix and the state vector are specified as follows:

$$Z = \begin{bmatrix} 1 & 0 & 0 & -1 & 0 & 0 & 0 \\ 2 & 0 & 0 & -1 & -1 & 0 & 0 \\ 1 & 0 & 0 & 0 & 0 & -1 & 0 \\ 2 & 0 & 0 & 0 & 0 & -1 & -1 \\ 0 & 1 & 0 & -1 & 0 & 0 & 0 \\ 0 & 2 & 0 & -1 & -1 & 0 & 0 \\ 0 & 1 & 0 & 0 & 0 & -1 & 0 \\ 0 & 2 & 0 & 0 & 0 & -1 & -1 \\ 0 & 0 & 1 & -1 & 0 & 0 & 0 \\ 0 & 0 & 2 & -1 & -1 & 0 & 0 \\ 0 & 0 & 1 & 0 & 0 & -1 & 0 \\ 0 & 0 & 2 & 0 & 0 & -1 & -1 \end{bmatrix} \quad \text{and} \quad \alpha_t = \begin{bmatrix} \theta_{1t} \\ \theta_{2t} \\ \theta_{3t} \\ \beta_{11} \\ \beta_{12} \\ \beta_{21} \\ \beta_{22} \end{bmatrix}. \quad (8.24)$$

The covariance matrix for this model is a block matrix given by

$$\Sigma_t = \begin{bmatrix} \Sigma_{1t} & & \\ 0 & \Sigma_{2t} & \\ 0 & 0 & \Sigma_{3t} \end{bmatrix}, \quad (8.25)$$

where each block $j = 1, \ldots, 3$ is given by

$$
\Sigma_{jt} = \begin{bmatrix} \mathrm{diag}[p_1(\theta_{jt})] - p_1(\theta_{jt})p_1(\theta_{jt})' & \\ 0 & \mathrm{diag}[p_2(\theta_{jt})] - p_2(\theta_{jt})p_2(\theta_{jt})' \end{bmatrix}, \qquad (8.26)
$$

where $\mathrm{diag}[p_i(\theta_{jt})]$, $i = 1, 2$ is a 2×2 diagonal matrix with the elements of the vector containing the item category probabilities $[p_i(\theta_{jt})]$ on the diagonal. The transition, selection, and state error covariance matrix can be formed by

$$
F = \begin{bmatrix} 0 & 0 & 0 & 0 & 0 & 0 & 0 \\ 0 & \varphi_1 & 0 & 0 & 0 & 0 & 0 \\ 0 & 0 & 1 & 0 & 0 & 0 & 0 \\ 0 & 0 & 0 & 1 & 0 & 0 & 0 \\ 0 & 0 & 0 & 0 & 1 & 0 & 0 \\ 0 & 0 & 0 & 0 & 0 & 1 & 0 \\ 0 & 0 & 0 & 0 & 0 & 0 & 1 \end{bmatrix}, \quad R = \begin{bmatrix} 1 \\ 1 \\ 1 \\ 0 \\ 0 \\ 0 \\ 0 \end{bmatrix}, \quad \text{and} \quad Q = \begin{bmatrix} \sigma_{\theta_1}^2 & & \\ 0 & \sigma_{\theta_2}^2 & \\ 0 & 0 & \sigma_{\theta_3}^2 \end{bmatrix}. \qquad (8.27)
$$

The process of the first person is stationary. For the process of Person 2 to be stationary, we constrain $|\varphi_1|$ to be less than 1. The process of the third person is not stationary. Note that the Kalman filtering and smoothing procedure we discuss next does not require the process under scrutiny to be stationary.

Estimation

The estimation of the discussed IRT models represented in state space form is performed by an iterative Kalman filtering and smoothing procedure as described by Fahrmeir and Wagenpfeil (1997). In this procedure, the mode of the posterior distribution of the states α_t is found by numerical approximations. The log-posterior for the state space model described earlier in the polytomous case is given by

$$
\log L(y; \theta; \beta) = \sum_{t=1}^{T} \sum_{j=1}^{N} \sum_{i=1}^{n} \sum_{k=1}^{q} y_{ijkt} \log[p_{ik}(\theta_{jt})]
$$

$$
+ \left(1 - \sum_{k=1}^{q} y_{ijkt}\right) \log\left(1 - \sum_{k=1}^{q} p_{ik}(\theta_{jt})\right)
$$

$$
- \frac{1}{2}(\alpha_0 - a_0)' R Q_0^{-1} R' (\alpha_0 - a_0)
$$

$$
- \frac{1}{2} \sum_{t=1}^{T} (\alpha_t - F\alpha_{t-1})' R Q^{-1} R' (\alpha_t - F\alpha_{t-1}), \qquad (8.28)
$$

where all individual latent processes $\theta_{jt}, j = 1, \ldots, N,$ individual means, and item parameters are stacked in the state vector α_t. The procedure consists of several steps, which we now describe in detail.

In discussing the steps of the KFS it is assumed that the elements of $Z, F,$ $a_0, Q_0, R,$ and Q are either fixed or known. Estimates of α_t and associated covariance matrices are denoted by $a_{t|t}$ and $V_{t|t}$ for the filter and by $a_{t|T}$ and $V_{t|T}$ for the smoother. Each iteration i of the KFS needs evaluation values for the complete latent state process, which are denoted by $\tilde{a}^i = (\tilde{a}_1^{i'}, \tilde{a}_2^{i'}, \ldots, \tilde{a}_T^{i'})'$. The filtering recursions consist of a prediction and correction step defined for $t = 1, \ldots, T$ by

1. Prediction:

$$a_{t|t-1} = Fa_{t-1|t-1}, \quad a_{0|0} = a_0,$$

$$V_{t|t-1} = FV_{t-1|t-1}F' + RQR', \quad V_{0|0} = RQ_0R'. \quad (8.29)$$

2. Correction:

$$V_{t|t} = \left(V_{t|t-1}^{-1} + B_t \right)^{-1},$$

$$a_{t|t} = a_{t|t-1} + V_{t|t}b_t, \quad (8.30)$$

where B_t and b_t are given by

$$B_t = Z'\Sigma_t Z,$$

$$b_t = Z'(y_t - h(Z\tilde{a}_t^i)) - B_t(a_{t|t-1} - \tilde{a}_t^i), \quad (8.31)$$

and Σ_t is evaluated at $\tilde{a}_t^i$. The filter predictions $a_{t|t-1}$ are a natural choice to start up the iterations, that is, $\tilde{a}_t^i = a_{t|t-1}$. If the procedure is terminated after a single iteration, it is equal to the generalized extended Kalman filter described by Fahrmeir (1992). The fixed interval smoother is initialized with the final estimates of the Kalman filter $a_{t|t}$ and $V_{t|t}$. For $t = T, \ldots, 2$, the smoother can be given by

$$a_{t-1|T} = a_{t-1|t-1} + G_t(a_{t|T} - a_{t|t-1}),$$

$$V_{t-1|T} = V_{t-1|t-1} + G_t(V_{t|T} - V_{t|t-1})G_t', \quad (8.32)$$

where

$$G_t = V_{t-1|t-1}F'V_{t|t-1}^{-1}. \quad (8.33)$$

After the smoother is applied the evaluation values are updated with the smoother estimates, that is, $\tilde{a}^i = (a_{1|T}', \ldots, a_{t|T}')'$. The procedure is repeated until some convergence criterion is reached. The stopping criterion used in this study is $\max|\tilde{a}^i - \tilde{a}^{i-1}| < 1^{-12}$. The KFS procedure just discussed resembles the procedure described by Durbin and Koopman (2001, Chapter 10).

When the KFS procedure is applied in a standard IRT setting some comparisons can be made with the estimation procedures described in the previous section. The KFS procedure resembles MML in that a distribution is assumed for θ, and so estimates can be obtained for extreme score patterns. However, the distributional assumption is part of the model and not of the estimation procedure (see also Holland, 1990). It differs from MML in that both item and person parameters are estimated simultaneously. This resembles the JML estimation procedure, yet that procedure iteratively estimates person and item parameters. The procedure shows similarities with that described by Tsutakawa and Johnson (1990) in which uncertainties in item parameter estimates are incorporated in the person parameter estimation procedure.

Evaluation

The same aspects of evaluating the fit of standard IRT models are involved in the case of dynamic IRT models. An important additional aspect is the dependence of the observations over time. In particular, the time dependence is explicitly accounted for by the specification of the model, and the extent to which this is successfully performed can be checked. A customary method is to inspect the autocorrelations or spectra of the residuals. Any substantial residual dependencies can then be interpreted as a misspecification of the transition equation. This inspection can be performed at the level of the individual. Together with the fit indices discussed earlier, which are now to be interpreted conditionally on y^*_{t-1}, an indication of the appropriateness of the model can be obtained at different levels.

The standardized residuals z_{ij} as defined in Equation 8.11 can now be extended with the time index t. The lag l $n \times n$ auto- and cross-correlation matrix of the standardized residuals of person j is denoted by C_{jl} and can be computed from the standardized residual z_{ijt} by

$$C_{jl} = \sum_{t=l+1}^{T} \frac{z_{jt} z'_{j,t-1}}{T}. \quad (8.34)$$

The lag zero correlation matrix can be used for inspection of any residual dependencies not accounted for by the model. If the model provides an accurate description, off-diagonal elements should be close to zero. Lagged correlation matrices can be used to inspect any residual time dependencies.

Examples

To provide an illustration of how the discussed models can be applied by making use of the state space framework, we analyzed two data sets: one obtained in a standard IRT setting and the other in a longitudinal setting. We performed the first analysis to compare the KFS estimation procedure with standard IRT estimation methods for the estimation of both person and item parameters. The second analysis illustrates the generality of the state space framework in a longitudinal setting where the number of persons is relatively small and the number of time points is relatively large.

Standard Item Response Theory: Law School Admission Test—6 Data

The first data set has been used frequently to illustrate and compare parameter estimation methods for the RM (see, e.g., Andersen & Madsen, 1977; Baker, 1991; Thissen, 1982). It consists of the responses of 1,000 persons to five figure classification items that formed Section 6 of the Law School Admission Test (LSAT) as described by Bock and Lieberman (1970). With these data, the item parameter estimation methods CML and MML are compared with the KFS. In addition, we compared BM estimation of θ with the output of the KFS. We should stress that with the KFS both person and item parameter estimates are obtained at the same time. The RM is used in the state space representation that we discussed in the previous section.

All analyses were performed with the free software package R (R Development Core Team, 2008). For CML and MML estimation of the item parameters, we used the R packages *extended Rasch modeling* (Mair & Hatzinger, 2007a, 2007b) and *latent trait modeling* (Rizopoulos, 2006), respectively. We also used the latent trait modeling package to produce BM estimates of the person parameter. We implemented the KFS estimation procedure in R.[1] In applying the MML and KFS procedures a standard normal distribution is assumed for θ. In comparing the methods for item parameter estimation, the mean item difficulty is fixed to zero.

Table 8.1 displays the five estimated item difficulties and standard errors of the CML, MML, and KFS estimation procedures. The CML and MML point estimates are very close to each other compared with those obtained with the KFS. The differences between the point estimates of the KFS and those of CML and MML are not large, yet not negligible, larger at the extremes, and can be interpreted as bias. The differences are most likely due to the fact that the KFS procedure uses a posterior and CML and MML a likelihood. The standard errors of all three methods are very close, although those of the KFS are slightly smaller.

In Table 8.2 the sum scores and associated person parameter estimates and standard errors are shown for the BM and KFS estimation procedures. BM estimation of θ is performed with fixed item parameters estimated with MML, whereas the KFS estimates of θ are obtained simultaneously with the item parameter estimates. The point estimates of the two methods have to be compared in view of the differences between MML and KFS for the estimation of item parameters, especially μ_θ. Keeping these differences in mind, the two methods can be considered to yield comparable point estimates. The standard errors of the KFS are substantially smaller than those obtained with BM estimation. This might be because the KFS simultaneously estimates item and person parameters.

We evaluated the goodness of fit of the RM with the Pearson chi-square and the likelihood ratio statistic G^2, as discussed earlier. For the LSAT data the results of the MML estimation procedure were used for computing

---

[1] The source code is available on request from Peter van Rijn (e-mail: Peter.vanRijn@cito.nl).

Table 8.1. Item Parameter Estimates of the Law School Admission Test Data Set

	CML		MML		KFS	
Parameter	Estimate	SE	Estimate	SE	Estimate	SE
β_1	−1.256	0.104	−1.255	0.104	−1.223	0.102
β_2	0.475	0.070	0.476	0.070	0.465	0.069
β_3	1.236	0.069	1.235	0.069	1.194	0.065
β_4	0.168	0.073	0.168	0.073	0.168	0.071
β_5	−0.623	0.086	−0.625	0.086	−0.604	0.084
μ_θ			1.475	0.052	1.417	0.051
σ_θ			0.755	0.069		

Note. CML = conditional maximum likelihood; MML = marginal maximum likelihood; KFS = Kalman filter and smoother.

the fit statistics, which resulted in $\chi^2(25, N = 1,000) = 18.33$ ($p = .83$), and $G^2 = 21.80$ ($df = 25$, $p = .65$), indicating a good fit. Because the fit is satisfactory, checking further item and person fit diagnostics is not deemed necessary for now.

To compare the results of the KFS estimation procedure in this situation with the CML and MML estimation procedures, we conducted a small study in which data are simulated on the basis of the LSAT analysis; that is, we simulated 1,000 replications of 1,000 responses to a test with five items. The parameters in this simulation are rounded for ease of comparison. The results of this study with respect to the item parameters are displayed in Table 8.3. One can see that the item parameters produced by KFS are biased. The pattern of the bias is the same as in Table 8.1. The differences in standard errors among the three methods are very small and can be neglected. The means and standard deviations of the fit measures were 27.32 and 11.26 for the G^2, and 25.88 and 10.76 for the chi-square, respectively, both with 25 degrees of freedom.

Table 8.4 shows the results of the simulations with respect to the person parameter estimates. Again, the results should be compared in view of the differences in the estimates of item parameters and the mean μ_θ. In this respect, the differences are not too large, except perhaps for sum score 5.

Table 8.2. Person Parameter Estimates of the Law School Admission Test Data Set

	BM		KFS	
Sum score	Estimate	SE	Estimate	SE
0	−0.432	0.790	−0.526	0.704
1	0.038	0.793	−0.038	0.696
2	0.516	0.801	0.448	0.701
3	1.007	0.816	0.950	0.720
4	1.519	0.836	1.490	0.754
5	2.058	0.862	2.095	0.804

Note. BM = Bayesian model estimation; KFS = Kalman filter and smoother.

Table 8.3. Results of Simulation With Respect to Estimation of Item Parameters

Parameter	Value	CML			MML			KFS		
		M	SE	SD	M	SE	SD	M	SE	SD
β_1	-1.25	-1.263	0.104	0.103	-1.262	0.106	0.106	-1.231	0.104	0.100
β_2	-0.50	-0.502	0.084	0.082	-0.504	0.084	0.092	-0.484	0.083	0.079
β_3	0.00	0.001	0.073	0.072	0.001	0.075	0.077	0.005	0.074	0.070
β_4	0.50	0.506	0.072	0.072	0.507	0.070	0.073	0.494	0.069	0.069
β_5	1.25	1.257	0.069	0.069	1.258	0.069	0.072	1.216	0.065	0.064
μ_θ	1.50				1.507	0.053	0.060	1.446	0.051	0.044
σ_θ	0.75				0.754	0.071	0.103			

Note.   CML = conditional maximum likelihood; MML = marginal maximum likelihood; KFS = Kalman filter and smoother.

Table 8.4. Results of Simulation With Respect to Estimation of Person Parameters

Sum score	BM			KFS		
	M	SE	SD	M	SE	SD
0	−0.402	0.791	0.128	−0.509	0.703	0.050
1	0.061	0.794	0.102	−0.027	0.692	0.051
2	0.542	0.803	0.090	0.461	0.701	0.047
3	1.027	0.818	0.067	0.962	0.721	0.049
4	1.544	0.838	0.067	1.507	0.756	0.046
5	2.082	0.864	0.067	2.112	0.807	0.046

Note. BM = Bayesian model estimation; KFS = Kalman filter and smoother.

Dynamic Item Response Theory: Borkenau and Ostendorf's (1998) Data

The second example consists of an application of a dynamic PCM as discussed in the Dynamic Item Response Theory section in regard to repeated administrations of a personality questionnaire. We used a selection of the data set that has already been used to illustrate dynamic models and associated estimation methods (Hamaker, Dolan, & Molenaar, 2005; Molenaar, 2004). The data were collected by Borkenau and Ostendorf (1998) and consist of the responses of 22 persons to a 30-item personality questionnaire on 90 consecutive days. The questionnaire was designed to measure the Big Five personality factors (i.e., Extraversion, Neuroticism, Agreeableness, Conscientiousness, and Openness to Experience), and the items were scored on a 7-point Likert scale. Because our interest lies in the illustration of a dynamic PCM we used only the responses to the six items that are indicative of the Extraversion factor. This scale consisted of three positively formulated and three negatively formulated items.

Because we have no knowledge about the individual latent processes for this type of analysis, our modeling starts out by assuming that each person follows a unidimensional, independent, normally distributed process with possibly different means. In other words, a measurement-invariant model is assumed over persons to start the analysis. Each individual's variance is fixed at 1 for now and, to reiterate, the item category parameters are assumed to be constant over time. In many practical situations one should investigate whether the assumptions of unidimensionality and (which types of) measurement invariance hold. A full discussion of these issues for this particular application surpasses the purpose of this chapter, however.

The specification of the dynamic PCM in state space form for this situation proceeds along similar lines as described in the Dynamic Item Response Theory section. A full description of the state space representation is given. If we define

$$Z_1 = \begin{bmatrix} 1 & 1 \\ 2 & 2 \\ \vdots & \vdots \\ 6 & 6 \end{bmatrix}, \quad \text{and} \quad Z_2 = \begin{bmatrix} -1 & 0 & \cdots & 0 \\ -1 & -1 & \cdots & 0 \\ \vdots & \vdots & \ddots & \vdots \\ -1 & -1 & \cdots & -1 \end{bmatrix}, \quad (8.35)$$

we can write the 792×80 design matrix Z for this example by

$$Z = [I_{22} \otimes (1_6 \otimes Z_1) \quad 1_{22} \otimes (I_6 \otimes Z_2)], \quad (8.36)$$

where I is an identity matrix of indicated dimension, 1 indicates an identity vector of indicated dimension, and $\otimes$ is the Kronecker product. The state vector containing the person and item parameters is given by

$$\alpha_t = (\theta_{1t}, \mu_{\theta_1}, \ldots, \theta_{22,t}, \mu_{\theta_{22}}, \beta_{11}, \beta_{12}, \ldots, \beta_{66})'. \quad (8.37)$$

The covariance matrix Σ_t can be built in an analogous manner as described earlier. If we continue by defining

$$F_1 = \begin{bmatrix} 0 & 0 \\ 0 & 1 \end{bmatrix}, \quad (8.38)$$

then the 80×80 transition matrix can be written as

$$F = \begin{bmatrix} I_{22} \otimes F_1 & 0 \\ 0 & I_{36} \end{bmatrix}. \quad (8.39)$$

Finally, if we define $R_1 = (1, 0)'$, then the 80×22 selection matrix can be written as

$$R = \begin{bmatrix} I_{22} \otimes R_1 \\ 0 \end{bmatrix}. \quad (8.40)$$

The model in the preceding representation is not identified, and at least one of the person means or item parameters needs to be fixed. We choose to fix the first person's mean at 0 for the present situation. The lengths and appropriate dimensions of all associated model vectors and matrices are then reduced by 1. The resulting lengths and dimensions of the model vectors and matrices are displayed in Table 8.5.

Table 8.6 displays the results of the KFS estimation procedure with respect to the item category parameters. The values of the category thresholds

Table 8.5. Model Dimensions for State Space Representation of Dynamic Partial Credit Model for Extraversion Data

Model vector	Dimension	Model matrix	Dimension
y_t	792	Z	792×79
α_t	79	F	79×79
ξ_t	22	R	79×22

Table 8.6. Item Category Parameter Estimates

i	k	β_{ik}	SE
1	1	−2.52	0.21
	2	−1.01	0.11
	3	−0.55	0.08
	4	0.65	0.06
	5	1.97	0.08
	6	3.50	0.14
2	1	−1.87	0.22
	2	−1.71	0.13
	3	−0.41	0.08
	4	0.09	0.07
	5	1.37	0.07
	6	2.33	0.09
3	1	−2.13	0.27
	2	−1.78	0.16
	3	−0.88	0.10
	4	−0.21	0.07
	5	1.06	0.07
	6	1.86	0.08
4	1	−1.82	0.23
	2	−1.91	0.15
	3	−0.43	0.09
	4	−0.08	0.07
	5	1.21	0.07
	6	2.31	0.09
5	1	−2.87	0.24
	2	−1.04	0.10
	3	−0.40	0.08
	4	0.50	0.07
	5	1.67	0.08
	6	2.72	0.11
6	1	−2.11	0.22
	2	−1.56	0.13
	3	−0.53	0.08
	4	0.43	0.07
	5	1.73	0.08
	6	2.41	0.10

are fairly spread out over the scale. Their overall mean is rescaled at 0 so that the individual latent processes can be related to the response scale. Except for the first two category thresholds of Item 4, all item category parameters are ordered within items. Note that the parameters of the outer categories have the largest standard errors, especially the lowest categories.

Table 8.7 displays the estimated person means, standard errors and person fit based on estimates $a_{t|T}$ (Fit$_t$) and on predictions $Fa_{t-1|T}$ (Fit$_{t-1}$) of the KFS procedure. It is clear that the differences in individual means are quite large, ranging from −0.47 for Person 3 to 2.72 for Person 6. The overall mean is equal to 0.68, indicating that the persons responded on the positive side of the scale

Table 8.7.   Estimated Person Means, Standard Error, and Fit

Person	$\bar{\theta}$	SE	Fit$_t$	Fit$_{t-1}$
1	0.26	0.11	0.42	0.92
2	0.09	0.11	0.37	0.88
3	−0.47	0.11	1.00	1.16
4	1.43	0.12	1.00	2.06
5	1.50	0.12	1.40	2.96
6	2.72	0.12	1.43	1.96
7	0.57	0.11	0.72	1.79
8	1.28	0.11	0.97	1.46
9	0.92	0.11	0.69	1.73
10	−0.07	0.11	0.54	1.31
11	1.49	0.12	0.77	1.57
12	0.68	0.11	0.39	0.95
13	1.25	0.12	0.94	2.15
14	0.80	0.12	0.85	5.68
15	0.09	0.11	0.58	1.32
16	0.22	0.11	0.42	0.65
17	0.47	0.11	0.64	1.30
18	0.66	0.11	0.76	0.87
19	0.51	0.11	0.94	2.05
20	0.85	0.11	0.67	1.02
21	−0.38	0.11	0.69	0.86
22	0.09	0.11	0.74	1.40

of the Extraversion items. No overall goodness-of-fit measures are calculated here, because chi-square approximations based on the contingency table of possible response patterns are likely to fail; that is, the total number of observations ($22 \times 90 = 1{,}980$) compared with the number of cells of this table is very small ($76 = 117{,}649$). The individuals who showed the largest sum of squared standardized residuals based on the estimates $a_{t|T}$ are Persons 5 and 6. The person fit indices based on the predictions give an indication of predictive value of the model for each individual. In general, they are somewhat larger than the indices based on $a_{t|T}$, which is explained by the independent normality of the individual processes in the model used. In addition, it is interesting that the difference between both indices varies substantially between individuals.

As a final illustration, we fitted first-order autoregressive latent processes to the time series of each person separately. The penalized likelihood of Equation 8.28 was optimized numerically with the L-BFGS-B method of the R function optim() (see Byrd, Lu, Nocedal, & Zhu, 1995). The item category thresholds were fixed at the values displayed in Table 8.6, the process was restricted to be stationary by restricting $|\varphi_1| < 1$, and again each individual's variance was fixed at 1. We investigated whether the individual fit improved. The results of this analysis are shown in Table 8.8. In inspecting point estimates and standard errors it can be said that in about one third of the cases a substantial autoregressive component is found. The change in person fit based on estimates $a_{t|T}$ is negligible in most cases. However, the fit based on the predictions improves substantially.

Table 8.8. Estimated Autoregressive Parameter, Standard Error, and Fit

Person	ϕ_1	SE	Fit_t	Fit_{t-1}
1	0.17	0.13	0.42	0.78
2	0.16	0.14	0.37	0.74
3	0.27	0.20	1.00	1.08
4	0.30	0.08	1.00	1.54
5	0.28	0.06	1.40	2.24
6	0.60	0.06	1.45	1.54
7	0.16	0.09	0.72	1.48
8	0.39	0.11	0.97	1.17
9	0.24	0.09	0.69	1.31
10	0.15	0.11	0.54	1.11
11	0.34	0.08	0.77	1.15
12	0.23	0.11	0.39	0.74
13	0.26	0.07	0.95	1.64
14	0.22	0.04	0.87	3.68
15	0.12	0.12	0.57	1.16
16	0.17	0.19	0.43	0.58
17	0.20	0.11	0.64	1.07
18	0.37	0.21	0.73	0.79
19	0.21	0.09	0.94	1.63
20	0.32	0.13	0.67	0.85
21	0.21	0.21	0.69	0.79
22	0.15	0.11	0.74	1.23

Discussion

The main purpose of this chapter was to apply state space methods to the modeling of item responses. Not only can these methods be applied in standard IRT settings, but also extensions to modeling repeated measurements are easily made within the same framework, and the same estimation methods can be used. An application of Kalman filtering and smoothing techniques to two example data sets illustrated the flexibility of the state space framework. The results of the first analysis indicated that the KFS can result in some bias in the estimation of item parameters. This can be related to the fact that a posterior distribution is optimized by the KFS estimation procedure, and this is known to produce bias (see Hoijtink & Boomsma, 1995; and Tsutakawa & Johnson, 1990). However, the standard errors are consistent with the two standard IRT estimation procedures CML and MML. The discussed framework can be easily equipped to perform typical IRT analyses such as multigroup and differential item functioning analyses.

The second example illustrated some possibilities of the state space approach to the modeling of repeated measurements. We applied the KFS estimation procedure to a data set to obtain item and person parameter estimates and again analyzed individual time series to investigate the strength of latent autoregressions. This procedure works reasonably well for the discussed situation and might be useful for analyzing various types of longitudinally observed item responses; however, an investigation into the quality of the produced estimates and fit diagnostics (e.g., by means of simulations) remains an important and interesting topic for future research.

We admit that many extensions of the discussed models and procedures remain to be explored. For instance, the inclusion of a discrimination parameter as in the two-parameter logistic model (Birnbaum, 1968) and generalized PCM (Muraki, 1992) is an interesting extension, because in many applications, the RM and its extensions do not fit very well to all item responses. In close connection with this is the extension to differing individual variances of the latent process in the case of repeated measurements. Fahrmeir and Wagenpfeil (1997) discussed an estimator for this case, but its quality is as yet unknown. Finally, extensions of the model to allow for time-varying parameters—for example, item parameters or person means (trends)—might be significant developments for the future, especially when the interest lies in the analysis of change.

In closing, all possible applications of the state space framework are interesting only when the different models and extensions can be compared and the differences can be tested; that is, reliable diagnostics and fit statistics are necessary to find a fit model, and finding appropriate ones is perhaps the biggest challenge.

References

Andersen, E. B. (1972). The numerical solution of a set of conditional estimation equations. *Journal of the Royal Statistical Society Series B: Methodological, 34,* 42–54.

Andersen, E. B. (1995). Polytomous Rasch models and their estimation. In G. Fischer & I. W. Molenaar (Eds.), *Rasch models: Foundations, recent developments, and applications* (pp. 271–292). New York, NY: Springer-Verlag.

Andersen, E. B., & Madsen, M. (1977). Estimating the parameters of the latent population distribution. *Psychometrika, 42,* 357–374. doi:10.1007/BF02293656

Andrich, D. (1978). A rating formulation for ordered response categories. *Psychometrika, 43,* 561–573. doi:10.1007/BF02293814

Baker, F. B. (1991). *Item response theory: Parameter estimation techniques.* New York, NY: Marcel Dekker.

Bertoli-Barsotti, L. (2005). On the existence and the uniqueness of JML estimates for the partial credit model. *Psychometrika, 70,* 517–531. doi:10.1007/s11336-001-0917-0

Birnbaum, A. (1968). Some latent trait models and their use in inferring an examinee's ability. In F. M. Lord & M. R. Novick (Eds.), *Statistical theories of mental test scores* (pp. 395–480). Reading, MA: Addison-Wesley.

Bock, R. D., & Lieberman, M. (1970). Fitting a response model for n dichotomously scored items. *Psychometrika, 35,* 179–197. doi:10.1007/BF02291262

Borkenau, P., & Ostendorf, F. (1998). The Big Five as states: How useful is the five-factor model to describe intraindividual changes over time? *Journal of Research in Personality, 32,* 202–221. doi:10.1006/jrpe.1997.2206

Borsboom, D., Mellenbergh, G. J., & van Heerden, J. (2003). The theoretical status of latent variables. *Psychological Review, 110,* 203–219. doi:10.1037/0033-295X.110.2.203

Byrd, R. H., Lu, P., Nocedal, J., & Zhu, C. (1995). A limited memory algorithm for bound constrained optimization. *SIAM Journal on Scientific Computing, 16,* 1190–1208. doi:10.1137/0916069

Durbin, J., & Koopman, S. J. (2001). *Time series analysis by state space methods.* New York, NY: Oxford University Press.

Eggen, T. J. H. M. (2000). On the loss of information in conditional maximum likelihood estimation of item parameters. *Psychometrika, 65,* 337–362. doi:10.1007/BF02296150

Embretson, S. E. (1991). A multidimensional latent trait model for measuring learning and change. *Psychometrika, 56,* 495–515. doi:10.1007/BF02294487

Embretson, S. E., & Reise, S. P. (2000). *Item response theory for psychologists.* Mahwah, NJ: Erlbaum.

Fahrmeir, L. (1992). Posterior mode estimation by extended Kalman filtering for multivariate dynamic generalized linear models. *Journal of the American Statistical Association, 87,* 501–509. doi:10.2307/2290283

Fahrmeir, L., & Tutz, G. (2001). *Multivariate statistical modeling based on generalized linear models* (2nd ed.). New York, NY: Springer-Verlag.

Fahrmeir, L., & Wagenpfeil, S. (1997). Penalized likelihood estimation and iterative Kalman smoothing for non-Gaussian dynamic regression models. *Computational Statistics & Data Analysis, 24,* 295–320. doi:10.1016/S0167-9473(96)00064-3

Fischer, G. (1989). An IRT-based model for dichotomous longitudinal data. *Psychometrika, 54,* 599–624. doi:10.1007/BF02296399

Fischer, G., & Molenaar, I. W. (Eds.). (1995). *Rasch models: Foundations, recent developments, and applications.* New York, NY: Springer-Verlag.

Glas, C. A. W., & Verhelst, N. D. (1995). Testing the Rasch model. In G. Fischer & I. W. Molenaar (Eds.), *Rasch models: Foundations, recent developments, and applications* (pp. 69–96). New York, NY: Springer-Verlag.

Hamaker, E. L., Dolan, C. V., & Molenaar, P. C. M. (2005). Statistical modeling of the individual: Rationale and application of multivariate time series analysis. *Multivariate Behavioral Research, 40,* 207–233. doi:10.1207/s15327906mbr4002_3

Hambleton, R. K., & Swaminathan, H. (1985). *Item response theory: Principles and applications.* Boston, MA: Kluwer.

Hamilton, J. D. (1994). *Time series analysis.* Princeton, NJ: Princeton University Press.

Hoijtink, H., & Boomsma, A. (1995). On person parameter estimation in the dichotomous Rasch model. In G. Fischer & I. W. Molenaar (Eds.), *Rasch models: Foundations, recent developments, and applications* (pp. 53–68). New York, NY: Springer-Verlag.

Holland, P. W. (1990). On the sampling theory foundations of item response theory models. *Psychometrika, 55,* 577–601. doi:10.1007/BF02294609

Kelderman, H., & Molenaar, P. C. M. (2007). The effect of individual differences in factor loadings on the standard factor model. *Multivariate Behavioral Research, 42,* 435–456.

Kempf, W. F. (1977). Dynamic models for measurement of "traits" in social behavior. In W. F. Kempf & B. H. Repp (Eds.), *Mathematical models for social psychology* (pp. 14–58). Bern, Switzerland: Hans Huber.

Lord, F. M., & Novick, M. R. (1968). *Statistical theories of mental test scores.* Reading, MA: Addison-Wesley.

Lütkepohl, H. (2005). *New introduction to multiple time series analysis.* Berlin, Germany: Springer-Verlag.

MacCallum, R., & Ashby, F. G. (1986). Relationships between linear systems theory and covariance structure modeling. *Journal of Mathematical Psychology, 30,* 1–27. doi:10.1016/0022-2496(86)90039-8

Mair, P., & Hatzinger, R. (2007a). CML based estimation of extended Rasch models with the eRm package in R. *Psychological Science, 49,* 26–43.

Mair, P., & Hatzinger, R. (2007b). Extended Rasch modeling: The eRm package for the application of IRT models in R. *Journal of Statistical Software, 20,* 1–20.

Masters, G. N. (1982). A Rasch model for partial credit scoring. *Psychometrika, 47,* 149–174. doi:10.1007/BF02296272

Masters, G. N., & Wright, B. D. (1997). The partial credit model. In W. J. van der Linden & R. K. Hambleton (Eds.), *Handbook of modern item response theory* (pp. 101–122). New York, NY: Springer-Verlag.

Molenaar, P. C. M. (2004). A manifesto on psychology as idiographic science: Bringing the person back into scientific psychology, this time forever. *Measurement: Interdisciplinary Research & Perspective, 2,* 201–218.

Muraki, E. (1992). A generalized partial credit model: Application of an EM algorithm. *Applied Psychological Measurement, 16,* 159–176.

Neyman, J., & Scott, E. L. (1948). Consistent estimates based on partially consistent observations. *Econometrika, 16,* 1–32.

Rasch, G. (1980). *Probabilistic models for some intelligence and attainment tests* (expanded ed.). Chicago, IL: University of Chicago Press. (Original work published 1960)

R Development Core Team. (2009). *R: A language and environment for statistical computing.* Retrieved from http://www.R-project.org

Rizopoulos, D. (2006). Ltm: An R package for latent variable modeling and item response theory analyses. *Journal of Statistical Software, 17,* 1–25.

Sage, A., & Melsa, J. (1971). *Estimation theory, with applications to communications and control.* New York, NY: McGraw-Hill.

Samejima, F. (1969). Estimation of latent ability using a response pattern of graded scores. *Psychometrika Monograph, 34*(Suppl.), 100–114.

Thissen, D. (1982). Marginal maximum likelihood estimation for the one-parameter logistic model. *Psychometrika, 47,* 175–186.

Tsutakawa, R. K., & Johnson, J. C. (1990). The effect of uncertainty of item parameter estimation on ability estimates. *Psychometrika, 55,* 371–390. doi:10.1007/BF02295293

van der Linden, W. J., & Hambleton, R. K. (Eds.). (1997). *Handbook of modern item response theory.* New York, NY: Springer-Verlag.

Verhelst, N. D., & Glas, C. A. W. (1993). A dynamic generalization of the Rasch model. *Psychometrika, 58,* 395–415. doi:10.1007/BF02294648

Warm, T. A. (1989). Weighted likelihood estimation of ability in item response models. *Psychometrika, 54,* 427–450. doi:10.1007/BF02294627

Wilson, M., & Masters, G. N. (1993). The partial credit model and null categories. *Psychometrika, 58,* 87–99. doi:10.1007/BF02294473

Part III _____

Modeling Issues

9

Regime-Switching Models to Study Psychological Processes

Ellen L. Hamaker, Raoul P. P. P. Grasman, and Jan Henk Kamphuis

In the 1980s, two extensions of the linear autogressive (AR) model were introduced: (a) the threshold autoregressive (TAR) model (Tong & Lim, 1980) and (b) the Markov-switching autoregressive (MSAR) model (Hamilton, 1989). Both models allow for recurrent switches between two or more distinct AR processes, each of which is characterized by its own parameters. These models have proved useful in economic research—for instance, to model certain features of the business cycle, such as the asymmetry between phases of expansion and decline (Clements & Krolzig, 1998).

Despite the models' popularity in economics, the TAR model has seen only a few applications in psychological research (Hamaker, 2009; Hamaker, Zhang, & Van der Maas, 2009; Warren, 2002; Warren, Hawkins, & Sprott, 2003), and, to our knowledge, the MSAR model has not been applied in psychological research. This is remarkable, because there are many psychological phenomena that are characterized by recurrent shifts between different psychological states; for instance, addiction can involve periods of recovery and relapse; posttraumatic stress disorder is characterized by episodes of intrusion and avoidance; premenstrual syndrome involves physiological and emotional symptoms in the luteal phase, which elevate after the onset of menses; and bipolar disorder is characterized by switches between episodes of mania and depression. Moreover, in cognitive tasks people may switch between different strategies (i.e., psychological states), such as performing a task quickly at the cost of making more mistakes versus being more accurate at the cost of performing it more slowly.

In this chapter we refer to such psychological states as *regimes*. Note that by *regime* we mean "the characteristic behavior or orderly procedure of a natural phenomenon or process" (from *Merriam-Webster's Collegiate Dictionary*, 2007, p. 1048). Hence, in contrast to the more popular use of the term, where *regime* refers to a form of government that is long lasting and typically not reoccurring, we use it to refer to a psychological state, which may alternate repeatedly with other psychological states. In this chapter we propose to describe such a psychological state

We gratefully acknowledge Liv Pijck for gathering the data. This work was supported by the Netherlands Organization for Scientific Research: Veni Grant 451-05-012, awarded to Ellen L. Hamaker, and Veni Grant 451-06-013, awarded to Raoul P. P. P. Grasman.

with a particular AR model, and we investigate the possibility that psychological processes that are characterized by recurrent shifts between distinct psychological states can be modeled using regime-switching models such as the TAR and MSAR models.

The purpose of this chapter is to introduce readers to the TAR model and the MSAR model and to illustrate the usefulness of these models for gaining more insight into the underlying dynamics of regime-switching processes such as the ones described earlier. In the first section we present these two models and discuss their main features and some important extensions. In the second section we present estimation procedures that can be used when there are missing data. In addition, we discuss the issue of model selection based on information criteria. The third section is an empirical application in which we compare the TAR and MSAR models with an ordinary AR model (i.e., a model without regime switching). To this end, we make use of daily mood scores obtained with the Positive Affect and Negative Affect Schedule (Watson & Clark, 1994) in an individual diagnosed with rapidly cycling bipolar disorder. Our aim was to determine whether there are two distinct regimes that represent a manic and a depressed state in this person's daily affect scores. In addition, we were interested in the actual regime-switching mechanism, that is, whether shifts from depression to mania and vice versa are triggered by affect levels themselves (as in a kind of feedback loop) or whether this is an autonomous mechanism that operates independently of the actual affect levels. We end this chapter with a brief discussion of the potential of these models for psychological research.

Regime-Switching Autoregressive Models

The TAR model and the MSAR model both consist of two or more distinct AR processes, referred to as *regimes*. At each occasion the system is in one of these regimes, meaning that one of the AR processes gave rise to the data. The difference between the TAR model and the MSAR model concerns the process that triggers the regime-switching. In the TAR model switching is modeled explicitly as a function of some manifest threshold variable. In contrast, in the MSAR model switching is regulated by a hidden Markov process and has to be inferred from the observed data. This has important implications for the substantive interpretation of these models, as we show later in this chapter.

Because we use vector extensions of the TAR and MSAR models in our illustration, we focus on the multivariate presentation. These multivariate models clearly include the univariate model as a specific case. We begin with the vector AR (VAR) model, because it forms the basis of both the vector TAR model and the vector MSAR model.

Vector Autoregressive Model

If $\mathbf{y}_t = (y_{t,1} \ldots y_{t,r})'$ denotes an r-variate observation at occasion t, the VAR(p) process is defined as

$$\mathbf{y}_t = \boldsymbol{\phi}_0 + \boldsymbol{\Phi}_1 \mathbf{y}_{t-1} + \cdots + \boldsymbol{\Phi}_p \mathbf{y}_{t-p} + \boldsymbol{\Omega} \mathbf{e}_t, \qquad (9.1)$$

where $\boldsymbol{\phi}_0$ is an r-variate vector with constants, and $\boldsymbol{\Phi}_1$ to $\boldsymbol{\Phi}_{p(j)}$ are $r \times r$ matrices with AR parameters on the diagonal and lagged cross-regressive parameters as off-diagonal elements (e.g., Hamilton, 1994, p. 257). An AR parameter relates a variable to itself at a preceding occasion, whereas a lagged cross-regressive parameter relates a variable to another variable at a previous occasion. The last term on the right-hand side of Equation 9.1 is an r-variate vector with residuals, that is, the parts of $\boldsymbol{y}_t$ that could not be predicted from previous realizations of the process. We use the (unconventional) notation $\boldsymbol{\Omega e}_t$, because this will prove useful when generalizing to the regime-switching models presented later in this chapter. It is assumed that the elements of e_t are standard normally distributed, such that the covariance matrix e_t is an identity matrix. As a result, the covariance matrix of the residuals can be denoted as $\boldsymbol{\Omega e}_t \sim N(\mathbf{0}, \boldsymbol{\Sigma})$, where $\boldsymbol{\Sigma} = \boldsymbol{\Omega}\boldsymbol{\Omega}'$, such that the residuals may be correlated within an occasion but are uncorrelated over time. For identification purposes, $\boldsymbol{\Omega}$ is constrained to be a lower triangular matrix (meaning that all elements above the diagonal are 0).

Vector Threshold Autoregressive Model

The univariate TAR model was introduced by Tong and Lim (1980) and has been extended by Koop, Pesaran, and Potter (1996) and Tsay (1998) to the multivariate case. All TAR models can be described as piecewise linear models in which the regime-switching is regulated by a manifest threshold variable z_t. Let $\{A_j\}$ be a nonoverlapping partitioning of the real line such that $A_j = (\tau_{j-1}, \tau_j)$, with $-\infty = \tau_0 < \tau_1 < \cdots < \tau_k = \infty$. Then τ_1 to τ_{k-1} are the thresholds of interest, which are used to distinguish between k distinct regimes. Let $I(z_{t-d} \in A_j)$ denote the indicator function, which takes on a value of 1 if z_{t-d} falls in A_j and is 0 otherwise. Note that for a specific occasion t, z_{t-d} will fall in one of the A_js, meaning that $I(z_{t-d} \in A_j)$ equals 1 for just one j. We refer to this j as the *regime* the system is in at occasion t.

The r-variate observation $\boldsymbol{y}_t$ is generated by a vector TAR($k, p^{(1)}, \ldots, p^{(k)}$) process if it can be written as

$$\boldsymbol{y}_t = \sum_{i=1}^{k} \left\{ \boldsymbol{\phi}_0^{(j)} + \boldsymbol{\Phi}_1^{(j)} y_{t-1} + \cdots + \boldsymbol{\Phi}_{p(j)}^{(j)} \boldsymbol{y}_{t-p(j)} + \boldsymbol{\Omega}^{(j)} e_t \right\} I\left(z_{t-d} \in A_j \right), \qquad (9.2)$$

where the vector $\boldsymbol{\phi}_0^{(j)}$ and the matrices $\boldsymbol{\Phi}_1^{(j)}$ to $\boldsymbol{\Phi}_{p(j)}^{(j)}$ play the same role as in Equation 9.1, except that they now depend on the regime the model is in, as indicated by the superscript (j). Furthermore, $e_t \sim N(0, Ir)$, such that the residuals for regime j are multivariate normally distributed, that is, $\boldsymbol{\Omega}^{(j)}e_t \sim N[0, \boldsymbol{\Sigma}^{(j)}]$, where $\boldsymbol{\Sigma}^{(j)} = \boldsymbol{\Omega}^{(j)}\boldsymbol{\Omega}^{(j)'}$.

Most publications on TAR modeling focus on the univariate case, which is obtained from Equation 9.2 by setting r equal to 1. An important aspect of the TAR model is the threshold variable, for which Tong and Lim (1980) suggested several options. First, one can use the same variable, that is, y_t. Such a TAR model is referred to as a *self-exciting TAR (SETAR) model* (Tong & Lim, 1980). Characteristic of this model is that there is a feedback loop that regulates the process when its output y_{t-d} becomes too extreme. In psychology research,

Warren and his colleagues have used the SETAR model to study self-regulation in sex offenders (Warren, 2002) and alcohol addicts (Warren et al., 2003).

Second, one can use an exogenous variable as the threshold variable. Tong and Lim (1980) referred to this as the *open-loop TAR system*. This model could prove useful in an experimental setting in which the experimenter continually varies some independent variable to study its effect on the dependent variable of interest within a single subject.

A third version of the TAR model consists of using two variables as each other's threshold variable. Such bivariate models have been referred to as a *closed-loop TAR system* (Tong & Lim, 1980) and have been used in modeling predator–prey cycles, where the size of the predator population serves as the threshold variable for the prey population and vice versa (Stenseth et al., 1998; Tong & Lim, 1980). In psychological research, closed-loop TAR systems have been used for modeling dyadic interactions in which each person serves as the other person's threshold variable (Hamaker et al., 2009).

Other extensions of the basic (univariate) TAR model consist of the following: including moving average relationships (see De Gooijer, 1998, for the threshold moving-average model; see Tong, 2003, for the threshold autoregressive moving-average model; Amendola, Niglio, & Vitale, 2006), adding (lagged) predictors (Tong & Lim, 1980), considering unit roots (Caner & Hansen, 2001), using the change (rather than the variable itself) as the threshold variable (momentum TAR model; Narayan, 2007), and having less sudden changes from one regime to another (smooth TAR model; Chan & Tong, 1986). Many of these extensions could be readily applied to the vector TAR model as well.

Markov-Switching Autoregressive Model

Just like the TAR model, the MSAR model is characterized by recurrent switches between two or more distinct AR processes. However, whereas the regime-switching in the TAR model is governed by an observed variable the regime-switching process in the MSAR model is governed by a finite state hidden Markov chain. The sequence of states of this hidden Markov chain is denoted as $\{s_t\}$, where s_t may take on any integer between 1 and k, with k being the total number of regimes. Let $I(s_t = j)$ denote the indicator function, which equals 1 if s_t equals j and is 0 otherwise (with $j = 1, \ldots, k$).

The multivariate MSAR $(k, p^{(1)}, \ldots, p^{(k)})$ model can be expressed as[1]

$$\boldsymbol{y}_t = \sum_{j=1}^{k} \left\{ \boldsymbol{\phi}_0^{(j)} + \boldsymbol{\Phi}_1^{(j)} \boldsymbol{y}_{t-1} + \cdots + \boldsymbol{\Phi}_{p(j)}^{(j)} \boldsymbol{y}_{t-p(j)} + \boldsymbol{\Omega}^{(j)} \boldsymbol{e}_t \right\} I(s_t = j), \qquad (9.3)$$

where the vectors and matrices have the same dimensions as the ones defined in multivariate TAR model in Equation 9.2. The only fundamental difference

---

[1]In the original presentation of this model by Hamilton (1989), the switching concerned the mean rather than the intercept. This leads to more abrupt switches than is the case in current presentation (see Frühwirth-Schnatter, 2006, pp. 360–361). Here, for comparability to the TAR model we use the MSAR model with switching intercept instead and allow all other model parameters to be regime dependent.

between this MSAR model and the TAR model is that in the latter the indicator function is based on an observed variable, whereas here it is based on the latent variable s_t.

The hidden Markov chain that governs the switching in the MSAR model is characterized by a matrix with transition probabilities, that is, the probabilities of switching from one regime to another. This matrix can be denoted as[2]

$$p = \begin{bmatrix} p_{11} & p_{21} \dots p_{k1} \\ p_{12} & p_{22} \dots p_{k2} \\ \dots \\ p_{1k} & p_{2k} \dots p_{kk} \end{bmatrix}, \quad (9.4)$$

where $p_{ij} = P[s_t = j | s_{t-1} = i]$ (with $i = 1, \dots, k$ and $j = 1, \dots, k$), that is, it is the chance of switching to regime j if the system was in regime i at the previous occasion. Here $\Sigma_{j=1}^k p_{ij} = 1$; that is, the conditional probabilities per column have to add to 1. Because of this constraint, there are only $k \times (k-1)$ free parameters in the matrix **p**.

A rather general extension of the MSAR model consists of the Markov-switching state space model proposed by Kim (1994; Kim & Nelson, 1999). Because many time series models can be formulated in state space format (e.g., Durbin & Koopman, 2001), this extension allows the researcher to consider a vast variety of models, including models with moving average relationships. Another extension of the MSAR model was proposed by Durland and McCurdy (1994). In their duration-dependent MSAR model the switching probabilities (i.e., Equation 9.4) depend on the time spent in a regime.

Model Estimation and Model Selection

Researchers typically are interested in comparing a number of models that represent rivaling theories. From the previous section it has become clear that the SETAR model and the MSAR model are characterized by different switching mechanisms. To determine which of these switching mechanisms is most likely to have generated the data, or that there actually is no switching mechanism operating in the data, we need to fit a number of different models (e.g., a linear AR model that represents no switching, an MSAR model with two regimes, etc.). We then have to decide which of these models gives the best description of the data. This procedure is referred to as *model selection* and is discussed at the end of this section.

Before we can focus on model selection we first need to estimate the model. Hence, we begin this section with a discussion of parameter estimation. For ease of presentation, we discuss parameter estimation of the multivariate

---

[2]The current presentation is based on Kim and Nelson's (1999) book. In many other presentations of the Markov model the transpose of this matrix is used, such that the row elements, rather than the column elements, sum to 1.

regime-switching models defined in Equations 9.2 and 9.3 for the specific case where the order of the VAR processes in each regimes is 1. However, we point out that the methods described here can be readily extended to models with higher order VAR processes.[3]

Estimation of (Multivariate) Self-Exciting Threshold Autoregressive Model

The standard procedure for estimating the parameters of a TAR model is through linear regression (e.g., Tong & Lim, 1980). Although this method is simple and fast, a drawback is that it does not handle missing data very efficiently. For every occasion that is missing there are two occasions that cannot be included in the least squares estimation: (a) the occasion that is missing and (b) the next occasion, when the missing occasion serves as a predictor. To overcome this problem, we propose to use an alternative estimation procedure based on the Kalman filter algorithm.

Let the qth element of $\boldsymbol{y}_{t-d}$ be the threshold variable, which we denote as $y_{t-d,q}$. For simplicity, we assume $d = 1$. Given a particular set of threshold values, this Kalman filter–based algorithm consists of the following steps. Set $y_{1|1} = y_1$, start at $t = 2$, and do the following:

1. Predict $\boldsymbol{y}_{t|t-1}$ from $\boldsymbol{y}_{t-1|t-1}$, depending on whether $y_{t-1|t-1,q} \in A_j$.
2. Determine the discrepancy $\boldsymbol{v}_t = \boldsymbol{y}_t - \boldsymbol{y}_{t|t-1}$.
3. Update the estimate $\boldsymbol{y}_{t|t-1}$ by $\boldsymbol{y}_{t|t} = \boldsymbol{y}_t$, and set $t = t + 1$.

These steps are repeated until the end of the series. Note that the update $\boldsymbol{y}_{t|t}$ forms the $\boldsymbol{y}_{t-1|t-1}$ in Step 1 of the next occasion. If the observation at t is missing we cannot determine the discrepancy in Step 2, and we cannot update our estimate in Step 3. Therefore, we will use $\boldsymbol{y}_{t|t} = \boldsymbol{y}_{t|t-1}$; that is, the update is the same as the prediction. This update is then used both as the value for the threshold variable and as the predictor at the next occasion (i.e., $\boldsymbol{y}_{t-1|t-1}$).[4]

The loglikelihood function for this model can be denoted as

$$\log L = \sum_{t=2}^{T} \log f(\mathbf{y}_t|\mathbf{Z}_{t-1}), \qquad (9.5)$$

---

[3]We used our own R code to estimate these models in the subsequent illustration. Currently, we are working on developing an R package that is an implementation of the algorithm developed by Kim (1994) for regime-switching state space models. The latter can be used to estimate MSAR models (see also Kim & Nelson, 1999). For more information, contact E. L. Hamaker at e.l.hamaker@uu.nl.
[4]The currently proposed method could be extended by taking the uncertainty of the predicted unobserved values into account; that is, instead of equating $y_{t|t-1,q} = y_{t|t,q}$ we could consider the prediction distribution $N[y_{t|t-1,q}, \sigma_q^{2(j)}]$ instead, where j depends on the regime the system is in at occasion t. When a prediction is made using this threshold value, one can make a prediction per regime that is then weighted by the proportion of the prediction distribution of the threshold value that falls in each of the regime areas. Although this would be a more sophisticated approach to the problem of missing data in SETAR models, it is beyond the scope of this chapter.

where $f(\mathbf{y}_t|\mathbf{Z}_{t-1})$ is the likelihood of $\mathbf{y}_t$ given all observed data up to the previous occasion, that is, $\mathbf{Z}_{t-1} = [\mathbf{y}'_1\,\mathbf{y}'_2,\,\ldots\,\mathbf{y}'_{t-1}]'$. In terms of the discrepancies $\boldsymbol{\nu}_{t|t-1}$, the log-likelihood can be written as follows:

$$\log f\,(\mathbf{y}_t|\mathbf{Z}_{t-1}) = \sum_{i=1}^{k}\left\{-\frac{r}{2}\log\,(2\pi)-\frac{1}{2}\log\left|\boldsymbol{\Sigma}^{(j)}\right|-\frac{1}{2}\boldsymbol{\nu}'_{t|t-1}\boldsymbol{\Sigma}^{(j)-1}\boldsymbol{\nu}_{t|t-1}\right\}\times I\,(y_{t-1,q}\in A_j). \qquad (9.6)$$

Note that when $\mathbf{y}_t$ is missing the discrepancy cannot be determined, such that this occasion will not contribute to the loglikelihood function in Equation 9.5. However, when $\mathbf{y}_t$ is missing we can still make a prediction for the next occasion, because we have the update $\mathbf{y}_{t|t} = \mathbf{y}_{t|t-1}$, which we can also use for the threshold value. As a result, a missing observation leads to only one missing occasion in the likelihood function using this procedure, in contrast to estimation based on linear regression.

To obtain estimates of the thresholds τ_1 to τ_{k-1}, we propose an exhaustive search considering all potential threshold values. Note that when we use $y_{t,q}$ as the threshold variable the thresholds can be estimated to equal only actual observed values of the threshold variable $y_{t,q}$; that is, we cannot differentiate between possible threshold values that have not been observed for the threshold variable.

Estimation of the Markov-Switching Autoregressive Model

A convenient way to estimate the parameters of an MSAR model is through the algorithm proposed by Kim (1994; Kim & Nelson, 1999). This is based on the Markov-switching state space model and consists of a combination of the well-known Kalman filter and the Hamilton filter. Here we present these filters in simplified form, because our states and our observations coincide (for a more detailed and general description of this procedure, see Kim & Nelson, 1999).

To allow for meaningful comparison to the multivariate SETAR model discussed earlier, we use the first observation only to regress onto, that is, $\mathbf{y}_1^{(j)} = \mathbf{y}_1$ for all j. Start at $t = 2$, and

1. Predict $\mathbf{y}_{t|t-1}^{(i,j)}$ from $\mathbf{y}_{t-1|t-1}^{(i)}$.

2. Determine the discrepancy $\boldsymbol{\nu}_t^{(i,j)} = \mathbf{y}_t - \mathbf{y}_{t|t-1}^{(i,j)}$.

3. Update the estimate $\mathbf{y}_{t|t}^{(i,j)}$ using the prediction $\mathbf{y}_{t|t-1}^{(i,j)}$ and the discrepancy $\boldsymbol{\nu}_t^{(i,j)}$.

4. Determine $P[s_{t-1}=i|s_t=j,\mathbf{Z}_t]$.

5. Collapse $\mathbf{y}_{t|t}^{(i,j)}$ into $\mathbf{y}_{t|t}^{(j)}$ using $\mathbf{y}_{t|t}^{(j)} = \sum_{i=1}\mathbf{y}_{t|t}^{(i,j)}P[s_{t-1}=i|s_t=j,\mathbf{Z}_t]$.

Note that the collapsed $\mathbf{y}_{t|t}^{(j)}$ forms the $\mathbf{y}_{t-1|t-1}^{(i,j)}$ at the next occasion. In case of missing data, we cannot determine the discrepancy in Step 2. Instead, our update will be equal to our prediction, that is, $\mathbf{y}_{t|t}^{(i,j)} = \mathbf{y}_{t-1|t-1}^{(i,j)}$. Moreover, because $\mathbf{Z}_t = \mathbf{Z}_{t-1}$, we propose to set $P[s_{t-1}=i|s_t=j,\,\mathbf{Z}_t] = P[s_{t-1}=i|s_t=j,\,\mathbf{Z}_{t-1}]$.

The loglikelihood function for this model is as defined in Equation 9.5, but now with

$$f(\mathbf{y}_t|\mathbf{Z}_{t-1}) = \sum_{i=1}^{k}\sum_{j=1}^{k} f(\mathbf{y}_t, s_{t-1} = i, s_t = j|\mathbf{Z}_{t-1})$$

$$= \sum_{i=1}^{k}\sum_{j=1}^{k} f(\mathbf{y}_t|s_{t-1} = i, s_t = j, \mathbf{Z}_{t-1}) P(s_{t-1} = i, s_t = j|\mathbf{Z}_{t-1}), \quad (9.7)$$

where

$$f(\mathbf{y}_t|s_{t-1} = i, s_t = j, \mathbf{Z}_{t-1}) = (2\pi)^{-r/2}\left|\mathbf{\Sigma}^{(j)}\right|^{-1/2} \exp\left\{-\frac{1}{2}\mathbf{v}_t^{(i,j)'}\mathbf{\Sigma}^{(j)-1}\mathbf{v}_t^{(i,j)}\right\}. \quad (9.8)$$

Note that the discrepancy $\mathbf{v}_t^{(i,j)}$ cannot be computed when $\mathbf{y}_t$ is missing. As a result, this occasion will not contribute to the likelihood function.

Model Selection

As indicated at the beginning of this section, researchers may be interested in discovering which model best describes the data at hand. To this end, the researcher has to fit several models to the data and determine which model fits the best. Model comparison and model selection typically are done using some sort of test statistic (e.g., the F test, or a loglikelihood difference test). However, the TAR model and the MSAR are not nested, and hence there is no statistical test that can be used to compare these models as rivaling hypotheses. Moreover, although the linear AR model is nested under both the TAR model and the MSAR model (i.e., it can be obtained by setting $k = 1$), one cannot compare these using standard tests because of nuisance parameters that are absent (or unidentified) under the null model. For instance, if one wishes to compare a one-regime model with a two-regime model one can simply constrain all parameters across the two regimes such that there are no differences between the regimes and hence it becomes one regime. However, in that case the threshold parameter (in case of a TAR model), or the switching probabilities (in case of an MSAR model), can take on any value. Hence, these parameters are unidentified under the one-regime model (which is the same as saying they are absent). A similar problem occurs in mixture modeling, if one is interested in comparing models with different numbers of components (see also Frühwirth-Schnatter, 2006, pp. 114–115, and Strikholm & Teräsvirta, 2006). As a result, the loglikelihood difference statistic has an unknown distribution.

Instead, one can make use of information criteria such as the Akaike information criterion (AIC; Akaike, 1973) and the Bayesian information criterion (BIC; Schwarz, 1978). Both criteria consist of –2 times the loglikelihood, plus a penalty for the number of parameters that are estimated in the model. Smaller values point to better models. To facilitate the interpretation of whether a difference between two models should be considered large or small, one can transform the information criteria into model weights. Model weights that are based on the BIC are also referred to as *posterior model probabilities* (see Burnham & Anderson, 2002, p. 290) and can be interpreted as the probability that this model generated the data, given the set of models that is considered.

When information criteria are used in the TAR literature, the threshold parameters are not penalized (e.g., Peña & Rodriguez, 2005; Strikholm & Teräsvirta, 2006), although no rationale for this decision has been given. In contrast, in the MSAR literature the estimated transition probabilities are penalized in the same way as all other model parameters. Hence, in comparing the two models discussed next we follow Clements and Krolzig (1998), who penalized all model parameters (including the threshold parameters in the TAR model), but we caution readers that there is no consensus on this issue.

Empirical Application

The data used in this illustration come from a diary study based on the Positive and Negative Affect Schedule (Watson & Clark, 1994). The individual analyzed was diagnosed with rapidly cycling bipolar disorder. The data, consisting of daily self-reported positive affect (PA) and negative affect (NA), are presented in Figure 9.1. Of the total of 91 days, 17 had missing scores.

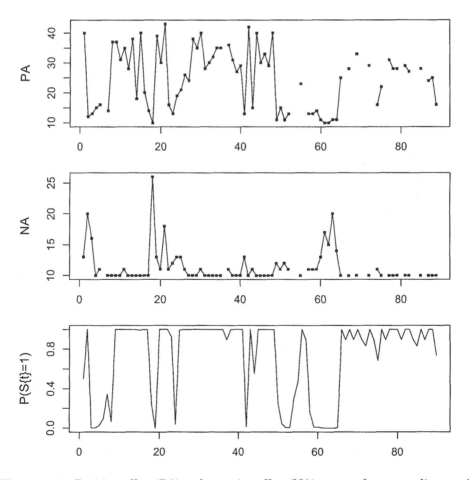

Figure 9.1.   Positive affect (PA) and negative affect (NA) scores of a person diagnosed with rapidly cycling bipolar disorder. At the bottom the probability of being in Regime 1 as estimated with a Markov-switching autoregressive (1) model is presented.

We expected this person to switch repeatedly between a manic regime and a depressed regime, and we wanted to investigate whether this switching was triggered by one of the variables in the system, (i.e., either by PA or NA) or whether it is governed by an autonomous latent process. To this end, we considered four models. Model 1 is a linear VAR(1) model, in which there is no regime-switching, which can be denoted as

$$
\begin{bmatrix} PA_t \\ NA_t \end{bmatrix} = \begin{bmatrix} \phi_{0,PA} \\ \phi_{0,NA} \end{bmatrix} + \begin{bmatrix} \phi_{11} & \phi_{12} \\ \phi_{21} & \phi_{22} \end{bmatrix} \begin{bmatrix} PA_{t-1} \\ NA_{t-1} \end{bmatrix} + \begin{bmatrix} \omega_{11} & \omega_{12} \\ \omega_{21} & \omega_{22} \end{bmatrix} \begin{bmatrix} e_{t,PA} \\ e_{t,NA} \end{bmatrix}, \tag{9.9}
$$

where the covariance matrix of the residuals of PA and NA is $\Sigma = \Omega\Omega'$, allowing for a correlation between the residuals at the same occasion. This model implies there is only one regime, meaning that there are no distinct states that can be recognized as mania and depression in the self-reported affect of this person.

Models 2 and 3 are multivariate SETAR(1) models: In Model 2, PA serves as the threshold variable, whereas in Model 3 NA is the threshold variable. In these models it is assumed that regime-switching is triggered by affect itself. For instance, if PA is the threshold variable, this model implies that as PA increases and reaches some critical value—the threshold—the system "surrenders," so to speak, to a different state, which is characterized by a high level of PA. Then, as PA decreases and drops below the threshold value, the system surrenders again to the previous state, which is characterized by a low level of PA. Such a feedback mechanism in affect regulation can be understood as maladaptive: Instead of restoring some (nonextreme) equilibrium after the system wanders too far from equilibrium (as one may expect in a healthy system), the switching mechanism just described implies a system that changes from one extreme to another, without the possibility of settling around some nonextreme equilibrium.

The last model, Model 4, is a multivariate MSAR(1) model. This model consists of two regimes, as is the case in Models 2 and 3, but the switching between the regimes is an exogenous mechanism, which is not influenced by affect itself.

To be able to make use of the AIC and BIC, we have to determine the number of parameters in each of the models. Model 1 contains 9 parameters (2 constants, 4 auto- and cross-regression parameters, and 3 elements in the covariance matrix of the residuals), Models 2 and 3 contain $(2 \times 9 =)$ 18 regular parameters and 1 threshold parameter, and Model 4 contains $(2 \times 9 =)$ 18 regular parameters and 2 transition probabilities. The results for these four models are presented in Table 9.1. Using the AIC and BIC to compare these models one can conclude there is overwhelming evidence that Model 4 is the most appropriate model among this set of models (cf. Burnham & Anderson, 2002, p. 78). From the model weights presented in the last column of the table one can conclude that the SETAR models are extremely unlikely to have generated the data. When one compares the linear model with the MSAR model one can state that the latter is more than 13 times more likely to have generated the data than the linear model $(0.9301/0.0699 = 13.3)$. From this we conclude that there is considerable evidence that the self-reported affect of this individual with rapidly cycling bipolar dis-

Table 9.1.   Results Obtained for Four Models

Model	−2logL	m	AIC	BIC	MW
1	443.1	9	461.1	481.9	.0699
2	427.1	19	465.1	509.9	<.0001
3	436.9	19	474.9	518.7	<.0001
4	390.6	20	430.6	476.7	.9301

Note.   The four models are the linear model (1), the self-exciting threshold autoregressive (SETAR) model with positive affect as the threshold variable (2), the SETAR model with negative affect as the threshold variable (3), and the Markov-switching autoregressive (MSAR) model (4). k = the number of parameters that are penalized; AIC = −2logL + 2k; AIC = Akaike information criterion; BIC = Bayesian information criterion (−2logL + log(T)k, where T is the number of observations); MW = the model weight based on the BIC.

order can be understood as coming from two distinct regimes. Moreover, switching between these regimes is regulated by an exogenous mechanism and is not influenced by either PA or NA.

To obtain more insight into the process that is inferred by Model 4, and to determine whether we can actually interpret one of the regimes as the manic state and the other as the depressed state, we simulated a time series of 100,000 data points to determine the means and variances of the two variables in each regime. In Regime 1, PA has a mean of 29.98 (SD = 7.27), and NA has a mean of 10.49 (SD = 1.30). In Regime 2, PA has a mean of 12.67 (SD = 1.84), and NA has a mean of 13.49 (SD = 4.05). From this we can conclude that Regime 1 is a positive regime with high scores on PA, and an absence of negative affect, whereas Regime 2 is a negative one, with very low PA scores and a slight increase in NA scores. Although the slight difference in NA between these regimes may seem curious, these results correspond with other reports that indicate that PA is more closely related to depression (i.e., low PA is associated with depression), whereas NA is more closely related to anxiety (Crawford & Henry, 2004; Jacques & Mash, 2004). Hence, we may interpret Regime 1 as the manic state and Regime 2 as the depressed state.

It is also interesting to note that PA scores vary a lot in Regime 1 but not in Regime 2, whereas for NA the reverse is true. In addition, the correlation between PA and NA is .14 in Regime 1 and −.65 in Regime 2. The auto- and lagged cross-regressive coefficients are close to 0 in both regimes. Finally, the estimated probabilities to remain in the same regime is higher for the positive regime than for the negative regime: .89 for Regime 1 versus .71 for Regime 2. From this we conclude that for this person the manic episodes (Regime 1) are a bit more persistent than the depressed episodes (Regime 2).

Finally, we estimated the probability that the person was in Regime 1, and we plotted these probabilities at the bottom of Figure 9.1. This shows that at many occasions the probability of being in Regime 1 is either very close to 1 or very close to 0, meaning we can be fairly sure of the regime this person was in at any particular occasion. Only at the end, when there are a lot of missing observations, does it become more difficult to determine whether the person was in Regime 1 or 2.

Discussion

In this chapter, we have discussed two regime-switching models that can be used to study psychological processes characterized by shifts between different psychological states. We have presented estimation procedures for both models that can be used when there are missing data (a common issue in diary data studies) and discussed how these models can be compared using information criteria. In our empirical application we compared multivariate SETAR models—which can be understood as regime-switching processes characterized by maladaptive regulation mechanisms—to a multivariate MSAR model—which is a regime-switching process that is characterized by a latent, exogenous switching process. We compared these models with a baseline model without regime-switching. The MSAR model proved the best description of the daily affect measurements of an individual with rapid cycling bipolar disorder.

To our knowledge, this is the first empirical study that shows that there are indeed two distinct psychological states in the affect of an individual with bipolar disorder. Moreover, we have shown that the switches from mania to depression, and vice versa, do not depend on affect itself but instead depend on an exogenous process. To obtain more insight into the nature of this process one could extend the MSAR model such that the transition probabilities can be regressed onto variables that are assumed to be important for the switching process. For instance, Frank et al. (2005) indicated that variables such as sleep quality, interpersonal stress, and disruptions in daily routines are crucial in the onset of manic episodes. The current MSAR model could be extended such that the switching probabilities are regressed onto such predictors. This would not only include the option of determining whether switching is triggered by these predictors but also allow one to investigate whether switching from the manic regime to the depressed regime depends on different variables than switching from the depressed regime to the manic regime. As such, these models allow for a detailed look at the underlying mood-regulating process and offer the opportunity to test specific hypotheses about this at the level of the individual. In addition, these models could be used to investigate whether mood regulation in other (related) disorders (e.g., borderline personality disorder), is governed by the same factors or whether this is actually a differentiating feature of disorders. If the latter proves to be the case, then investigating the specific regime-switching process in self-reported affect may become a useful tool in diagnostics in the future.

We believe the models discussed in this chapter have strong potential for elucidating underlying dynamics of psychological processes in general, including psychopathology as illustrated here. Although the interpretation of these models may (in part) depend on the actual application, we hope that the current presentation is sufficiently general and detailed that it inspires readers to consider the use of these techniques in their own fields of expertise.

References

Akaike, H. (1973). Information theory and an extension of the maximum likelihood principle. In B. N. Petrov & F. Caski (Eds.), *Proceedings of the Second International Symposium on Information Theory* (pp. 267–281). Budapest, Hungary: Akademiai Kaido.

Amendola, A., Niglio, M., & Vitale, C. (2006). Multi-step SETARMA predictors in the analysis of hydrological time series. *Physics and Chemistry of the Earth, 31,* 1118–1126.

Burnham, K. P., & Anderson, D. R. (2002). *Model selection and multi-model inference: A practical information–theoretic approach* (2nd ed.). New York, NY: Springer.

Caner, M., & Hansen, B. E. (2001). Threshold autoregression with unit root. *Econometrica, 69,* 1555–1596. doi:10.1111/1468-0262.00257

Chan, K. S., & Tong, H. (1986). On estimating thresholds in autoregressive models. *Journal of Time Series Analysis, 7,* 179–190. doi:10.1111/j.1467-9892.1986.tb00501.x

Clements, M. P., & Krolzig, H.-M. (1998). A comparison of the forecast performance of Markov-switching and threshold autoregressive model of US GPN. *Econometrics Journal, 1,* C47–C75. doi:10.1111/1368-423X.11004

Crawford, J. R., & Henry, J. D. (2004). The Positive and Negative Affect Schedule (PANAS): Construct validity, measurement properties and normative data in a large non-clinical sample. *British Journal of Clinical Psychology, 43,* 245–265. doi:10.1348/0144665031752934

De Gooijer, J. G. (1998). On threshold moving-average models. *Journal of Time Series Analysis, 19,* 1–18. doi:10.1111/1467-9892.00074

Durbin, J., & Koopman, S. J. (2001). *Time series analysis by state space methods.* New York, NY: Oxford University Press.

Durland, J. M., & McCurdy, T. H. (1994). Duration-dependent transitions in a Markov model of U.S. GPN growth. *Journal of Business & Economic Statistics, 12,* 279–288. doi:10.2307/1392084

Frank, E., Kupfer, D. J., Thase, M. E., Mallinger, A. G., Swartz, H. A., Fagiolini, A. M., . . . Monk, T. (2005). Two-year outcomes for interpersonal and social rhythm therapy in individuals with bipolar I disorder. *Archives of General Psychiatry, 62,* 996–1004. doi:10.1001/archpsyc. 62.9.996

Frühwirth-Schnatter, S. (2006). *Finite mixture and Markov switching models.* New York, NY: Springer.

Hamaker, E. L. (2009). Using information criteria to determine the number of regimes in threshold autoregressive models. *Journal of Mathematical Psychology, 53,* 518–529. doi:10.1016/j.jmp. 2009.07.006

Hamaker, E. L., Zhang, Z., & Van der Maas, H. L. J. (2009). Using threshold autoregressive models to study dyadic interactions. *Psychometrika, 74,* 727–745. doi:10.1007/s11336.009-9113-4.

Hamilton, J. D. (1989). A new approach to the economic analysis of nonstationary time series and the business cycle. *Econometrica, 57,* 357–384. doi:10.2307/1912559

Hamilton, J. D. (1994). *Time series analysis.* Princeton, NJ: Princeton University Press.

Jacques, H. A. K., & Mash, E. J. (2004). A test of the tripartite model of anxiety and depression in elementary and high school boys and girls. *Journal of Abnormal Child Psychology, 32,* 13–25. doi:10.1023/B:JACP.0000007577.38802.18

Kim, C.-J. (1994). Dynamic linear models with Markov-switching. *Journal of Econometrics, 60,* 1–22. doi:10.1016/0304-4076(94)90036-1

Kim, C.-J., & Nelson, C. R. (1999). *State–space models with regime switching: Classical and Gibbs-sampling approaches with applications.* Cambridge, MA: MIT Press.

Koop, G., Pesaran, M. H., & Potter, S. N. (1996). Impulse response analysis in nonlinear multivariate models. *Journal of Econometrics, 74,* 119–147. doi:10.1016/0304-4076(95)01753-4

Merriam-Webster, Inc. (2007). *Merriam-Webster's collegiate dictionary* (11th ed.). Springfield, MA: Author.

Narayan, P. K. (2007). Are nominal exchange rates and price levels co-integrated? New evidence from threshold autoregressive and momentum-threshold autoregressive models. *The Economic Record, 83,* 74–85. doi:10.1111/j.1475-4932.2007.00377.x

Peña, D., & Rodriguez, J. (2005). Detecting nonlinearity in time series by model selection criteria. *International Journal of Forecasting, 21,* 731–748. doi:10.1016/j.ijforecast.2005.04.014

Schwarz, G. (1978). Estimating the dimension of a model. *Annals of Statistics, 6,* 461–464. doi:10. 1214/aos/1176344136

Stenseth, N. C., Falck, W., Chan, K.-S., Bjørnstad, O. N., O'Donoghue, M., Tong, H., . . . Yoccoz, N. G. (1998). From patterns to processes: Phase and density dependencies in the Canadian lynx cycle. *Proceedings of the National Academy of Sciences, USA, 95,* 15430–15435. doi:10.1073/pnas.95.26.15430

Strikholm, B., & Teräsvirta, T. (2006). A sequential procedure for determining the number of regimes in a threshold autoregressive model. *The Econometrics Journal, 9,* 472–491. doi:10.1111/j.1368-423X.2006.00194.x

Tong, H. (2003). *Non-linear time series: A dynamic system approach*. Oxford, England: Oxford Science Publications.

Tong, H., & Lim, K. S. (1980). Threshold autoregression, limit cycles and cyclical data. *Journal of the Royal Statistical Society, B, 42,* 245–292.

Tsay, R. S. (1998). Testing and modeling multivariate threshold models. *Journal of the American Statistical Association, 93,* 1188–1202. doi:10.2307/2669861

Warren, K. (2002). Thresholds and the abstinence violation effect: A nonlinear dynamic model of the behaviors of intellectually disabled sex offenders. *Journal of Interpersonal Violence, 17,* 1198–1217. doi:10.1177/088626002237402

Warren, K., Hawkins, R. C., & Sprott, J. C. (2003). Substance abuse as a dynamical disease: Evidence and clinical implications of nonlinearity in a time series of daily alcohol consumption. *Addictive Behaviors, 28,* 369–374. doi:10.1016/S0306-4603(01)00234-9

Watson, D., & Clark, L. A. (1994). *The PANAS-X: Manual for the Positive and Negative Affect Schedule—Expanded Form*. Retrieved from http://www.psychology.uiowa.edu/faculty/Clark/PANAS-X.pdf

10

Standard Error Estimation in Stationary Multivariate Time Series Models Using Residual-Based Bootstrap Procedures

Guangjian Zhang and Sy-Miin Chow

A *univariate time series* consists of a number of repeated measurements made on a single individual and a single variable over a period of time. For example, an individual's ratings of her anxiety over a 3-month period constitute a time series. If repeated measurements are made on several variables at each time point, the resultant measurements form a multivariate time series. For example, the individual's repeated ratings of both her anxiety and depression give rise to a multivariate time series—also referred to as *P-data* in Cattell's (1951) data box heuristic. The promises brought by such intensive repeated measurement data have been articulated by several researchers across a variety of modeling contexts (Ford & Lerner, 1992; Nesselroade & Ford, 1985; Walls & Schafer, 2006).

Traditionally used in the natural sciences, engineering, and economics, time series analysis has gained increased recognition among social and behavioral scientists in the last two decades (Browne & Nesselroade, 2005; Ferrer & Zhang, 2008; West & Hepworth, 1991). For instance, multivariate time series analysis has been used for studying perceived control, effort, and academic performance (Schmitz & Skinner, 1993), the effectiveness of psychotherapy (Borckardt et al., 2008), intimate relationships (Ferrer & Nesselroade, 2003), brain imaging (Kim, Zhu, Chang, Bentler, & Ernst, 2007), and Parkinson's disease (Chow, Nesselroade, Shifren, & McArdle, 2004). A key feature of time series is that observations at adjacent time points tend to correlate with each other. This lack of independence among observations makes estimating time series models a nontrivial task; specifically, because longitudinal data in social and behavioral science applications are typically of small to moderate lengths, standard asymptotic theory used to derive standard errors and test statistics no longer holds. In such cases bootstrap procedures provide a viable alternative for deriving these measures.

Our goal in this chapter is to provide an overview of the use of bootstrap procedures to derive standard error estimates in time series models. The bootstrap was originally proposed for independent data (Efron, 1979), and it has to be modified for time series data (Singh, 1981, Remark 2.1). One possible adaptation is to use residual-based bootstrap procedures to circumvent the issue of time dependency (see Lütkepohl, 2005, p. 421; see also Bühlmann, 2002; Stoffer & Wall, 1991). The central idea behind these procedures is to fit a parametric model to a set of time series data and then use the residuals from this model to construct bootstrap samples from which standard errors or other accuracy measures for the statistical estimates of interest are derived.

This chapter is organized as follows. We first describe a commonly used multivariate time series model, the vector autoregressive moving average (VARMA) model. This model serves as the parametric model in one of the residual-based bootstrap approaches considered herein. We then present the details associated with two residual-based bootstrap procedures: (a) the *sieve bootstrap* and (b) the *bootstrap of state space models*. We illustrate the sieve bootstrap using an empirical data set.

Vector Autoregressive Moving Average Models

A popular model for multivariate time series is the VARMA model, written as

$$\boldsymbol{y}_t = \sum_{i=1}^{p} \boldsymbol{A}_i \boldsymbol{y}_{t-i} + \boldsymbol{u}_t + \sum_{j=1}^{q} \boldsymbol{B}_j \boldsymbol{u}_{t-j}, \qquad (10.1)$$

where $\mathbf{y}_t$ is a vector of manifest observations at time t, p is the lag order of the autoregressive (AR) process, and q is the lag order of the moving average (MA) process. $\boldsymbol{A}_i$ is an AR weight matrix representing the influence of $\boldsymbol{y}_{t-i}$ on the current process vector $\boldsymbol{y}_t$, $\boldsymbol{B}_j$ is an MA weight matrix representing the influence of $\boldsymbol{u}_{t-j}$ on $\mathbf{y}_t$, and $\boldsymbol{u}_t$ is the shock vector driving the VARMA process. Different components of the shock vector can be correlated within the same time points, but not across different time points. If $q = 0$, the process becomes a pure AR process; if $p = 0$, the process becomes a pure MA process. The process depicted in Equation 10.1 is generally referred to as a *VARMA (p,q) process*.

In the present context we consider only stationary cases of the VARMA process. If all statistical properties of a multivariate time series remain the same over time, the time series is said to be stationary. MA processes are generally stationary, but AR processes may manifest signs of nonstationarity in specific parameter ranges (e.g., "explosive" processes whose variances increase as opposed to remaining constant over time; Hamilton, 1994). Stationary VARMA processes have invariant mean and covariance functions over time. It is important to note that even when constrained to reside in the stationary region, the VARMA model still includes many other dynamic models as special cases (e.g., the cyclic model; Harvey, 1993). Its flexibility has rendered it particularly suited to representing a broad array of phenomena in the social and behavioral sciences. Examples include dyadic interaction (Beebe et al., 2007), mood and cognitive fluctuations (Chow, Hamagami, & Nesselroade, 2007), and longitudinal mediation processes (Cole & Maxwell, 2003). Many nonstationary time series can also be transformed to stationary time series by removing the trend or seasonal component. Alternatively, techniques for representing nonstationary change processes also exist (Boker, Xu, Rotondo, & King, 2002; Chow, Hamaker, Fujita, & Boker, 2009; Weber, Molenaar, & Van der Molen, 1992).

When a multivariate time series is normally distributed one can perform maximum likelihood estimation of the VARMA model using the raw data (see Lütkepohl, 2005, Chapter 12, and Brockwell & Davis, 1991, pp. 430–432). Maximizing the likelihood function directly with raw time series data can be difficult, however, because the time series contains dependent data and the likelihood function cannot be separated into individual terms. In practice, maximum likelihood estimation of VARMA model with normal time series is often carried out with prediction errors instead of the raw data. The prediction errors are independent; therefore, the likelihood function can be written as the product of independent terms.

Alternatively, the VARMA model can be expressed as a state space model. One can use the Kalman filter and the associated prediction error decomposition function (Harvey, 1989; Schweppe, 1965) to derive maximum likelihood estimates using the raw data when the time series is normally distributed. Implementing the Kalman filter requires specification of an initial state vector and its covariance matrix. When the time series is long, the initial state vector specification has little influence on the estimates; when the time series is short, the initial state vector specification has substantial influence on the estimates (De Jong, 1991; Oud, Jansen, van Leeuwe, Aarnoutse, & Voeten, 1999).

The VARMA models can also be estimated as structural equation models (du Toit & Browne, 2007; Hamaker, Dolan, & Molenaar, 2002; Van Buuren, 1997). In one structural equation modeling (SEM) approach, a lagged correlation (or alternatively, a lagged covariance) matrix is first computed from a time series and subsequently used for model-fitting purposes. Du Toit and Browne (2007) derived the covariance structure of the VARMA process. Their derivation involves an initial state vector whose covariance matrix reflects preconceived notions regarding the stationarity of the VARMA process of interest.[1]

Fitting the VARMA model within the SEM framework has several advantages. First, the VARMA model can be used to characterize the dynamic inter-relationships among latent variables (Browne & Nesselroade, 2005; Browne & Zhang, 2007; Molenaar, 1985). Second, because of social and behavioral researchers' general familiarity with SEM techniques, SEM formulation of the VARMA model helps make time series modeling accessible to a broader audience. Third, SEM provides a convenient framework for specifying and comparing different variations of the VARMA model.

In sum, the general VARMA (p,q) model provides a flexible platform for representing a variety of different change processes. Its potential utility is evidenced by its widespread use across multiple disciplines and model-fitting traditions. However, asymptotic standard errors for the VARMA process require that the

---

[1]For instance, it is an appropriate representation for stationary VARMA processes that started in the distant past, stationary VARMA processes that come into existence only at the first observed time point, or processes that started before the first time point but just become a stationary VARMA process at the first time point. Among the three conditions, the first one is directly related to the VARMA models of a single subject.

multivariate time series is long and normally distributed. It is not uncommon that these assumptions are unattainable in the social and behavioral sciences. We next describe procedures for bootstrapping time series data when these assumptions do not hold.

The Bootstrap of Time Series Data

When a multivariate time series is normally distributed and is long enough, standard error of maximum likelihood estimates can be obtained analytically (Lütkepohl, 2005, pp. 692–697). However, analytical standard errors for maximum likelihood estimates are derived under the conditions that the time series is normally distributed, the time series length is long, and the model of interest is the true model. These assumptions may be violated in empirical settings.

The bootstrap (Efron & Tibshirani, 1993) is a computer-intensive method for estimating measures of accuracy of point estimates. One common use of the bootstrap is in the estimation of standard errors. It is particularly suitable for deriving standard errors in cases involving non-normal data, small sample sizes, and imperfect models. The basic idea behind the bootstrap is to simulate the mechanism by which the data are generated from the population using the computer; specifically, when data are independently and identically distributed bootstrap samples are obtained by means of sampling with replacement from the original data, and the bootstrap replications obtained from the bootstrap samples are used as the basis for computing standard error estimates and constructing confidence intervals. The quality of bootstrap standard errors or confidence intervals depends on how closely the estimated data-generating mechanism approximates the "true" data-generating mechanism. In this chapter, we refer to this bootstrap procedure as the *independent bootstrap*. It is well known that the independent bootstrap provides accurate standard error estimates when the data are independent. However, a blind use of the independent bootstrap with time series fails miserably: A time series consists of dependent data, but the independent bootstrap destroys the dependence (Singh, 1981, Remark 2.1).

Effective bootstrap procedures for time series data have received much attention in statistics (Bühlmann, 2002; Lahiri, 2003; Lütkepohl, 2005). Among some of the proposed approaches is the *block bootstrap* (Künsch, 1989), a nonparametric approach for bootstrapping time series data. The block bootstrap is based on the assumptions that the correlation between two observations tends to be substantial if they are close in time and that the correlation tends to be negligible if they are far away from each other. It is a nonparametric approach because it makes no assumption about the distribution of the time series or the true underlying data-generating model. This approach involves forming blocks of observations from the raw data and subsequently drawing samples with replacement from the blocks rather than individual observations. The sampled blocks are then connected to form a bootstrap sample or time series. Repeating this process a large number of times—say, for B replications—yields B bootstrap time series and B corresponding sets of statistics or estimates, known as *bootstrap replications*. Examples of such statistics or estimates may include lagged correlations and AR weights. Standard errors and confidence intervals for the parameters of interest can then be computed from the B bootstrap replications (Efron & Tibshirani, 1993).

Directly contrary to nonparametric approaches such as the block bootstrap is the *parametric bootstrap*. This approach assumes that a specific time series model gives rise to the data and that the data conform to a certain distribution. The parametric bootstrap is like a Monte Carlo study in which the population values are parameter estimates obtained from the original sample. Zhang (2006) used both the block bootstrap and the parametric bootstrap to estimate standard errors and test statistics for dynamic factor analysis models. The results from random sampling experiments suggest that both bootstrap methods provide satisfactory standard error estimates when their respective assumptions are met.

In this chapter, we describe in detail two semiparametric residual-based procedures: (a) the sieve bootstrap and (b) the bootstrap of state space models. In both approaches a parametric model is first fitted to the original time series. The resultant parameter estimates are then used to construct bootstrap time series by sampling with replacement from the original residuals. These procedures are semiparametric because they assume that a certain model gives rise to the data, but they make no assumption about the corresponding data distribution.

The Sieve Bootstrap

The sieve bootstrap is based on the property that any VARMA process can be expressed as a VAR(p^*) process (Lütkepohl, 2005, p. 421):

$$y_t = \sum_{i=1}^{\infty} A_i y_{t-i} + u_t. \qquad (10.2)$$

In this bootstrap procedure a VAR(p^*) model is used as the parametric model for constructing bootstrap time series. Doing so requires a researcher to determine a finite number p^*, so the VAR(p^*) model can adequately approximate the true time series process. It is important to note that because a VAR(p^*) model can essentially approximate any process because p^* tends to ∞, a finite-order VAR model with a sufficiently high lag can still provide a reasonable approximation even though the true time series process is not a VAR process.

The first step of the sieve bootstrap is to fit a VAR(p^*) model to the sample time series $y_1, y_2, \ldots, y_T$. Let $\hat{A}_1, \hat{A}_2, \ldots, \hat{A}_{p^*}$ be the AR weight matrices. The residuals $u_{p^*+1}, u_{p^*+2}, u_{p^*+3}, \ldots, u_T$ are calculated by

$$u_t = (y_t - \bar{y}) - \sum_{i=1}^{p^*} \hat{A}_i (y_{t-i} - \bar{y}). \qquad (10.3)$$

Here $\bar{y}$ is the mean vector of the sample time series.

If the mean vector of the residuals $u_{p^*+1}, u_{p^*+2}, \ldots, u_T$ is not a null vector, the mean vector should be removed from the residuals,

$$e_t = u_t - \frac{1}{T - p^*} \sum_{1=p^*+1}^{T} u_i. \quad (10.4)$$

The residuals $e_{p^*+1}, e_{p^*+2}, e_{p^*+3}, \ldots, e_T$ are referred to as the *centered residuals*. Note that Equation 10.3 requires observations from p^* previous time points to calculate the residuals at time t, but no actual y_t can be used to obtain the first p^* residuals (i.e., $u_1, \ldots, u_{p^*}$). Thus, we only use residuals from $p^* + 1$ to T.

After obtaining the centered residuals, a bootstrap sample of residuals—$e_1^*, e_2^*, e_3^*, \ldots, e_T^*$—is drawn with replacement from the centered residuals. A bootstrap time series, $y^* = [y_1^*, y_2^*, \ldots, y_T^*]'$, is then constructed from the bootstrap residuals and AR weight matrices as

$$y_t^* = \hat{A}_1 y_{t-1}^* + \hat{A}_2 y_{t-2}^* + \cdots + \hat{A}_{p^*} y_{t-p^*}^* + e_t^*. \quad (10.5)$$

The equation requires values at the p^* previous time points before the first time point, $y_0^*, y_{-1}^*, \ldots, y_{-p^*+1}^*$. One solution is to start the process from the remote past, for example, $t = -1{,}000$ and set $y_{-1{,}000}^*, y_{-999}^*, \ldots, y_{-1{,}001+p}^*$ to be null vectors. With sufficient iterations, Equation 10.5 will eventually produce a stationary process. The first 1,000 time points are then discarded as burn-ins, and the last T time points, $y_1^*, y_2^*, \ldots, y_T^*$ constitute the bootstrap time series.

One important issue in the implementation of the sieve bootstrap pertains to the selection of p^*, the order of the VAR(p^*) model. Ideally, p^* is large enough to adequately approximate the true process and small enough at the same time so the VAR(p^*) can be accurately estimated by the sample time series. Model selection criteria such as the Akaike Information Criterion (AIC; Akaike, 1974) or the Bayesian Information Criterion (BIC; Schwarz, 1978) can be used to strike a balance between these two needs.

The sieve bootstrap involves estimating B bootstrap replications of the VAR model. The VAR(p^*) model can be estimated by solving the multivariate Yule–Walker equation (Lütkepohl, 2005, pp. 85–86). The Yule–Walker estimators are asymptotically equivalent to maximum likelihood estimators, but the former require far less computation. However, solving the Yule–Walker equation directly for a k-variate time series involves the inversion of a $p^* \times k$ by $p^* \times k$ lagged correlation matrix. Numerical difficulties may arise when the dimension of this matrix becomes large. In such cases, the Whittle algorithm (Brockwell & Davis, 1991, pp. 421–423) can be used to avoid inverting the big matrix. The Yule–Walker estimates are then plugged into the likelihood function to provide the AIC or BIC value.

The sieve bootstrap is consistent with the notion that "all models are wrong, but some are useful" (Box, 1976). This semiparametric approach involves fitting a VAR(p^*) model to the sample time series: It is just an approximation of the "true" model. If the length of the sample time series T increases, more data points will support a more complex model: The order of the VAR process p^* increases, and a more accurate approximation is achieved.[2] Because the bootstrap residuals are sampled with replacement from residuals in the original

---

[2]This is only for theoretical interest. In application, the time series length T is a fixed number.

sample, standard error estimates obtained from the sieve bootstrap should be valid for nonnormal time series.

The Bootstrap of State Space Models

The state space model (Harvey, 1989) is essentially a general modeling framework, and many time series models, including the VARMA model, can be formulated within this framework. The state space model consists of two equations: (a) the measurement equation, which relates the latent state vector to observed variables, and (b) the transition equation, which specifies that the current state vector depends only on the previous state vector. When the multivariate time series is normally distributed, one can obtain maximum likelihood estimates of the modeling parameters using the Kalman filter. The Kalman filter also produces standard error estimates. The Kalman filter standard error estimates are appropriate if the time series is long and normally distributed and the VARMA model is the true model.

Stoffer and Wall (1991) described a residual-based bootstrap for estimating standard errors in state space models. It is particularly useful for finite time series or non-normal time series. In the bootstrapping state space model it is convenient to express the state space model in the innovations form as

$$\epsilon_t = \mathbf{y}_t - \mathbf{G}\mathbf{s}_t^{t-1}, \qquad (10.6)$$

$$\mathbf{s}_{t+1}^t = \mathbf{F}\mathbf{s}_t^{t-1} + \mathbf{K}_t\epsilon_t, \qquad (10.7)$$

$$\mathbf{y}_t = \mathbf{G}\mathbf{s}_t^{t-1} + \epsilon_t, \qquad (10.8)$$

where Equation 10.7 defines the transition model and Equation 10.8 is the measurement model; s_t^{t-1} denotes the predicted value of the state vector at time t based on all the manifest observations up to time $t-1$ (i.e., $\mathbf{y}_1, \mathbf{y}_2, \ldots, \mathbf{y}_{t-1}$), $\mathbf{F}$ is the transition matrix, $\mathbf{G}$ is the factor loading matrix, ϵ is a vector of innovations capturing the discrepancies between actual and predicted manifest observations, and $\mathbf{K}_t$ denotes the Kalman gain matrix premultiplied by the transition matrix.

Let $\hat{\mathbf{F}}$ and $\hat{\mathbf{G}}$ be the estimated transition and factor loading matrices obtained from fitting the state space model in Equations 10.8 and 10.7 to the raw data using the prediction error decomposition likelihood function (Harvey, 1989; Schweppe, 1965), and let $\hat{\mathbf{K}}_t$ be the Kalman gain matrix that is premultiplied by the estimated transition matrix. The Kalman filter also produces estimates of the state vector, s_t^{t-1}, and the corresponding innovations,

$$\hat{\epsilon}_t = \mathbf{y}_t - \hat{\mathbf{G}}\mathbf{s}_t^{t-1}, \qquad (10.9)$$

which are standardized to yield

$$e_t = \sum_t^{-1/2} \hat{\epsilon}_t, \qquad (10.10)$$

where Σ is the covariance matrix associated with the estimated state vector, s_t^{t-1}, available from running the Kalman filter.

The bootstrap procedure is implemented as follows. First, a bootstrap sample of standardized residuals, $e_1^*, e_2^*, e_3, \ldots, e_T^*$, is obtained by sampling with replacement from the standardized innovations, $e_1, e_2, e_3, \ldots, e_T$, available from Equation 10.10. A bootstrap time series is then constructed by using the following equations:

$$y_t^* = \hat{G}s_t^{t-1*} + \sum\nolimits_t^{1/2} e_t^*, \quad (10.11)$$

and

$$s_{t+1}^{t*} = \hat{F}s_t^{t-1*} + \hat{K}_t \sum\nolimits_t^{1/2} e_t^*. \quad (10.12)$$

Equations 10.11 and 10.12 are similar to the state space representation in Equations 10.8 and 10.7 except that the parameter matrices are replaced by their sample estimates and the innovations are replaced by the bootstrap samples of innovations. One can initiate the bootstrap sample–generating procedure using a diffuse initial condition; that is, the initial state vector can be specified to be a null vector and its covariance matrix a diagonal matrix with large diagonal elements. To ensure that the bootstrap time series is stationary, however, a researcher can start the process at a distant past (e.g., $t = -1,000$) and retain only the last T observations by discarding the initial burn-in samples.

The bootstrap of state space model is not robust against model misspecification, but it is robust against the violation of the normality assumption. Stoffer and Wall (1991) showed that the bootstrap approach provides more accurate standard error estimates than asymptotic standard errors when time series are of short to moderate lengths (e.g., $T = 50$).

Illustration

We now illustrate the sieve bootstrap using a bivariate time series described in the classic textbook *Time Series Analysis: Forecasting and Control* (Box & Jenkins, 1976, pp. 409–412). The first component is the sales of a product, and second component is the leading indictor. The raw series contains 150 time points and is nonstationary. A new series is constructed by differencing the raw series,

$$Z_t = Y_t - Y_{t-1}. \quad (10.13)$$

Here, Y_t is the original series, and Z_t is the new series. We will use the sieve bootstrap to estimate standard errors of lagged cross-correlations between the two components of Z_t. Figure 10.1 displays the time series: The top panel plots the indicator, and the bottom panel plots the sales. A quick look at Figure 10.1 shows that the two series are very similar.

Sales Data

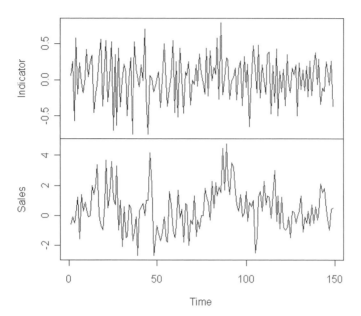

Figure 10.1.   Sales with a leading indicator: the differences.

Figure 10.2 displays the autocorrelations and cross-correlations of these two series. As shown in the lower left panel, the lagged cross-correlations $r_{1,2}(0)$, $r_{1,2}(-1)$, $r_{1,2}(-2)$, and $r_{1,2}(-3)$ are $-.00$, $.07$, $-.38$, and $.72$. They are correlations between the series of sales with the series of indicator at the current time point, one time point earlier, two time points earlier, and three time point earlier. It is interesting to note that the lag 0 correlation and the lag 1 correlation are small, but the lag 2 correlation and the lag 3 correlation are substantial. We illustrate how to estimate their standard errors using the sieve bootstrap.

We fitted a sequence of VAR models to the bivariate time series $\mathbf{Z}_1, \mathbf{Z}_2, \ldots,$ $\mathbf{Z}_{149}$ and selected the AR(5) model according to the AIC. The AR matrices are

$$\hat{\mathbf{A}}_1 = \begin{bmatrix} -0.52 & 0.24 \\ -0.02 & -0.05 \end{bmatrix}, \hat{\mathbf{A}}_2 = \begin{bmatrix} -0.19 & -0.02 \\ 0.05 & 0.25 \end{bmatrix}, \hat{\mathbf{A}}_3 = \begin{bmatrix} -0.07 & 0.01 \\ 4.68 & 0.21 \end{bmatrix},$$

$$\hat{\mathbf{A}}_4 = \begin{bmatrix} -0.03 & -0.01 \\ 3.66 & 0.00 \end{bmatrix}, \text{and } \hat{\mathbf{A}}_5 = \begin{bmatrix} 0.02 & 0.01 \\ 1.30 & 0.03 \end{bmatrix}.$$

We computed the residuals $\hat{\boldsymbol{u}}_6, \hat{\boldsymbol{u}}_7, \ldots, \hat{\boldsymbol{u}}_{149}$ using

$$\hat{\boldsymbol{u}}_t = \left(\mathbf{Z}_t - \bar{\mathbf{Z}} \right) - \sum_{i=1}^{i=5} \hat{\mathbf{A}}_i \left(\mathbf{Z}_{t-i} - \bar{\mathbf{Z}} \right). \qquad (10.14)$$

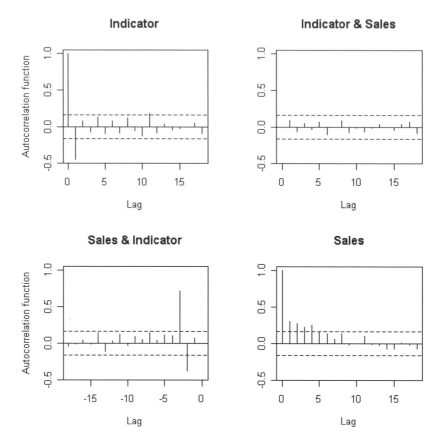

Figure 10.2.   Autocorrelations and cross-correlations.

Here $\bar{\mathbf{Z}}$ is the mean vector. Let $\hat{\mathbf{e}}_6, \hat{\mathbf{e}}_7, \ldots, \hat{\mathbf{e}}_{149}$ be the centered residuals as in Equation 10.4. We construct the bootstrap time series using

$$\mathbf{Z}_t^* = \sum_{i=1}^{i=5} \hat{\mathbf{A}}_i \mathbf{Z}_{t-i}^* + \hat{\mathbf{e}}_t^*. \quad (10.15)$$

Here $\hat{\mathbf{e}}_t^*$ is sampled with replacement from the centered residuals. We start the VAR(5) process in Equation 10.15 at $t = -150$. The time series at the five previous time points $\mathbf{Z}_{-155}^*$, $\mathbf{Z}_{-154}^*$, $\mathbf{Z}_{-153}^*$, $\mathbf{Z}_{-152}^*$, and $\mathbf{Z}_{-151}^*$ are set to be null vectors. We discarded the first 150 time points and kept $\boldsymbol{\epsilon}_1^*$, $\boldsymbol{\epsilon}_2^*$, $\ldots$, and $\boldsymbol{\epsilon}_{149}^*$ as a bootstrap time series.

The illustration involves a bootstrap sample size $B = 1,000$. Figure 10.3 displays the scatter plot of $r_{1,2}(-3)$ in the sample and the corresponding scatter plots in the first three bootstrap time series.

Let θ be the parameter of interest. Each bootstrap time series contributes a bootstrap replication of $\hat{\theta}_i^*$. The bootstrap standard error is estimated using the standard deviation of the B bootstrap replications,

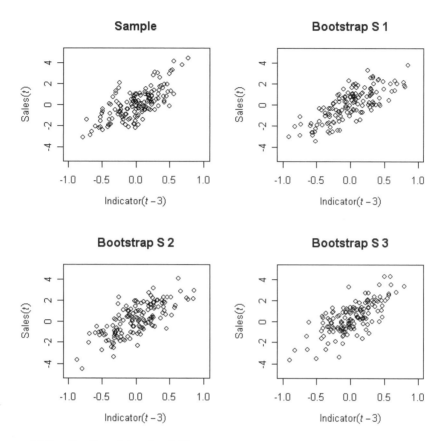

Figure 10.3. Scatter plots of $r_{1,2}(-3)$

$$\widehat{SE}_{\hat{\theta}} = \sqrt{\frac{\left(\sum_{i=1}^{B} \hat{\theta}_i^* - \overline{\hat{\theta}^*}\right)^2}{B-1}}. \qquad (10.16)$$

The bootstrap standard error estimates for the correlations $r_{1,2}$ at lag 0, lag 1, lag 2, and lag 3 are .08, .08, .07, and .02, respectively. Therefore, one can conclude that the correlations at lag 2 ($\hat{r}_{1,2}(3) = -.38$) and lag 3 ($\hat{r}_{1,2}(2) = .72$) are significantly different from zero.

Conclusion

We have reviewed two residual-based bootstrap approaches: (a) the sieve bootstrap and (b) the state space bootstrap. Although we included an empirical illustration using only the sieve bootstrap, some commonalities between the two can be noted. For instance, both of these approaches involve fitting a parametric model but make no assumption concerning the normality of the data.

The sieve bootstrap makes use of a general VAR(p^*) model that can approximate any process up to an arbitrary degree of accuracy when p^* is sufficiently large. In contrast, by embedding bootstrap procedures within the general state space framework, the state space bootstrap approach allows researchers to select their parametric models of interest from a rich array of modeling possibilities. This approach, however, does assume that the state space model of choice is the true model.

A practical issue for any computer-intensive procedure, of course, is how computationally intensive the procedure is. With the widespread availability of inexpensive computing resources, the demand for computing seems to be a less important issue. For example, our empirical illustration using the sieve bootstrap with $B = 1,000$ replications takes just a few seconds on a Lenovo X60 laptop.

One caveat pertaining to the sieve approach is worth noting. When the multivariate time series is short and is composed of many manifest variables, the sieve bootstrap may not be the most appropriate choice. Specifically, the order of the VAR(p^*) model is selected according to some model comparison criteria, such as the AIC and the BIC. These model selection criteria consist of two parts: (a) the loglikelihood function value and (b) a penalty for model complexity. The penalty for model complexity dominates the model selection criteria for short and high-dimensional time series, thus prompting these criteria to always favor lower selection orders. Other bootstrap procedures should thus be considered in such cases.

Multivariate time series models offer a unique way to study the dynamics of human behaviors, but time series models and the idiographic framework in general have not been widely adopted in the social and behavioral sciences. In our view, one reason stems in part from the lack of appropriate tools for handling computational issues inherent to the time series modeling framework. Fitting models of change to non-normal time series of finite lengths is a commonly encountered challenge. Standard error estimation simply constitutes one aspect of this challenge. Nevertheless, such issues have to be resolved, albeit one small step at a time, and this chapter provides one set of possible ways to tackle this specific issue.

References

Akaike, H. (1974). A new look at the statistical model identification. *IEEE Transactions on Automatic Control, 19,* 716–723. doi:10.1109/TAC.1974.1100705

Beebe, B., Jaffe, J., Buck, K., Chen, H., Cohen, P., Blatt, S., . . . Andrews, H. (2007). Six-week postpartum maternal self-criticism and dependency and 4-month mother–infant self- and interactive contingencies. *Developmental Psychology, 43,* 1360–1376. doi:10.1037/0012-1649.43.6.1360

Boker, S. M., Xu, M., Rotondo, J. L., & King, K. (2002). Windowed cross-correlation and peak picking for the analysis of variability in the association between behavioral time series. *Psychological Methods, 7,* 338–355. doi:10.1037/1082-989X.7.3.338

Borckardt, J. J., Nash, M. R., Murphy, M. D., Moore, M., Shaw, D., & O'Neil, P. (2008). Clinical practice as natural laboratory for psychotherapy research: A guide to case-based time-series analysis. *American Psychologist, 63,* 77–95. doi:10.1037/0003-066X.63.2.77

Box, G. E. P. (1976). Science and statistics. *Journal of the American Statistical Association, 71,* 791–799. doi:10.2307/2286841

Box, G. E. P., & Jenkins, G. M. (1976). *Time series analysis: Forecasting and control* (revised ed.). San Francisco, CA: Holden-Day.

Brockwell, P. J., & Davis, R. A. (1991). *Time series: Theory and methods* (2nd ed.). New York, NY: Springer-Verlag.

Browne, M. W., & Nesselroade, J. R. (2005). Representing psychological processes with dynamic factor models: Some promising uses and extensions of ARMA time series models. In A. Maydeu-Olivares & J. J. McArdle (Eds.), *Advances in psychometrics: A* festschrift *for Roderick P. McDonald* (pp. 415–452). Mahwah, NJ: Erlbaum.

Browne, M. W., & Zhang, G. (2007). Developments in the factor analysis of individual time series. In R. Cudeck & R. C. MacCallum (Eds.), *Factor analysis at 100: Historical developments and future directions* (pp. 265–291). Mahwah, NJ: Erlbaum.

Bühlmann, P. (2002). Bootstraps for time series. *Statistical Science, 17,* 52–72.

Buuren, S. van (1997). Fitting ARMA time series by structural equation models. *Psychometrika, 62,* 215–236. doi:10.1007/BF02295276

Cattell, R. (1951). On the disuse and misuse of P, Q, Qs, and O techniques in clinical psychology. *Journal of Clinical Psychology, 7,* 203–214.

Chow, S.-M., Hamagami, F., & Nesselroade, J. R. (2007). Age differences in dynamical cognition–emotion linkages. *Psychology and Aging, 22,* 765–780.

Chow, S.-M., Hamaker, E. J., Fujita, F., & Boker, S. M. (2009). Representing time-varying cyclic dynamics using multiple-subject state–space models. *British Journal of Mathematical and Statistical Psychology, 62,* 683–716.

Chow, S.-M., Nesselroade, J., Shifren, K., & McArdle, J. J. (2004). Dynamic structure of emotions among individuals with Parkinson's disease. *Structural Equation Modeling, 11,* 560–582. doi:10.1207/s15328007sem1104_4

Cole, D. A., & Maxwell, S. E. (2003). Testing mediational models with longitudinal data: Questions and tips in the use of structural equation modeling. *Journal of Abnormal Psychology, 112,* 558–577. doi:10.1037/0021-843X.112.4.558

De Jong, P. (1991). The diffuse Kalman filter. *Annals of Statistics, 19,* 1073–1083. doi:10.1214/aos/1176348139

du Toit, S., & Browne, M. W. (2007). Structural equation modeling of multivariate time series. *Multivariate Behavioral Research, 42,* 67–101.

Efron, B. (1979). Bootstrap methods: Another look at the jackknife. *Annals of Statistics, 7,* 1–26. doi:10.1214/aos/1176344552

Efron, B., & Tibshirani, R. J. (1993). *An introduction to the bootstrap.* New York, NY: Chapman and Hall.

Ferrer, E., & Nesselroade, J. R. (2003). Modeling affective process in dyadic relations via dynamic factor analysis. *Emotion, 3,* 344–360. doi:10.1037/1528-3542.3.4.344

Ferrer, E., & Zhang, G. (2008). Time series models for examining psychological processes: Applications and new developments. In R. E. Millsap & A. Madeu-Olivares (Eds.), *Handbook of quantitative methods in psychology* (pp. 637–657). Newbury Park, CA: Sage.

Ford, D. H., & Lerner, R. M. (1992). *Developmental systems theory: An integrative approach.* Newbury Park, CA: Sage.

Hamaker, E. L., Dolan, C. V., & Molenaar, P. C. M. (2002). On the nature of SEM estimates of ARMA parameters. *Structural Equation Modeling, 9,* 347–368.

Hamilton, J. D. (1994). *Time series analysis.* Princeton, NJ: Princeton University Press.

Harvey, A. C. (1989). *Forecasting, structural time series models and the Kalman filter.* Cambridge, England: Cambridge University Press.

Harvey, A. C. (1993). *Time series models* (2nd ed.). Cambridge, MA: MIT Press.

Kim, J., Zhu, W., Chang, L., Bentler, P. M., & Ernst, T. (2007). Unified structural equation modeling approach for the analysis of multisubject, multivariate functional MRI data. *Human Brain Mapping, 28,* 85–93.

Künsch, H. R. (1989). The jackknife and the bootstrap for general stationary observations. *Annals of Statistics, 17,* 1217–1241. doi:10.1214/aos/1176347265

Lahiri, S. N. (2003). *Resampling methods for dependent data.* New York, NY: Springer-Verlag.

Lütkepohl, H. (2005). *New introduction to multiple time series analysis.* New York, NY: Springer-Verlag.

Molenaar, P. C. M. (1985). A dynamic factor analysis model for the analysis of multivariate time series. *Psychometrika, 50,* 181–202. doi:10.1007/BF02294246

Nesselroade, J. R., & Ford, D. H. (1985). P-technique comes of age: Multivariate, replicated, single-subject designs for research on older adults. *Research on Aging, 7,* 46–80. doi:10.1177/0164027585007001003

Oud, J. H. L., Jansen, R. A. R. G., van Leeuwe, J. F. L., Aarnoutse, C. A. J., & Voeten, M. J. M. (1999). Monitoring pupil development by means of the Kalman filter and smoother based upon SEM state space modeling. *Learning and Individual Differences, 11,* 121–136. doi:10.1016/S1041-6080(00)80001-1

Schmitz, B., & Skinner, E. (1993). Perceived control, effort, and academic performance: Interindividual, intraindividual, and multivariate time series analysis. *Journal of Personality and Social Psychology, 64,* 1010–1028.

Schwarz, G. (1978). Estimating the dimension of a model. *Annals of Statistics, 6,* 461–464.

Schweppe, F. (1965). Evaluation of likelihood functions for Gaussian signals. *IEEE Transactions on Information Theory, 11,* 61–70. doi:10.1109/TIT.1965.1053737

Singh, K. (1981). On the asymptotic accuracy of Efron's bootstrap. *Annals of Statistics, 9,* 1187–1195. doi:10.1214/aos/1176345636

Stoffer, D. S., & Wall, K. D. (1991). Bootstrapping state-space models: Gaussian maximum likelihood estimation and the Kalman filter. *Journal of the American Statistical Association, 86,* 1024–1033. doi:10.2307/2290521

Walls, T. H., & Schafer, J. L. (2006). *Models for intensive longitudinal data.* Oxford, England: Oxford University Press.

Weber, E. J., Molenaar, P. C., & Van der Molen, M. W. (1992). A nonstationarity test for the spectral analysis of physiological time series with an application to respiratory sinus arrhythmia. *Psychophysiology, 29,* 55–62. doi:10.1111/j.1469-8986.1992.tb02011.x

West, S. G., & Hepworth, J. T. (1991). Statistical issues in the study of temporal data: Daily experiences. *Journal of Personality, 59,* 609–662. doi:10.1111/j.1467-6494.1991.tb00261.x

Zhang, G. (2006). *Bootstrap procedures for dynamic factor analysis.* Unpublished doctoral dissertation, Ohio State University.

11

Modeling Resilience With Differential Equations

Steven M. Boker, Mignon A. Montpetit, Michael D. Hunter, and Cindy S. Bergeman

A concept that has been bouncing around the psychological literature for some time is that of *resilience,* the idea that individuals can exhibit positive adaptation in the process of experiencing adverse life events. Simply put, one might say resilient people bounce back from negative events. *The New Shorter Oxford English Dictionary* (1993) contains the following definitions of *resilience:*

> 1 a The action or act of rebounding or springing back. b Recoil from something; revolt. 2 Elasticity; spec. the amount of energy per unit volume that a material absorbs when subjected to strain. 3 The ability to recover readily from, or resist being affected by, a setback, illness, etc. (p. 2562)

These definitions constitute an interesting overlap of physical and psychological meanings. This overlap creates an intentional metaphor of elasticity when used to describe a short-term, intraindividual psychological process. However, *positive adaptation* and *elasticity* may have subtly differing meanings.

In this chapter, we examine some models that can describe two physical properties, elasticity and damping, that are used to describe resilient physical systems. We propose that models such as these are important to consider if one wishes to make a claim of construct validity for the overlap between the physical and psychological meanings of resilience. In other words, our argument is that if we wish to measure how someone "bounces back," we need models that can parameterize the bounce. If we fit models describing components of physical elasticity to intraindividual psychological adaptation in the presence of stress and find that parts of the model do not provide explanatory power, then we would like to know what parts of the physical elasticity metaphor for resilience should be modified or discarded. Finally, by taking the physical elasticity metaphor seriously, we introduce a language for expressing differences between models that can help clarify our thinking about different forms of intraindividual adaptation to stress.

Funding for this work was provided in part by National Institute on Aging Grant 5R01AG023571 and National Institutes of Health Grant 1R21DA024304. Any opinions, findings, and conclusions or recommendations expressed in this chapter are those of the authors and do not necessarily reflect the views of the National Science Foundation or the National Institutes of Health.

Before we examine models for elasticity and damping, let us very briefly review some ways that resilience has been treated in the psychology literature (but for more thorough reviews, see Luthar, Cicchetti, & Becker, 2000; Ong & Bergeman, 2004; Reich, Zautra, & Davis, 2003). The notion of resilience as a traitlike characteristic grew out of work concerning vulnerability to morbidity (e.g., Anthony, 1974; Garmezy, 1971) and studies of at-risk children (e.g., Werner, Bierman, & French, 1971; Werner & Smith, 1982). The fact that some at-risk children thrived despite adverse conditions led to research on a variety of stressors and populations. Luthar et al. (2000) suggested that characteristics leading to resilience can be categorized into attributes of the children, of the families, and of the wider social environments. Although the early work on resilience focused on children, recently there has been increasing interest in the maintenance of resilience in older adults (e.g., Ong, Bergeman, Bisconti, & Wallace, 2006; Ryff, 1995; Staudinger, Marsiske, & Baltes, 1993).

One way of conceptualizing adaptation is as a self-regulatory system (Carver & Scheier, 1998) in which stress evokes negative emotional arousal and adaptive processes account for the return to homeostasis. Such a view fits well with the physical metaphor of elasticity. Individual differences in this intra-individual adaptive mechanism may account for observed individual differences in resistance to adversity as well as adaptive responses to positive life events (Zautra, Affleck, Tennen, Reich, & Davis, 2005). Masten and Coatsworth (1998) concluded that "converging evidence suggests that the same powerful adaptive systems protect development in both favorable and unfavorable environments" (p. 205). In the next sections we explore some dynamical systems models that could be candidates for representing these ideas of resilience, models that are used to understand the physical properties associated with elasticity. To gain an intuition into how these models behave, we first spend some time thinking about attractors.

Equilibria and Basins of Attraction

To define resilience, let us first consider what is meant by *equilibrium*. Suppose some life event is the proximal cause for stress in an individual. We might observe that the individual's state exhibits changes for some period of time but eventually returns to equilibrium. However, there are many kinds of equilibria. Homeostasis is sometimes considered to be a point equilibrium, that is, one postulates an ideal state around which an individual's moment-to-moment states are fluctuating. If an individual in a state near the point equilibrium tends to move toward the equilibrium as time progresses, such a point equilibrium is termed a *point attractor*. It is as if the homeostatic state attracts the individual's state toward it.

Attractors can be visualized as surfaces in three-dimensional space in which the slope with respect to the vertical represents the acceleration that the system would undergo at any combination of two variables x and y. This has an intuitive interpretation because one can then think about attractors as physical objects in a gravitational field. Suppose we are wondering how a person's state might change if he or she were self-regulating in a way consistent with a point attractor. Consider placing a marble somewhere on the surface of the bowl shape in Figure 11.1a. The marble would accelerate down the side of the bowl to the bottom, would then roll up some on the other side, and would continue rolling back and forth until it eventually came to rest in the middle of the bowl. As long as the bowl is not itself accelerating, the marble would always come to rest in the middle of the bowl. This metaphor of a bowl has proven so useful that the region surrounding an equilibrium is often called a *basin of attraction*. Basins of attraction may take on many shapes, and distinguishing between shapes of basins attraction is critical to identifying individual differences in the dynamics of systems.

Next consider a bowl with a flat bottom, such as the one shown in Figure 11.1b. A marble placed on the side of the bowl would roll down the slope to the flat bottom, roll up the other side, and eventually come to rest somewhere on the flat bottom. However, now we do not know exactly where the ball would come to rest. All of the points on the flat bottom have a slope of 0, and so no one point is any more likely to be the resting point of the ball than any other point. In psychological terms, we might think of this as a *comfort zone*. Within the comfort zone there may be no need for regulation; one state is just as comfortable as the next. Once outside of the comfort zone, however, regulation begins to act so as to bring the person back into her or his comfort zone. For this reason, we call these *zone attractors:* attractors in which the equilibrium has a finite area, that is, an *equilibrium zone*.

A third type of attractor basin is illustrated in Figure 11.1c. In this basin of attraction the slope of the basin is not linearly related to the distance from the equilibrium; instead, the slope becomes greater as the displacement from equilibrium becomes smaller; that is, the slope is inversely proportional to the displacement from equilibrium. We call this a *well attractor,* because if a marble were placed on the attractor's surface it would accelerate more and more rapidly toward the equilibrium, similar to dropping the marble down a well.

We have considered three different shapes for basins of attraction. These shapes affect how a marble would roll (i.e., the dynamics of a marble) if it were placed on the surface. Suppose the attractor surface were invisible and our data consisted of snapshots of the marble taken with a high speed camera—we could still reconstruct what the basin looked like. We would be able to tell the

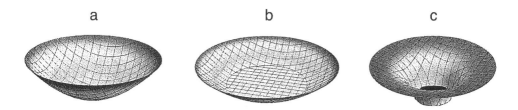

Figure 11.1. Visualizations of three attractors. Panel a: a point attractor with a linear relationship between the displacement from the equilibrium point and acceleration. Panel b: a zone attractor with a linear relationship between displacement and acceleration once the system is outside of the equilibrium zone. Panel c: a well attractor with an inverse relationship between the displacement from the equilibrium zone and acceleration.

difference among the three basins of attraction in Figure 11.1. In the dynamical systems literature this is known as *reconstructing the geometry of the attractor.* When analyzing intraindividual data we will use model-based regression techniques to estimate the shape of the attractor and the data residuals from the attractor surface. The regression estimation can be relatively straightforward if we have a good model for the intraindividual dynamics. Much of this chapter focuses on developing appropriate models.

Other types of attractors are also common in dynamical systems. Some that may be of interest to psychological researchers are forms of *periodic attractors,* also called *limit cycles.* When an individual's state is perturbed away from a limit cycle attractor, he or she tends to return to the cycle as time progresses. If the cycle does not exactly repeat itself, one calls these *quasi-periodic attractors.* Common examples of periodic or quasi-periodic attractors in human behavior are wake–sleep cycles, hunger–feeding cycles, and monthly hormonal cycles.

Finally, equilibria and basins of attraction may themselves be subject to change. For instance, if one takes an airline trip to a distant time zone in another part of the world, the previous wake–sleep and hunger–feeding cycles no longer are synchronized with the day–night cycle. After a few days of adjustment, one's wake–sleep and hunger–feeding cycles become resynchronized with the day–night cycle in the new time zone: The individual's limit cycle has adjusted. So too may other homeostatic equilibria adjust according to context, or may change in the course of long-term development. As we create models for resilience we would like to distinguish between *longer term adaptive changes* in location of an equilibrium or shape of the attractor basin and the *shorter term adaptation* that returns the individual to the equilibrium, that is, the self-regulation that is due to the current shape of the attractor. In fact, both types of adaptation are likely to be occurring simultaneously, and we would hope that our methods and models can capture these types of intraindividual change. Referring back to the first paragraph of the chapter, we wish to be able to distinguish between bouncing back and other forms of positive adaptation.

Resilience as Linear Damping

Let us next consider what would be necessary conditions for a regulatory system that would respond to changes in state relative to an equilibrium and act to bring the individuals back to equilibrium. First, the regulatory system would need to be able to detect the displacement from equilibrium. It would then need to be able to react in such a way that change in the individual's state led to a decrease in the displacement. To make a smooth transition back to equilibrium it would be useful to have one more property of the regulatory system: When the individual's state is far from equilibrium, the change in state should be larger than when the individual's state is near equilibrium.

This leads to perhaps the simplest model for resilience: The change in state with respect to time is a linear function of the displacement from equilibrium. Such a regulatory system can be expressed as a first-order differential equation:

$$\dot{y}(t) = \zeta y(t) \qquad (11.1)$$

where $y(t)$ is the displacement from equilibrium at time t, ζ is a constant less than 0 called the *damping parameter,* and $\dot{y}(t)$ is the instantaneous change with respect to time at time t, that is, the slope of the individual's curve at time t. An easy way to think about this is model is by anthropomorphizing it: "The farther I am from equilibrium, the faster I want to return to equilibrium." This type of system results in a negative exponential curve, because as the system reduces the displacement from equilibrium the slope is also reduced. Figure 11.2a plots the trajectory that results from starting Equation 11.1 at −20 and allowing it to evolve for 100 time steps. Change similar to this can be seen in self-report data such as the daily ratings of the Mental Health Inventory (Veit & Ware, 1983) from a recently bereaved widow plotted in Figure 11.2b (data from Bisconti, Bergeman, & Boker, 2004). Inspection of these two plots lets us conclude that there is at least one case when such a simple model of regulation is not entirely implausible. Later in the chapter we fit statistical models to gain a better understanding of how well different models for resilience fit patterns of within-individual change.

Let us take a closer look at Equation 11.1. Nowhere in this equation is the initial condition specified. Figure 11.2a plots a trajectory that starts at $x(0) = -20$, but Equation 11.1 simply gives the relationship between slope and displacement from equilibrium for any time t. Thus, one may say that the model for resilience expressed in Equation 11.1 specifies a family of curves: If an individual experiences an event that perturbs her or his state away from equilibrium, this model expresses how the individual regulates back to equilibrium. In observed data we may find that there are individual differences in initial conditions leading to apparently different trajectories, as in Figure 11.3a. However, these trajectories differ only in their initial conditions; the damping parameter ζ is the same for each of these curves.

On the other hand, there may be individual differences in the damping parameter ζ leading to different curves even if there are no individual differences

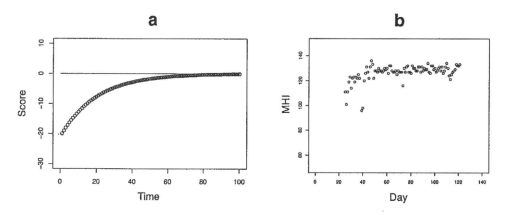

Figure 11.2. First-order linear differential equation model of resilience. Panel a: the effect of starting Equation 11.1 at an initial condition of −20 and allowing the system to regulate back to equilibrium. Panel b: Mental Health Inventory scores from 90 days of self-report from a recent widow, where loss of spouse occurred on Day 0.

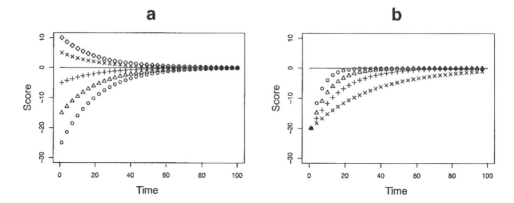

Figure 11.3.   First-order linear differential equation model with individual differences. Panel a: the effect of individual differences in initial conditions for Equation 11.1, but keeping the parameter ζ the same for each individual. Panel b: the effect of individual differences in the parameter ζ while starting each individual at the same initial condition.

in initial conditions. Four such trajectories are plotted in Figure 11.3b. Opportunity for such individual differences in regulation can be incorporated into our model by specifying

$$\dot{y}(t) = \zeta_i y(t) \qquad (11.2)$$

where ζ_i is the damping parameter for individual i. If there are individual differences in the parameters of the differential equation then, given the same perturbation, different individuals might regulate differently.

In our models for regulation we wish to distinguish between individual differences in *initial conditions* and individual differences in *regulation*. Individual differences in initial conditions are not particularly relevant to how the regulatory system responds; they are simply conditions to which the regulatory system is responding. On the other hand, regulation parameters are intrinsic to the person and express how that person might respond to a given level of stress. In studying resilience we wish to make this distinction, because we wish to be able to distinguish between traitlike characteristics that exist independent of exposure to adversity and adaptations that occur because of exposure to adversity.

Resilience as a Perfect Zero-Length Spring

In the previous section we examined a model for resilience that produces regulation that returns an individual to a point equilibrium. However, this is not a model for elasticity. If we are to take seriously the metaphor of resilience as being similar to elasticity, we should examine a physical model for elasticity and determine whether it might lead to behavior that is similar to what we mean when we see resilient human behavior. If so, it would make sense to see how well such a model might fit intraindividual data.

Elasticity is a property of an object that relates how the object changes shape (i.e., deforms) under stress. The deformation is a displacement from equilibrium and the stress is a force. In the so-called *elastic regime* of an object there is close to a linear relationship between the force exerted on the object and the displacement from equilibrium (Halliday & Resnick, 1967). This relationship, known as *Hooke's Law,* is attributed to Robert Hooke (see Andrade, 1960, for some interesting history on Hooke). The customary way of thinking about linear elastic relationships is the perfect zero-length spring, a spring that exerts force proportional to its displacement when it is stretched any amount at all,

$$F(t) = \eta x(t) \qquad (11.3)$$

where $F(t)$ is the force exerted by the spring at time t, η is a constant called the *stiffness parameter,* and $x(t)$ is the displacement from equilibrium.

Because force is related to acceleration through Newton's second law of motion, $F = ma$, force is equal to the mass of an object times its acceleration. We can thus rewrite Equation 11.3 as

$$F(t) = \eta x(t)$$

$$ma = \eta x(t)$$

$$m\ddot{x}(t) = \eta x(t)$$

$$\ddot{x}(t) = \frac{\eta}{m} x(t) \qquad (11.4)$$

where m is mass and $\ddot{x}(t)$ is acceleration, the second derivative of $x(t)$ with respect to time.

Assume that the mass of a human regulatory system is equal to 1: We argue that the scale for mass is arbitrary in the context of human resilience. We can then write Hooke's Law of elasticity as a simple linear second-order differential equation: The second derivative of the displacement from equilibrium is proportional to the displacement from equilibrium

$$\ddot{x}(t) = \eta x(t) \qquad (11.5)$$

where $x(t)$ is the displacement from equilibrium at time t; η is a constant less than 0 called the *stiffness parameter* in the context of elasticity; and $\ddot{x}(t)$ is the second derivative with respect to time at time t, that is, the curvature of the individual's trajectory at time t. Once again, it may help one's intuition if we anthropomorphize this equation: "The farther I am from equilibrium, the more I want to accelerate back toward equilibrium." The parameter η can be interpreted as the stiffness of this perfect zero-length spring. The spring is perfect because there is no dissipation of energy: Once it starts bouncing, it will continue indefinitely as shown in the trajectory plots in Figure 11.4. The spring is zero length because the acceleration is nonzero at all displacements except at the point equilibrium, $x(t) = 0$. The trajectory produced will oscillate at a wavelength, λ (i.e., the elapsed time between peaks of the variable's trajectory), that is dependent on the stiffness of the spring η such that

$$\lambda = \frac{2\pi}{\sqrt{-\eta}}. \qquad (11.6)$$

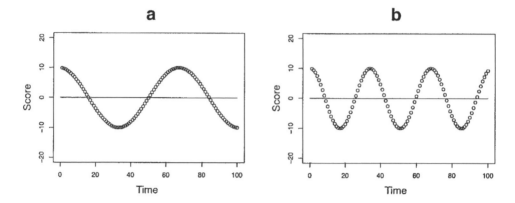

Figure 11.4. Second-order linear differential equation model of resilience as a perfect zero-length spring oscillating with a wavelength that is dependent on the stiffness parameter η. Panel a: Slow oscillations result from a spring with less stiffness. Panel b: Faster oscillations result from greater spring stiffness.

The trajectories in Figure 11.4 seem somewhat less than satisfying as a way of describing resilience. Although this oscillating system does not stray far from the equilibrium, the system never "settles down" to an equilibrium. For instance, if we were to choose an initial value of $x(0) = -30$, the system would oscillate between 30 and −30 forever. This seems contrary to the psychological sense of the definition of resilience. We have put "bounce" into our model, which seems to fit, but a perfect spring violates the intuitive notion of resilience bouncing back *to* something. The next model combines the two previous models to form a model of linear elasticity with linear damping.

Resilience as a Zero-Length Spring With Linear Damping

A real spring, or rubber ball, or other physical system that exhibits resilience, tends to dissipate stress into heat. In other words, the elasticity of the system is not perfect: It is damped by friction or a mechanism such as viscosity; the rubber ball tends to eventually stop bouncing. One might consider these properties to be similar to an automobile's springs and shock absorbers. The springs act quickly to absorb bumps in the road and turn them into oscillations, while the shock absorbers damp the bouncing springs back to equilibrium. In a car with a good match between springs and shock absorbers, one may ride over a bumpy road without being jostled about in one's seat. This spring and shock absorber system could serve as a reasonable metaphor for self-regulation leading to resilience: Adaptation is made to short-term stressors and negative life events in such a way that the long-term equilibrium remains relatively unaffected.

To combine the damping and the spring models, we will need to put Equation 11.1 into a form in which the second derivative of $x(t)$ is the variable on the left-hand side. Suppose $y(t) = \dot{x}(t)$. We can now substitute into Equation 11.1 as follows:

$$\dot{y}(t) = \zeta y(t)$$
$$\ddot{x}(t) = \zeta \dot{x}(t). \qquad (11.7)$$

So Equation 11.1 can also be expressed as a relationship between the first and second derivatives with respect to time. We now can create a linear combination that combines linear elasticity with linear damping as a model of a zero-length spring with damping:

$$\ddot{x}(t) = \zeta \dot{x}(t) + \eta x(t). \qquad (11.8)$$

In this model we may think of the stiffness of the springs as being represented by η and the damping of the shock absorber as being represented by ζ. Again, to gain intuition about this system allow us to anthropomorphize when $\zeta < 0$ and $\eta < 0$: "The farther I am from equilibrium, the more I want to turn and go back toward equilibrium, but at the same time, the faster I go, the more I want to slow down."

As long as both $\zeta < 0$ and $\eta < 0$, when an external stressor is applied to this system the system will self-regulate in such a way as to return to equilibrium, as shown in Figure 11.5a. A second example of self-report Mental Health Inventory data from a recent widow is plotted in Figure 11.5b, where both oscillation and damping appear to be at work. The zero-length spring with damping—that is, the spring and shock absorber model—is not an implausible model for these data. However, the linear damping model alone does not appear to be plausible, because linear damping alone never leads to oscillations. To test these appearances, we will fit plausible candidate models to intra-individual data.

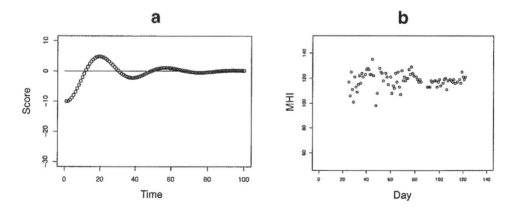

Figure 11.5. Second-order linear differential equation model of resilience. Panel a: the effect of starting Equation 11.5 at –10 and allowing the system to regulate back to equilibrium. Panel b: Mental Health Inventory scores from 90 days of self-report from a recent widow, where loss of spouse occurred on Day 0.

Individual differences in the parameters of Equation 11.8 may lead to very different types of trajectories. If $\eta < 0$ and $4\eta + \zeta^2 < 0$, the regulating system will undergo oscillation with a wavelength of

$$\lambda = \frac{2\pi}{\sqrt{-(\eta + \zeta^2/4)}}. \qquad (11.9)$$

When $4\eta + \zeta^2 > 0$ the system is called *overdamped* and leads to trajectories that look very much like the first-order linear damping model without elasticity. When the damping parameter, ζ, is 0 the results are trajectories such as those depicted in Figure 11.4. When $\zeta < 0$ and the system is not overdamped, we see trajectories such as those plotted in Figures 11.5a and 11.6a. When $\zeta > 0$ the regulatory system acts as an amplifier, magnifying the initial conditions into larger and larger oscillations, as plotted in Figure 11.6b. Depending on initial conditions, overdamped systems can either appear as if they are simple linear damping,

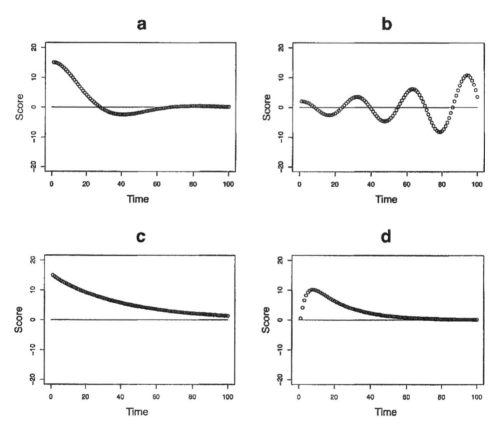

Figure 11.6.   Second-order linear differential equations with individual differences in stiffness and damping parameters. Panel a: A slow frequency with high damping may cross the equilibrium only once. Panel b: A positive ζ coefficient leads to amplification of oscillations instead of damping. Panel c: An overdamped system does not cross the equilibrium at all. Panel d: an overdamped system with the same parameters as in Panel c, but with initial conditions that start with displacement at 0 but with a high positive slope.

as in Figure 11.6c, or as more obviously regulated by elasticity, as plotted in Figure 11.6d.

To gain a better intuitive understanding of how individual differences in the regulation parameters might act it may be useful to think about three different automobiles in which you have ridden. First, consider a sports car with very stiff springs and very high damping shock absorbers. The car's body does not sway relative to the road, but this results in a ride during which you feel every little bump. Second, consider the other end of the spectrum, an old pickup truck with worn springs and shock absorbers that blew out long ago. When you hit just the right bump in the road, the body of the truck bounces up and down for a long time, and you may be thrown up into the air. However, small bumps are taken up by the soft springs, and you don't feel them as much as in the sports car. Finally, consider a new luxury sedan in which the springs are precisely matched with the shock absorbers and the mass of the body of the car so that most bumps in the road pass unnoticed. Each of these automobiles exhibits resilience, but there are individual differences in how the self-regulation adapts to the stressors in the road.

Keeping in mind the shock absorber and spring system, let us think again about how it may apply to resilience in a psychological context. An optimal spring and shock absorber system dissipates kinetic energy in a way that produces a minimal disturbance on the occupants of the automobile. How does it do this? The spring portion of the system absorbs the kinetic energy from a bump in the road quickly, effectively storing the kinetic energy in the oscillations of the spring. The shock absorber dissipates the kinetic energy in the spring relatively slowly but without transferring energy to the body of the automobile.

How would a resilient psychological system work if it were to use a similar mechanism? We expect to find two parts to the system: (a) one that operates on a relatively short time scale and that might produce oscillations and (b) one that operates on a longer time scale and exhibits damping. The faster responding part of the system would react quickly to an environmental stressor, directly absorbing the stress. The slower acting part of the system would act to reduce high rates of change in the system, damping those changes back to equilibrium.

What variables might be candidates for variations on an elasticity/damping model of resilience? One possibility might be the sympathetic and parasympathetic responses to stress (Appelhans & Luecken, 2006). The sympathetic nervous system reacts quickly to stress, up-regulating cardiovascular response and other homeostatic systems. On the other hand, the parasympathetic nervous system acts to damp these responses back to homeostatic equilibrium. Researchers from a variety of fields have begun to propose models that include reactivity and inhibition in a dynamical systems framework (e.g., Davies, Sturge-Apple, Cicchetti, & Cummings, 2007; Thayer & Lane, 2000).

Emotions are another candidate for modeling by an elasticity-damping model of resilience. For instance, negative emotions may increase shortly after a stressor and then be damped back to equilibrium at a slower rate. Individuals with higher scores on a dispositional resilience scale may differ either in the stiffness or damping parameters of models fit to intraindividual measurement of negative emotions. We examine this assertion further in the example later in this chapter.

Some Other Possibilities for Models of Resilience

The linear elasticity and damping model provides some satisfactory linguistic overlap between the physical and psychological meanings for resilience. Fitting such a model gives us a way of testing the degree to which we should be willing to accept the physical metaphor of elasticity for psychological resilience. However, a simple model for resilience will inevitably prove to be inadequate in some regards. It is wise to recall the advice of G. E. P. Box (1976), "Since all models are wrong the scientist must be alert to what is importantly wrong. It is inappropriate to be concerned about mice when there are tigers abroad" (p. 792). With that in mind, we next consider some potential ways that linear elasticity and damping might provide only an incomplete understanding, even if a model were to provide acceptable fit to data.

In the models we have discussed so far, the equilibrium itself has been assumed to be unchanging. However, it seems reasonable that individuals' equilibria may undergo longer term adaptation. For instance, a negative life event might result in oscillations about an equilibrium, but if the life event were particularly traumatic the equilibrium itself might be shifted and recover its former value only over a longer period of time. Such a system is plotted in Figure 11.7a, where the equilibrium itself undergoes damping to an asymptotic value. Any curve might describe the long-term change in equilibrium; for instance, in Figure 11.7b, linear growth in the equilibrium value is plotted. This type of system can be modeled by using a compound model where the change in equilibrium is modeled using one growth function and the residuals from that equilibrium are modeled by an elasticity and damping model. In the example data we will be making assumptions about the stability of the equilibrium that are, for simplicity of presentation in this chapter, untested. A more complete analysis would test for changes in the position of the equilibrium; however, this type of change may evolve over a long time span, so multiple bursts of measurement may be required (see the "Statistical

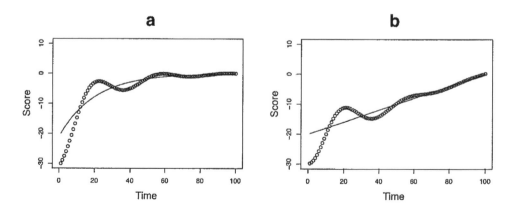

Figure 11.7. Composite models with short-term linear elasticity and damping to an equilibrium that itself is changing. Panel a: long-term linear damping of the short-term equilibrium. Panel b: linear change in the short-term equilibrium.

Modeling of Differential Equations" section for a description of burst measurement designs).

A second plausible alternative model is the nonzero length spring with damping. This results in a zone attractor as plotted in Figure 11.1b. One might think of this as a rubber band attached to a post. Suppose the rubber band has a nonzero length, ε, when it is not under stress. Thus, as long as the position of the end of the rubber band is within ε of the post, there is no force applied because of elasticity. However, once the end of the rubber band is of a distance d greater than ε from the post, the force is proportional to $d - \varepsilon$. One might say that the rubber band system in its "comfort zone" when $d < \varepsilon$. Comfort zone models may be applicable in a wide variety of psychological settings, but to our knowledge they have not yet been applied to psychological data using models of elasticity.

A third plausible extension to the elasticity and damping model involves transition to inelasticity; that is, if one stretches a rubber band past a certain point, it may break, or if one stretches a spring too far, it may lose some of its elasticity. Models for these types of nonlinear transitions are well known in physics and may have application to psychological resilience. Models of this type change their parameters over time and are dependent on the context. Most physical models have focused on properties of elasticity that weaken with time or use; however, psychological models need to consider the possibility of elasticity strengthening over time. Resilience might be strengthened by some life experiences just as muscles may adapt and grow stronger in response to a weight lifting regimen.

Finally, one may consider resilience from the standpoint of how several systems are coupled together. Two variables might each self-regulate but might also regulate each other. Montpetit, Bergeman, Deboeck, Tiberio, and Boker (2009) discussed resilience in the context of coupling between damped spring models for perception of stress and negative emotion. Coupling between stress and emotion might be thought of as being similar to a transfer function that transfers energy from one system to another. This transfer might be adaptive or maladaptive depending on which variables and what context is being modeled.

Statistical Modeling of Differential Equations

To estimate parameters and fit statistics for the models proposed in the previous sections, we need to think about the data requirements and methods for estimating the parameters. We first examine issues with respect to sampling the data and then choose an example method to fit some models. Then we discuss how to prepare the data for modeling and, finally, we estimate parameters for some candidate models.

Experimental Design and Data Requirements

To fit the proposed differential equations models for resilience to intraindividual data, we need to have appropriate data and methods to estimate the parameters of interest. To fit a differential equation, repeated observations on each individual are necessary. For most methods, equal intervals of elapsed time between occasions of measurement are preferred, but unequal intervals can be accommodated by most estimation methods. The main requirement for this type of modeling is that it should be an intensive longitudinal design; without a minimum of 10 observations per individual one cannot begin to estimate the within-person portion of the model so that between-person differences can be estimated. Fewer observations per individual can be used, but then one begins to be forced to assume that all individuals have the same attractor in order to estimate an attractor shape. The problem here is that the average attractor may or may not be representative of individuals in the sample, and there is no way to test this assumption of ergodicity. In the worst case, the average attractor might not represent the dynamics of any individual in the sample (see Molenaar, 2000, for a discussion of this issue). There is also surprising statistical power in intensive within-person measurement when one is interested in modeling intraindividual regulation (von Oertzen & Boker, in press).

The time scale of intraindividual sampling is critical to having sufficient information to estimate the regulation and adaptation in which one is interested. One ideally should have a small enough interval that four occasions of measurement can occur within one wavelength (interval of time between successive peaks) of a suspected oscillation. There is a limit, commonly known as the *Nyquist limit* (see Luke, 1999, for a discussion of the history of the Sampling Theorem), such that any wavelength smaller than or equal to the interval between three successive measurements will be not be recovered. A fourth observation within a single cycle allows an additional degree of freedom that can help identify estimates of measurement error relative to the signal.

Regulation typically happens at a faster time scale than adaptation. It may happen in a time scale of a few days, whereas adaptation may happen at a time scale of a few years. It would be costly (and exhausting to the individual) to record measurements daily for years at a time. For this reason, burst measurement (Nesselroade, 1991) may be an acceptable alternative. In burst measurement more than one time scale is considered: A single burst has sufficiently short time interval between occasions of measurement and sufficient occasions to capture the regulation of behavior over a short time span, and then several bursts are arranged over a longer time span so that adaptation in the shape and/or location of the attractor can also be estimated. For instance, a measurement burst might consist of daily self-reports for a period of 4 weeks in order to capture regulation. One then might arrange for bursts to occur at yearly intervals over a 5-year span to capture change in the shape and location of the attractor basin.

Estimation Methods

Once the data are in hand, one has a number of options for estimating the parameters of differential equations models (see H. Oud & Singer, 2008, for a discussion of some of the available methods). For instance, Singer (1993) developed the *exact discrete method,* and J. H. L. Oud and Jansen (2000) developed the *approximate discrete method,* both of which are based on work in stochastic differential equations (Bergstrom, 1966; Itô, 1951). Ramsay and colleagues have developed the *functional data analysis method* (Ramsay, Hooker, Campbell, & Cao, 2007; Ramsay & Silverman, 1997), which uses splines as a pathway to estimating the differential equations. Others have used variations on Kalman filtering (Kalman, 1960) to estimate the coefficients of differential equations (e.g., Chow, Hamaker, Fujita, & Boker, 2009; Molenaar & Newell, 2003). For the purposes of this chapter we use a variation of generalized local linear approximation (Boker, Deboeck, Edler, & Keel, 2010), an adaptation of Savitzky–Golay filtering (Savitzky & Golay, 1964) and time-delay embedding (Takens, 1985), to estimate multilevel linear differential equations.

Equilibrium Position

One needs to consider what to do about the position of the equilibrium when preparing data for differential equation modeling. The value of 0 in the data will be considered to be the center of the basin of attraction, although the model need not imply a point attractor. If one knows where the center of the basin of attraction is from knowledge about the experiment, then by all means he or she should use that knowledge and center the data around that value. If, for instance, the system was perturbed near the beginning of the time series, is regulating back to an equilibrium over the course of the time series, and might be a different equilibrium position for each individual, then an estimate of the equilibrium as the mean of the last 10 or so measurements for each individual might provide a good estimate of the individual's equilibrium. The example analysis in this chapter will take this approach.

If the equilibrium position is expected to be stable over the course of the experiment, one might center the data relative to a constant. However, if the equilibrium position itself is thought to be changing over the course of the measured time series one might model the differential equations with data that are residuals from the fit of a regression line or form of growth curve (see Boker & Bisconti, 2006, for some further ideas about estimating changing equilibrium position).

Time-Delay Embedding

Time-delay embedding is a way of preparing data for analysis. When estimating a longitudinal multilevel model, one commonly places each occasion of measurement on a separate row along with an identifier column so that the mixed-effects modeling software of your choice (e.g., R's lme package) can account for the between-row dependency grouped by individual. Time-delay embedding takes this one step further by extracting short snips of time dependency from each person and placing each of these on a row. The idea is to capture, within each row, the time dependency of the variables at a given time. Thus, the time dependency itself has the opportunity to change over time. To the extent that an individual's time dependency is stable, we say that their dynamics are *stationary,* that is, each row is a representative sample of the dynamics. When this condition is met, all of the individual's time dependency rows can be thought of as samples that define a single attractor surface. When this condition does not hold, the attractor surface itself may be changing over time.

Time-delay embedding is a simple operation. Given a starting index j in an individual's time series $\mathbf{x}$ and an integer lag τ, we select a sequence of D observations from the time series $\{x_j, x_{j+\tau}, x_{j+2\tau}, \ldots, x_{j+(D-1)\tau}\}$ and place it into D columns of the jth row for person i of a time-delay–embedded matrix. In so doing, we say we have created $\mathbf{X}^{(D)}$, a D-dimensional time-delay embedding of the time series $\mathbf{x}$.

As an example, suppose we wish to make a $D = 5$ dimensional time-delay–embedded matrix from a time series $\mathbf{x}$ with a lag of $\tau = 1$. If the original time series X is ordered by occasion $j = \{1, \ldots, P\}$ within individual $i = \{1, \ldots, N\}$, then the series of all observations $x_{(i,j)}$ can be written as a vector of scores

$$X = \{x_{(1,1)}, x_{(1,2)}, \ldots x_{(1,P)}, x_{(2,1)}, x_{(2,2)}, \ldots x_{(2,P)}, \ldots, x_{(N,1)}, x_{(N,2)}, \ldots x_{(N,P)}\}. \quad (11.10)$$

A five-dimensional time-delay–embedded matrix $\mathbf{X}^{(5)}$ of order $M \times 5$ where $\tau = 1$ can then be written as a matrix with three columns such that

$$\mathbf{X}^{(5)} = \begin{bmatrix} x_{(1,1)} & x_{(1,2)} & x_{(1,3)} & x_{(1,4)} & x_{(1,5)} \\ x_{(1,2)} & x_{(1,3)} & x_{(1,4)} & x_{(1,5)} & x_{(1,6)} \\ \vdots & \vdots & \vdots & & \\ x_{(1,P-4)} & x_{(1,P-3)} & x_{(1,P-2)} & x_{(1,P-1)} & x_{(1,P)} \\ x_{(2,1)} & x_{(2,2)} & x_{(2,3)} & x_{(2,4)} & x_{(2,5)} \\ x_{(2,2)} & x_{(2,3)} & x_{(2,4)} & x_{(2,5)} & x_{(2,6)} \\ \vdots & \vdots & \vdots & & \\ x_{(2,P-4)} & x_{(2,P-3)} & x_{(2,P-2)} & x_{(2,P-1)} & x_{(2,P)} \\ \vdots & \vdots & \vdots & & \\ x_{(N,1)} & x_{(N,2)} & x_{(N,3)} & x_{(N,4)} & x_{(N,5)} \\ x_{(N,2)} & x_{(N,3)} & x_{(N,4)} & x_{(N,5)} & x_{(N,6)} \\ \vdots & \vdots & \vdots & & \\ x_{(N,P-4)} & x_{(N,P-3)} & x_{(N,P-2)} & x_{(N,P-1)} & x_{(N,P)} \end{bmatrix}. \quad (11.11)$$

Note that the number of observations per individual need not be constant as in this example; that is, each individual may have a different number of rows in the time-delay–embedded matrix.

Derivative Estimation With Generalized Local Linear Approximation

Generalized local linear approximation is a linear filter–based approach for estimating derivatives from data (Boker et al., in press). The basic idea is that one wishes to find a transformation matrix that, when multiplied by the data, produces a least squares estimate of the displacement and derivatives of the data. If one uses a latent growth curve decomposition to specify the relationship between an $N \times 5$ time-delay embedded data matrix, $\mathbf{X}^{(5)}$, and an $N \times 3$ matrix of derivatives, $\mathbf{Y}$, where the columns of $\mathbf{Y}$ are the displacement, first derivative, and second derivative respectively,

$$\mathbf{X}^{(5)} = \mathbf{Y}\mathbf{L}' \quad (11.12)$$

where $\mathbf{L}$ is a 5×3 matrix of fixed loadings. The derivatives' relationship to the indicators is established by setting the loadings for the displacement to be equal to 1, the loadings for the first derivative to be increasing linearly with a step of $\tau \Delta t$ centered at the middle row, and the loadings for the second derivative to be the indefinite integral of the loadings for the second latent variable. These fixed loadings are specified for our example five-dimensional time-delay embedding as

$$\mathbf{L} = \begin{bmatrix} 1 & -2\tau\Delta t & (-2\tau\Delta t)^2/2 \\ 1 & -1\tau\Delta t & (-1\tau\Delta t)^2/2 \\ 1 & 0 & 0 \\ 1 & 1\tau\Delta t & (1\tau\Delta t)^2/2 \\ 1 & 2\tau\Delta t & (2\tau\Delta t)^2/2 \end{bmatrix}. \qquad (11.13)$$

Now, if $\mathbf{L'L}$ is nonsingular, we can solve for $\mathbf{Y}$ while accounting for the possibility that $\mathbf{L}$ might not be square by the following:

$$\mathbf{X}^{(5)} = \mathbf{YL'} = \mathbf{YL'L} \qquad (11.14)$$

$$\mathbf{X}^{(5)}\mathbf{L}(\mathbf{L'L})^{-1} = \mathbf{Y}(\mathbf{L'L})(\mathbf{L'L})^{-1} \qquad (11.15)$$

$$\mathbf{X}^{(5)}\mathbf{L}(\mathbf{L'L})^{-1} = \mathbf{Y} \qquad (11.16)$$

So, if

$$\mathbf{W} = \mathbf{L}(\mathbf{L'L})^{-1} \qquad (11.17)$$

we have a created a transformation matrix $\mathbf{W}$ such that it can be postmultiplied by the data and produce a least squares estimate of the derivatives of $\mathbf{X}^{(5)}$.

$$\mathbf{Y} = \mathbf{X}^{(5)}\mathbf{W} \qquad (11.18)$$

R codes for producing a time-delay embedded data matrix and the matrix $\mathbf{W}$ for any arbitrary embedding dimension D, elapsed time between observations Δt and time-delay lag τ can be downloaded from Stephen M. Boker's website (http://people.virginia.edu/~smb3u).

Model Specification

Now that we have created a matrix $\mathbf{Y}$ that contains estimates of the displacement, first, and second derivatives of the data, we are ready to specify some candidate models for resilience. Given that we expect there to be individual differences in the regulation parameters, we will specify multilevel models grouped by individual. We may also be interested in whether other characteristics of the individual predict the regulation parameters. These interests lead us to specify the three models we have discussed as multilevel models where in each case the first level is the model of regulation and the second level predicts the random coefficients in the first level model. For a step-by-step introduction to modeling differential equations using multilevel models, see Maxwell and Boker (2007).

We can specify the second-order differential equation with only linear damping as

$$\ddot{x}_{it} = \zeta_i \dot{x}_{it} + e_{it} \qquad (11.19)$$

$$\zeta_i = c_{10} + c_{11} z_i + u_{i1} \qquad (11.20)$$

where $\dot{x}$ and $\ddot{x}$ can be found in the columns of $\mathbf{Y}$, each individual i has multiple occasions of measurement t, and each individual has an individual characteristics variable z_i. In Equation 11.19 ζ_i is a random coefficient; that is, each individual may have his or her own damping parameter, and the distribution of these damping parameters is assumed to be normal. The coefficient c_{10} represents the sample mean of the parameter ζ, the coefficient c_{11} is the regression coefficient relating the individual characteristic variable z_i to ζ. The residual term e_{it} in Equation 11.19 is an estimate of the overall unexplained variance and the residual term u_{i1} in Equation 11.20 is an estimate of the unexplained variance in the random coefficient ζ.

Similarly, we can specify the second-order differential equation for the perfect zero-length spring as

$$\ddot{x}_{it} = \eta_i x_{it} + e_{it} \qquad (11.21)$$

$$\eta_i = c_{20} + c_{21} z_i + u_{i2} \qquad (11.22)$$

where x and $\ddot{x}$ can be found in the columns of $\mathbf{Y}$, each individual i has multiple occasions of measurement t, and each individual has an individual characteristics variable z_i. In Equation 11.21 η_i is a random coefficient; that is, each individual may have his or her own damping parameter and the distribution of these damping parameters is assumed to be normal. The coefficient c_{20} represents the sample mean of the parameter η, the coefficient c_{21} is the regression coefficient relating the individual characteristic variable z_i to η. The residual term e_{it} in Equation 11.21 is an estimate of the overall unexplained variance, and the residual term u_{i2} in Equation 11.22 is an estimate of the unexplained variance in the random coefficient η.

Finally, we can specify the second-order differential equation for the zero-length spring with linear damping as

$$\ddot{x}_{it} = \zeta_i \dot{x}_{it} + \eta_i x_{it} + e_{it} \qquad (11.23)$$

$$\zeta_i = c_{10} + c_{11} z_i + u_{i1} \qquad (11.24)$$

$$\eta_i = c_{20} + c_{21} z_i + u_{i2} \qquad (11.25)$$

where the terms are defined as for Equations 11.19 through 11.22 in the preceding two paragraphs.

Example Analysis

For the example analysis, we will fit the three models just discussed to data from the Notre Dame Longitudinal Study of Aging (Montpetit, 2007). Participants in the study were older adults (M age = 79 years, 83% were female, 54% lived alone, 37% were married) from a midsize midwestern city. Participants were likely to be White (90% White, 5% Black, 5% Hispanic) and have post–high school education (98% had completed high school, 64% had some post–high school education).

Participants ($N = 101$) first completed questionnaires on traitlike individual characteristics, including the Dispositional Resilience Scale (DRS; Bartone, Ursano, Wright, & Ingraham, 1989). The scale assesses three factors of resilience: (a) control, (b) commitment, and (c) challenge (Cronbach's α = .88). Items on this scale are Likert scaled from 1 (*not at all*) to 4 (*completely true*) for phrases such as "Planning ahead can help me avoid most future problems," "Trying your best at everything you do really pays off in the end," and "I like it when things are uncertain and unpredictable."

Daily self-reports of negative affect were completed by participants ($N = 66$) over a period of 56 days with packets counterbalanced into 1-, 2-, and 3-week lengths to reduce the possibility that packet length might contribute to periodicity in the data. Negative affect was measured by the 10-item Negative Affect (NA) subscale (Cronbach's α = .90) of the Positive and Negative Affect Schedule (Watson, Clark, & Tellegen, 1988). Of the 66 participants who began the daily Positive and Negative Affect Schedule measures, 52 completed the DRS, and at least 80% of the daily measures and were included in the present analysis.

Because there was no a priori reason to think that the equilibrium position or shape was changing over time, we performed the example analysis with the assumption that the equilibrium was invariant over the 56 days of the study. We used the mean of the last one third of each person's daily affect data to estimate the position of each person's attractor and centered each person's daily negative affect data relative to that value. Next, we constructed a $D = 5$ dimensional time-delay–embedding matrix with a lag of $\tau = 1$ and used a generalized local linear approximation filter to estimate the displacement, first, and second derivative for each row of the data matrix with complete observations. This resulted in a derivative matrix with 2,070 total observations grouped by the 52 individuals contributing data. The data matrix submitted to the analysis thus included five columns: (a) person ID, (b) DRS score, (c) NA displacement, (d) first derivative of NA, and (e) second derivative of NA. As many as 48 rows of the data matrix might be contributed by any single individual.

We modeled the data matrix using the R function lme(), a linear mixed-effects function found in the contributed library called *nlme*. This function fits a mixed-effects model (Pinheiro & Bates, 2000) that can be grouped by individual and with random effects so that each individual may have her or his own damping and stiffness parameters. We fit the models from Equations 11.19 through 11.25 where the variable x_{it} is the NA negative affect score on day t for person i and the second-level predictor variable z_i is individual i's DRS resilience score. Note that ζ_i and η_i are the random effects in this model but that there is no first-level intercept term. We thus are required to force the first-level intercept to zero in the call to the lme function.

Table 11.1. Linear Damping, Perfect Spring, and Damped Spring Models With Resilience Predicting the Random Effects

Parameter	Models		
	Linear Damping[a]	Perfect Spring[b]	Damped Spring[c]
Fixed effects			
Damping	−0.070		−0.105
SE	0.0349		0.0365
t	−2.005		−2.879
p	.045		.004
Stiffness		−0.472	−0.472
SE		0.0218	0.0195
t		−21.69	−24.15
p		< .001	< .001
Damping × Resilience	−0.050		−0.056
SE	0.0277		0.0310
t		−1.806	−1.805
p		.071	.071
Stiffness× Resilience	−0.038		−0.046
SE		0.0191	0.0170
t		−1.99	−2.689
p		.047	.007
Random effects			
Intercept *SD*	0.000	0.217	0.221
Damping *SD*	0.044		0.155
Stiffness *SD*		0.116	0.100
Corr(Stiffness, Damping)			−.707
Residual *SD*	1.284	0.905	0.893
Fit statistics			
Akaike information criterion	6932.9	5592.7	5573.0
Bayesian information criterion	6966.7	5626.5	5634.9
Estimated R^2	.005	.520	.535

Note. Sample included 52 individuals and 2,070 total observations. Corr = correlation.
[a]See Equations 19 and 20 in the text. [b]See Equations 21 and 22 in the text. [c]See Equations 23 through 25 in the text.

The results of the three models are presented in Table 11.1. The model with only linear damping accounted for virtually none of the variance in the second derivative of negative affect. Although the damping parameter achieved significance at the .05 level, we find this model to be unsatisfying because of its lack of explanatory power. The model of the perfect spring with no damping fit much better than the damping-only model. The improvement in the Akaike information criterion (AIC) and Bayesian information criterion (BIC) scores is large, and the explained variance in the second derivative is now $R^2 = .52$. This model is clearly a big improvement over the model with only linear damping.

Also note that dispositional resilience predicts the stiffness of the spring as shown in the interaction term Stiffness × Resilience. The sign of this term is negative, so higher scores on resilience are associated with stiffer springs.

Finally, in the rightmost column of Table 11.1 are the results of fitting a model with both linear damping and a spring. There is only a very small increase in R^2 over the perfect spring model, and the AIC and BIC provide conflicting evidence (the AIC score is smaller, but the BIC score is larger) as to whether to prefer the damped spring model over the perfect spring model. In the damped spring model the fixed effects for damping and stiffness are both significant, and the coefficient values are negative. The period of the oscillation implied by the fixed effects can be calculated as

$$\lambda = \frac{2\pi}{\sqrt{-(\eta + \zeta^2/4)}}$$

$$= \frac{2\pi}{\sqrt{-(-.472 - .105^2/4)}}$$

$$= 9.1 \text{ days.}$$

The damped spring model also exhibits a relationship between resilience and the stiffness of the spring such that greater resilience is associated with stiffer springs. There is also a trend toward an association between greater resilience and greater damping, but this did not achieve significance at the .05 level.

Note that there is interesting information in the standard deviations of the random effects. The individual differences in the damping parameter are relatively large in comparison to its mean value. Thus, we expect that some individuals in this sample have positive damping parameters and are thus amplifying instead of damping negative affect. Also, note that there is a strong negative correlation between individuals' stiffness and damping parameters; that is, if an individual's spring has greater stiffness then the damping tends to be weaker.

Conclusions

Many potentially valuable psychological constructs have only verbal embodiment and so lack the rigor necessary to be evaluated and incorporated into sound, empirically based theory. This is especially true for constructs that imply complex patterns of change, at least in part because of the necessary technical description and notation. In this chapter, we have presented a way of testing whether the theoretical construct "resilience" exhibits characteristics of physical resilience. We have presented three simple differential equation models for resilience that have physical analogs in a spring and shock absorber system similar to that in an automobile. We have also presented an example data set to give an idea of how these models can be estimated and the results presented. The analysis of the example data set provided results consistent with an association between a self-reported measure of dispositional resilience and the stiffness of a linear spring model estimated from daily self-reported negative affect.

The intent of this chapter is to explore ways in which resilience might be modeled and not to present a definitive empirical result. We believe a great deal of work remains in modeling of intraindividual data before theoretical conclusions can be drawn about how resilience should best be viewed. For instance, in this chapter we have not explored models for coupling between perceived stress and negative affect, modeled nonlinearities such as transitions to inelasticity, or explored how the position and shape of an individual's attractor might change or adapt over time. The current work is merely a stepping-stone on a much longer path. However, it is our hope that these pages may put a bounce in the step of researchers interested in protective processes that allow individuals to adapt to the stresses of life.

References

Andrade, E. N. C. (1960). Robert Hooke, F. R. S. *Notes and Records of the Royal Society of London, 15,* 137–145. doi:10.1098/rsnr.1960.0013

Anthony, E. J. (1974). The syndrome of the psychologically vulnerable child. In E. J. Anthony & C. Koupernik (Eds.), *The child in his family: Children at psychiatric risk* (pp. 3–10). New York, NY: Wiley.

Appelhans, B. M., & Luecken, L. J. (2006). Heart rate variability as an index of regulated emotional responding. *Review of General Psychology, 10,* 229–240. doi:10.1037/1089-2680.10.3.229

Bartone, P., Ursano, R., Wright, K., & Ingraham, L. (1989). The impact of a military air disaster on the health of assistance workers: A prospective study. *Journal of Nervous and Mental Disease, 177,* 317–328. doi:10.1097/00005053-198906000-00001

Bergstrom, A. R. (1966). Nonrecursive models as discrete approximations to systems of stochastic differential equations. *Econometrica, 34,* 173–182. doi:10.2307/1909861

Bisconti, T. L., Bergeman, C. S., & Boker, S. M. (2004). Emotional well-being in recently bereaved widows: A dynamical systems approach. *The Journals of Gerontology. Series B, Psychological Sciences and Social Sciences 59,* 158–167.

Boker, S. M., & Bisconti, T. L. (2006). Dynamical systems modeling in aging research. In C. S. Bergeman & S. M. Boker (Eds.), *Quantitative methodology in aging research* (pp. 185–229). Mahwah, NJ: Erlbaum.

Boker, S. M., Deboeck, P. R., Edler, C., & Keel, P. K. (2010). Generalized local linear approximation of derivatives from time series. In S.-M. Chow, E. Ferrar, & F. Hsieh (Eds.), *Statistical methods for modeling human dynamics: An interdisciplinary dialogue.* Boca Raton, FL: Taylor & Francis.

Box, G. E. P. (1976). Science and statistics. *Journal of the American Statistical Association, 71,* 791–799. doi:10.2307/2286841

Carver, C. S., & Scheier, M. F. (1998). *On the self-regulation of behavior.* New York, NY: Springer-Verlag.

Chow, S.-M., Hamaker, E. L., Fujita, F., & Boker, S. M. (2009). Representing time-varying cyclic dynamics using multiple-subject state-space models. *British Journal of Mathematical and Statistical Psychology, 62,* 683–716.

Davies, P. T., Sturge-Apple, M. L., Cicchetti, D., & Cummings, E. M. (2007). The role of child adrenocortical functioning in pathways between interparental conflict and child maladjustment. *Developmental Psychology, 43,* 918–930. doi:10.1037/0012-1649.43.4.918

Garmezy, N. (1971). Vulnerability research and the issue of primary prevention. *American Journal of Orthopsychiatry, 41,* 101–116.

Halliday, D., & Resnick, R. (1967). *Physics.* New York, NY: Wiley.

Itô, K. (1951). On stochastic differential equations. *American Mathematical Society Memoirs, 4,* 1–51.

Kalman, R. E. (1960). A new approach to linear filtering and prediction problems. *Transactions of the ASME Journal of Basic Engineering, 82,* 35–45.

Luke, H. D. (1999, April). The origins of the sampling theorem. *IEEE Communications Magazine*, 106–108.

Luthar, S. S., Cicchetti, D., & Becker, B. (2000). The construct of resilience: A critical evaluation and guidelines for future work. *Child Development, 70*, 543–562.

Masten, A., & Coatsworth, J. D. (1998). The development of competence in favorable and unfavorable environments: Lessons from research on successful children. *American Psychologist, 53*, 205–220.

Maxwell, S. E., & Boker, S. M. (2007). Multilevel models of dynamical systems. In S. M. Boker & M. J. Wenger (Eds.), *Data analytic techniques for dynamical systems in the social and behavioral sciences* (pp. 161–187). Mahwah, NJ: Erlbaum.

Molenaar, P. C. M. (2000). A manifesto on psychology as idiographic science: Bringing the person back into scientific psychology, this time forever. *Measurement: Interdisciplinary Research & Perspective, 2*, 201–218.

Molenaar, P. C. M., & Newell, K. M. (2003). Direct fit of a theoretical model of phase transition in oscillatory finger motions. *British Journal of Mathematical and Statistical Psychology, 56*, 199–214.

Montpetit, M. A. (2007). *Negative affect and stress: A dynamical systems analysis.* Unpublished doctoral dissertation, University of Notre Dame, South Bend, IN.

Montpetit, M. A., Bergeman, C. S., Deboeck, P. R., Tiberio, S. S., & Boker, S. M. (2009). *Resilience-as-process: Negative affect, stress, and coupled dynamical systems.* Manuscript submitted for publication.

Nesselroade, J. R. (1991). The warp and woof of the developmental fabric. In R. Downs, L. Liben, & D. S. Palermo (Eds.), *Visions of aesthetics, the environment, and development: The legacy of Joachim F. Wohlwill* (pp. 213–240). Hillsdale, NJ: Erlbaum.

The New Shorter Oxford English Dictionary. (1993). Oxford, England: Oxford University Press.

Ong, A., & Bergeman, C. S. (2004). Resilience and adaptation to stress in later life: Empirical perspectives and conceptual implications. *Aging International, 29*, 219–246.

Ong, A., Bergeman, C. S., Bisconti, T. L., & Wallace, K. A. (2006). Psychological resilience, positive emotions, and successful adaptation to stress in later life. *Journal of Personality and Social Psychology, 91*, 730–749.

Oud, H., & Singer, H. (2008). Editorial introduction. *Statistica Neerlandica, 62*, 1–3.

Oud, J. H. L., & Jansen, R. A. R. G. (2000). Continuous time state space modeling of panel data by means of SEM. *Psychometrica, 65*, 199–215.

Pinheiro, J. C., & Bates, D. M. (2000). *Mixed-effects models in S and S-Plus.* New York, NY: Springer-Verlag.

Ramsay, J. O., Hooker, G., Campbell, D., & Cao, J. (2007). Parameter estimation for differential equations: A generalized smoothing approach. *Journal of the Royal Statistical Society B, 69*, 774–796.

Ramsay, J. O., & Silverman, B. W. (1997). *Functional data analysis.* New York, NY: Springer-Verlag.

Reich, J. W., Zautra, A. J., & Davis, M. C. (2003). Dimensions of affect relationships: Models and their integrative implications. *Review of General Psychology, 7*, 66–83.

Ryff, C. D. (1995). Psychological well-being in adult life. *Current Directions in Psychological Science, 4*, 99–104.

Savitzky, A., & Golay, M. J. E. (1964). Smoothing and differentiation of data by simplified least squares. *Analytical Chemistry, 36*, 1627–1639.

Singer, H. (1993). Continuous-time dynamical systems with sampled data, errors of measurement and unobserved components. *Journal of Time Series Analysis, 14*, 527–545.

Staudinger, U. M., Marsiske, M., & Baltes, P. B. (1993). Resilience and levels of reserve capacity in later adulthood: Perspectives from life-span theory. *Development and Psychopathology, 5*, 541–566.

Takens, F. (1985). Detecting strange attractors in turbulence. In A. Dold & B. Eckman (Eds.), *Lecture notes in mathematics 1125: Dynamical systems and bifurcations* (pp. 99–106). Berlin, Germany: Springer-Verlag.

Thayer, J. F., & Lane, R. D. (2000). A model of neurovisceral integration in emotion regulation and dysregulation. *Journal of Affective Disorders, 61*, 201–216.

Veit, C. T., & Ware, J. E. (1983). The structure of psychological distress and well-being in general populations. *Journal of Consulting and Clinical Psychology, 51,* 730–742.

von Oertzen, T., & Boker, S. M. (in press). Time delay embedding increases estimation precision of models of intraindividual variability. *Psychometrika.*

Watson, D., Clark, L. A., & Tellegen, A. (1988). Development and validation of brief measures of positive and negative affect: The PANAS scales. *Journal of Personality and Social Psychology, 54,* 1063–1070.

Werner, E. E., Bierman, J. M., &French, F. E. (1971). *The children of Kauai: A longitudinal study from the prenatal period to age ten.* Honolulu: University of Hawaii Press.

Werner, E. E., & Smith, R. (1982). *Vulnerable but invincible: A study of resilient children.* New York, NY: McGraw-Hill.

Zautra, A. J., Affleck, G. G., Tennen, H., Reich, J. W., & Davis, M. C. (2005). Dynamic approaches to emotions and stress in everyday life: Bolger and Zuckerman reloaded with positive as well as negative affects. *Journal of Personality, 73,* 1–28.

Part IV

Reflections and Prospects

12

On an Emerging Third Discipline of Scientific Psychology

John R. Nesselroade

Cronbach (1957, 1975) identified and discussed two disciplines of scientific psychology—(a) *experimental psychology* and (b) *correlational* or *differential psychology*—in an appealing and straightforward way that captured well their essential differences. The thrust of the experimental approach is to create variation under controlled conditions to test hypothesized cause–effect relationships, whereas the differential approach emphasizes the analysis of existing variation found among individuals to discover and explicate relationships among important variables. Sandwiched between Cronbach's two articles is Cattell's (1966) article, in which he elaborated the distinction and warmed up the discussion with an historical account of what he termed the *multivariate experimental psychology movement* that derived mostly from differential psychology.

Both the experimental and correlational approaches have as their scientific goal the articulation of lawful relationships of some generality concerning the nature of behavior. Experimental psychology relies heavily on manipulative research designs that typically lead to some application of the analysis of variance, so much so that for decades the teaching of analysis of variance in psychology graduate school has often occurred in courses labeled *experimental design*. Differential psychologists have adapted, developed, and used a variety of analytical techniques (correlation and regression, factor analysis, structural equation modeling, etc.) to decompose measured variance in meaningful ways.

In the experimental approach, different individuals are viewed as randomly equivalent replicates of one another, and the differences found among individuals who receive the same combination of treatments in an experiment are assigned to the *error term*—variation for which there is no other accounting. The error term provides a base against which to evaluate the magnitude of the variation produced by the treatment. In the differential approach, individuals are not considered to be randomly equivalent, and the differences among individuals found to exist in nature are the targets for analysis with the tools of correlational research. Both disciplines have enjoyed long histories, have continued to develop their favored methodological approaches, and have fostered much theoretical and empirical work pertaining to the study of behavior.

This work was supported by The Institute for Developmental and Health Research Methodology at the University of Virginia.

Surveying the behavioral science landscape from an early 21st century vantage point, I believe that a third discipline of scientific psychology is emerging that features two defining characteristics that set it apart from the experimental and differential ones discussed by Cronbach (1957, 1975). First, the focal unit of analysis is the individual, but each individual is attended to in his or her own right, and it is the identification of similarities among individuals as much as the assessment of their differences that directs empirical research. Second, the primary source of variation under scrutiny is *intraindividual*—the varying of a person over time and/or situations and conditions—and typically is modeled at the latent variable level, which is possible with data arising from repeated multivariate measurement.

Perhaps from a Hegelian perspective some synthesis of the two traditions described by Cronbach (1957, 1975) would be predicted to occur sooner or later, but I believe what is happening should not be so simply construed. Instead, this third discipline that is now being recognized has its own distinct roots, some of them reaching as deeply into psychology's past as those of the experimental and differential traditions. In this chapter I want to identify some of these key antecedents, readily admitting that no doubt there are others that could be included in a wholly comprehensive retrospective.

Because methodological advances are intimately involved in shaping and discriminating among disciplines, I will trace some of the antecedents for this emerging third discipline of scientific psychology to help place into perspective the methodological tools that have been rather quietly developing, tools that I believe already provide powerful underpinnings for the demanding empirical work required by this third discipline. Other chapters in this volume present some of these methodological innovations, as do recent volumes by Chow, Ferrer, and Hsieh (2009); Maydeu-Olivares and McArdle (2005); Bergeman and Boker (2006); and Boker and Wenger (2007).

The Individual as the Unit of Analysis

A clear focus on the individual as the unit of analysis is a central defining characteristic of the emerging third discipline of scientific psychology. One of the taproots feeding this developing discipline traces back to the old distinction between *idiographic* and *nomothetic* approaches to the study of behavior, both aspects of which have taken on a variety of guises over the past century or so. Idiographic concerns emphasize the uniqueness of the individual, whereas nomothetic concerns emphasize generality in behavioral lawfulness (e.g., Allport, 1937; Lamiell, 1981, 1988; Molenaar, 2004; Rosenzweig, 1958, 1986; van Kampen, 2000; Zevon & Tellegen, 1982). The distinction has markedly influenced the shape and development of behavioral research over the past century, both implicitly and explicitly, with current, related manifestations including such contrasts as that between single-subject versus group designs and person-centered versus variable-centered research orientations (see e.g., Bergman, Magnusson, & El-Kouri, 2003; Magnusson, 2003).

Indeed, many writers over many years have called for a stronger emphasis on the individual as the unit of analysis for studying behavior. Cattell (1963) promoted the application of the factor analysis model (*P-technique factor analysis*) to intensive measurements of the individual (multivariate time series) as a way of identifying individual traits. Carlson (1971) asked "Where is the person in personality research?" Lamiell (1981, 1988) has proposed an idiothetic approach to blend the strengths of individual- and group-based analyses. Zevon and Tellegen (1982) illustrated putting the idiographic emphasis to the service of the nomothetic approach by focusing first on individual-level structuring of behavior and then looking for common patterns across these individual structures at a more abstract level. More recently Molenaar (2004), in a technically elegant way based on the ergodicity theorems of classical mechanics, made the case for elevating the individual to prime status as the unit of analysis for behavioral science. He ardently pleaded for a focus on intraindividual variability with the individual as the unit of analysis by demonstrating that in nonergodic behavioral systems (which include developmental phenomena) synthesizing the differences among individuals (the differential approach) cannot serve as a substitute for studying the actual functioning of individuals over time.

Other researchers have cautioned against regarding the individual as the unit of analysis for reasons of reliability and precision. For example, Salthouse, Kausler, and Saults (1986) argued for the importance of increased reliability of measurement at any given occasion and more occasions of measurement if the individual were to be the unit of analysis in cognitive aging studies. Estabrook and Grimm (2006) presented evidence favoring the use of many occasions of measurement if reliable indicators of intraindividual variability were to be obtained. These arguments are not against the use of individuals as the unit of analysis per se but rather warnings regarding important measurement issues not being taken for granted.

Individual-level analyses are certainly not limited to single-subject designs. As demonstrated by Lebo and Nesselroade (1978) and Zevon and Tellegen (1982), and argued for by Nesselroade and Ford (1985), as multivariate, replicated, single-subject, repeated measures designs, individual-level analyses can (and should) be carried out simultaneously on multiple participants and with deliberate regard for rapprochement between idiographic and nomothetic emphases (see also Zevon and Tellegen, 1982, in this regard). The key idea is that a more thorough understanding of the behaviors of interest as they occur at the individual level (what P-technique provides) can usefully inform attempts to articulate lawful relationships that pertain to the multiple participants. This means ferreting out the similarities amid the differences among individuals, another key feature of the emerging third discipline.

Obviously, the matter of seeking lawful relationships across individuals is closely bound to concerns with data aggregation and generalizability. The P-technique is not being promoted purely as a single-subject approach but instead as an effective basis for creating informed aggregations of information across multiple participants. It can be argued that aggregation as performed in the usual differential approach has not done a particularly effective job of resynthesizing the individual from all of the individual differences that have been examined (see e.g., Lamiell, 1988; Molenaar, 2004, on this point). Instead, the argument is that aggregation can and should be informed, rather than blind, as in the tradition of group-based analyses performed on haphazardly drawn samples. For a long time now, aggregating different subsamples merely to produce a large number of observations on which to base parameter estimates, for instance, has been known to be problematic (see, e.g., Guilford, 1952). Currently popular techniques such as spline regression and mixture modeling are stark reminders that aggregates often are not homogeneous and cannot be effectively represented as if they were.

Readers will see that the notion of informed aggregation is extended in critical ways as the arguments develop. I advocate that a more general approach to the study of the individual better serves the articulation of lawful relationships that apply to the collective as opposed to the somewhat more pragmatic matter of how to aggregate information based on individuals for more effective, group-based analyses of the differential tradition.

Focusing on Intraindividual Variability

An investigator whose raw material is variation and whose unit of analysis is the individual is pretty much constrained to gathering and analyzing repeated measurements. The history of studying intraindividual variability and change, which is also as old as the systematic study of behavior (see, e.g., Wundt, 1897, on the topic of emotions), provides important precedents, both substantive and methodological, that emphasize individual-level empirical research. Since the classic article by Fiske and Rice (1955) categorizing kinds of intraindividual variation, and especially in the past couple of decades, a great deal of interest has developed in the study of a rich variety of intraindividual variability phenomena (e.g., Hultsch, Hertzog, Dixon, & Small, 1998; Moskowitz & Hershberger, 2002; Nesselroade, 1988).

The study of intraindividual variability has resulted in a wide array of valuable conceptions of relatively short-term change, such as states versus traits (Cattell & Scheier, 1961; Hamaker, Nesselroade, & Molenaar, 2007), aspects of stress and coping (DeLongis, Folkman, & Lazarus, 1988), and more dynamic definitions of the concept of personality consistency (e.g., Mischel, 1991). This interest has blossomed methodologically as well, with a number of new and powerful techniques being promulgated for analyzing such data, as the chapters in this volume attest.

P-technique factor analysis has played a key role in regard to the study of intraindividual variability and the individual as the unit of analysis. For more than two decades, proposals for a blending of the idiographic and nomothetic research perspectives have implicated P-technique factor analysis (Nesselroade & Ford, 1985; Zevon & Tellegen, 1982) as a valuable tool for this purpose. In the interim, P-technique factor analysis has sired some important new methodological developments that I believe are ready to play a critical role in unlocking the secrets of behavior within the purview of the emerging third discipline of scientific psychology.

What is P-technique factor analysis? It fundamentally involves applying one of the main tools of individual differences research (factor analysis) to variation within an individual over time in lieu of variation over individuals at one occasion of measurement. Named by Cattell (1952, 1963), P-technique, more specifically, involves the application of the common factor model to multivariate time series representing frequently repeated measurements on individual participants. Its purpose is to identify patterns of covariation within the intraindividual variation observed over time.

Bereiter (1963) referred to P-technique as the "logical technique for studying the interdependencies of measures" (p. 15). The outcome of a P-technique analysis is a set of regression-like weights (factor loadings) that describe each observed variable in terms of a few latent variables or factors. Because the variation analyzed is within the person over time, these patterns of factor loadings tell a story of systematic "ups and downs" experienced (or at least reported) by the participant for the interval along which observations are made. However, the important ups and downs are on the unobserved factors instead of directly on the observed variables, thus making the former useful tools of theory. These factors may or may not be correlated with each other. As noted earlier, I identify and discuss here some of the important extensions of P-technique that are intimately involved in defining the emerging third discipline of concern.

Developmental Systems Theory

There is another important set of roots that I believe has fundamentally nurtured this emerging discipline from a substantive perspective and is beginning to have a strong methodological impact as well. These roots are embedded firmly in the rich soil of general systems theory (von Bertalanffy, 1968). A more direct articulation of living systems theory (e.g., Ford, 1987) and its application directly to the study of development (see e.g., Ford & Lerner, 1992) exemplify how important inroads have been made into conceptualizing the study of the individual from a substantive developmental perspective. An important facet has been the emphasis on organized, systematic changes over time, the empirical study of which demands the collection and modeling of longitudinal data. The longitudinal data emphasis ties in closely not only with newer methodological developments but also with an emphasis on examining interindividual similarities in patterns of intraindividual change (Baltes & Nesselroade, 1979).

Important methodological developments have ensued from the general systems orientation. Arising from the earlier P-technique modeling, for example, are now readily available statistical tools, including software, for dynamic factor analysis (Browne & Nesselroade, 2005; Browne & Zhang, 2005, 2007; Molenaar, 1985). Moreover, sophisticated quantitative modeling of the individual as a dynamical system enables the capturing of behavior in terms of rates of change and changes in rates of change (Boker & Nesselroade, 2002; Nesselroade & Boker, 1994; Zhang, McArdle, & Nesselroade, 2009). This, in turn, has spurred new interest in the explicit modeling of processes based on intraindividual variability.

In the area of psychological measurement, the influence of this general orientation has led to a proposal for preventing idiosyncratic features of individual behavior from hiding what is common in behavior across individuals (Nesselroade, Gerstorf, Hardy, & Ram, 2007). This proposal involved fitting an invariant measurement framework at the more abstract level of higher order factors, using first-order factors to filter out idiosyncrasies in the manifest variables. Nesselroade et al. (2007) illustrated their points with self-report data collected in a replicated P-technique factor analysis design (Lebo & Nesselroade, 1978), but there are other content domains that seem to be just as vulnerable to the sabotage

of idiosyncrasy. For example, concern with specificity of response in the auto-
nomic nervous system reflects an awareness of the way idiosyncratic learning and
conditioning histories "tune" the individual's patterns of response to stimuli that
arouse him or her. By structuring the concept of measurement invariance at the
individual level and anchoring it at the level of relationships among factors,
instead of at the level of the relationships between manifest and latent variables,
one has a way to make operational developmentally important concepts such as
heterotypic continuity and discontinuity (Kagan, 1980).

Influences of the Experimental and Correlational Disciplines

What about the more direct influences of the experimental and correlational traditions on this emerging third discipline? They clearly are in evidence, and it
seems that the most important of these are the emphasis on the individual as the
unit of analysis deriving from the experimentalist's orientation and the emphasis on nonmanipulative, *in situ,* naturalistic measurement of multiple variables
that arises mainly from the correlationalist's approach. The analytical tools
underpinning the third discipline are primarily those of the correlational persua-
sion, but selected use of manipulative, experimental design and analysis procedures can certainly be brought to bear on particular research questions. The use
of discriminant function analysis, for example, a multivariate technique once
popular within the individual-differences tradition, is very closely tied to multivariate analysis of variance, an appropriate tool for analyzing many experimental designs involving multiple dependent variables.

Fleshing Out the Third Discipline

My sense is that there is a more acute awareness than in the past that several
kinds of individual differences have to be acknowledged and dealt with, carefully,
if the study of behavior and behavior change is to advance. Tucker (1966), for
example, distinguished between the *extent* and the *quality* of individual differences. One of the arguments made by Nesselroade et al. (2007) is that, because of
idiosyncratic features, some individual differences (in quality, to use Tucker's
term) actually get in the way of finding lawful relationships in (the extent of)
individual differences among important variables.

As one begins to home in more effectively on modeling processes with more
elaborate procedures even greater care must be taken with individual differences
because, for a given question, there are some kinds of individual differences that
need to be filtered out rather than studied for their own sake. For example, what
is actually the same process can play out at different rates for different people.
It might take one person 6 days to get over a cold, another person 7 days, and
a third person 8 days, but most people would agree that the process is the same.
Individual differences in some aspects of rate may not be critical to understanding the nature of the process. Thus, one may need dynamical models
that can idiographically filter the nature of lagged relationships. Suppose, for
instance, that people are measured daily and a lag 1 model is fitted to their data.
For some individuals that may be optimal, but for others the proper lag 1 should

be an interval of 2 days, and so on. Individual differences in rates represent another example in which distortions may need to be set aside rather than studied per se. This in no way negates the importance of modeling lagged relationships, but artificially forcing individuals to progress at the same rate may constrain relationships to invariance that should not be so constrained. This appears be the same generic problem as the one with which Nesselrode et al. (2007) tried to deal in higher order invariance: the disentangling of relevant and irrelevant variation, given one's research focus. One may need to cede invariance at the level of individual differences in order to rediscover it at some level of individual similarities.[1]

Methodological Developments

Important by-products of the research on intraindividual variability that bear on the present discussion include the realization that rigorous and systematic research can be conducted at the individual level with a focus on intraindividual variability. As many of the chapters in this volume attest, there are already several analytical tools available for modeling behavior at the individual level as the first step to looking for commonalities across individuals in aspects of their behavior. Thus, the "informed aggregation" Molenaar (2004) called for has not only become feasible but also is underwritten by powerful and relatively new modeling procedures, including several variants of dynamic factor analysis, dynamical systems models, and so on. Easily accessible computer software is available for researchers who are willing to invest in collecting appropriate data and learning to use the programs. However, disciplines have a voracious appetite for analytical tools, and other, still more promising ones for this third discipline are already coming into evidence.

Beginning with P-technique factor analysis, a long series of adaptations and improvements have brought us to a level of analytic prowess today that is quite impressive. Among these are dynamic factor analysis models that extend the power and versatility of P-technique factor analysis while maintaining its original purpose of studying how an individual varies over time (Browne & Zhang, 2005; Molenaar, 1985; Nesselrode, McArdle, Aggen, & Meyers, 2002). One of the central by-products is a genuine interest in modeling process. I believe that it is to this general line of approach that we must turn to provide the basis for a more informed aggregation of data as we try to accommodate both

---

[1]Molenaar (2004) agreed that interindividual differences in the rate of what is otherwise an invariant across subjects may seriously distort any analysis of interindividual differences and that such differences should be filtered out at the individual level before attempting analyses focused on nomothetic relationships. He likened it to the standard procedure in brain imaging: Before comparing source maps across differences, the maps of each subject (obtained by means of dedicated time series analysis) are warped onto a common brain structure. There are procedures that provide a way to warp interindividual differences in time (and, hence, rate) onto a common metric. The end result of this filtering/warping operation then would be a better starting point to look for nomothetic relationships by means of standard interindividual differences approaches. With the rapid increases in imaging work we are witnessing, the possible benefits of these kinds of modeling advances to neuroscience are substantial.

idiographic and nomothetic concerns in behavioral research (see e.g., Nesselroade & Molenaar, 1999).

Conclusion

What I have been referring to as an emerging third discipline in scientific psychology has been evolving, but it seems not with great urgency, over many decades. For several reasons, it now appears a somewhat more urgent matter. The array of available tools is clearly more impressive now than at any time in the history of behavioral science and, as noted earlier, disciplines thrive with their methodological strengths and innovations. What the telescope did for astronomy and the microscope for biology bear elegant testimony to this fact. Our newer methods may lack the drama provided by those earlier optical innovations, but there is good reason for enthusiasm and optimism regarding what may be accomplished next.

Although we have had thousands of active researchers implicitly working for decades on developing it, in the early 21st century one is hard-pressed to articulate a list of "The Top 10 Lawful Relationships of Scientific Psychology" that is impressive in both its scope and precision. Therefore, it seems that encouraging the further elaboration of some new directions is surely not a potential waste of resources. Instead, I am optimistic that more concerted efforts to focus the study of behavior in the ways I have been discussing have the potential to pay a new round of dividends.

It is clear, as the chapters in this volume indicate, that an innovative set of methodological tools is at our service, and a remarkable cohort of younger scientists is ably wielding them. To nudge our long-standing traditions over even a little bit to give some more operating room seems an effort well worth making.

References

Allport, G. W. (1937). *Personality: A psychological interpretation*. New York, NY: Holt, Rinehart and Winston.

Baltes, P. B., & Nesselroade, J. R. (1979). History and rationale of longitudinal research. In J. R. Nesselroade & P. B. Baltes (Eds.), *Longitudinal research in the study of behavior and development* (pp. 1–39). New York, NY: Academic Press.

Bereiter, C. (1963). Some persisting dilemmas in the measurement of change. In C. Harris (Ed.), *Problems in measuring change* (pp. 3–20). Madison: University of Wisconsin Press.

Bergeman, C. S., & Boker, S. M. (Eds.). (2006). *Quantitative methods in aging research*. Mahwah, NJ: Erlbaum.

Bergman, L. R., Magnusson, D., & El-Kouri, B. M. (2003). *Studying individual development in an interindividual context*. Mahwah, NJ: Erlbaum.

Bertalanffy, L. V. (1968). *General systems theory*. New York, NY: George Braziller.

Boker, S. M., & Nesselroade, J. R. (2002). A method for modeling the intrinsic dynamics of intraindividual variability: Recovering the parameters of simulated oscillators in multi-wave data. *Multivariate Behavioral Research, 37,* 127–160. doi:10.1207/S15327906MBR3701_06

Boker, S. M., & Wenger, M. J. (Eds.). (2007). *Data analytic techniques for dynamical systems in the social and behavioral sciences*. Mahwah, NJ: Erlbaum.

Browne, M. W., & Nesselroade, J. R. (2005). Representing psychological processes with dynamic factor models: Some promising uses and extensions of ARMA time series models. In A. Maydeu-Olivares & J. J. McArdle (Eds.), *Psychometrics: A Festschrift to Roderick P. McDonald* (pp. 415–452). Mahwah, NJ: Erlbaum.

Browne, M. W., & Zhang, G. (2005). *User's guide: DyFA: Dynamic factor analysis of lagged correlation matrices* [Computer software]. Columbus: Department of Psychology, Ohio State University.

Browne, M. W., & Zhang, G. (2007). Developments in the factor analysis of individual time series. In R. Cudeck & R. MacCallum (Eds.), *100 years of factor analysis: Historical developments and future directions* (pp. 265–291). Mahwah, NJ: Erlbaum.

Carlson, R. (1971). Where is the person in personality research? *Psychological Bulletin, 75,* 203–219. doi:10.1037/h0030469

Cattell, R. B. (1952). The three basic factor-analytic research designs—Their interrelations and derivatives. *Psychological Bulletin, 49,* 499–520. doi:10.1037/h0054245

Cattell, R. B. (1963). The structuring of change by P-technique and incremental R-technique. In C. W. Harris (Ed.), *Problems in measuring change* (pp. 167–198). Madison: University of Wisconsin Press.

Cattell, R. B. (1966). Multivariate behavioral research and the integrative challenge. *Multivariate Behavioral Research, 1,* 4–23. doi:10.1207/s15327906mbr0101_1

Cattell, R. B., & Scheier, I. H. (1961). *The meaning and measurement of neuroticism and anxiety.* New York, NY: Ronald Press.

Chow, S.-Y., Ferrer, E., & Hsieh, F. (Eds.). (2009). *Statistical methods for modeling human dynamics: An interdisciplinary dialogue.* New York,. NY: Taylor & Francis.

Cronbach, L. J. (1957). The two disciplines of scientific psychology. *American Psychologist, 12,* 671–684. doi:10.1037/h0043943

Cronbach, L. J. (1975). Beyond the two disciplines of scientific psychology. *American Psychologist, 30,* 116–127. doi:10.1037/h0076829

DeLongis, A., Folkman, S., & Lazarus, R. S. (1988). The impact of daily stress on health and mood: Psychological and social resources. *Journal of Personality and Social Psychology, 54,* 486–495. doi:10.1037/0022-3514.54.3.486

Estabrook, C. R., & Grimm, K. J. (2006, November). *Reliability of individual standard deviations.* Paper presented at the annual meeting of the Gerontological Society of America, Washington, DC.

Fiske, D. W., & Rice, L. (1955). Intra-individual response variability. *Psychological Bulletin, 52,* 217–250. doi:10.1037/h0045276

Ford, D. H. (1987). *Humans as self-constructing living systems.* Hillsdale, NJ: Erlbaum.

Ford, D. H., & Lerner, R. M. (1992). *Developmental systems theory: An integrative approach.* Newbury Park, CA: Sage.

Guilford, J. P. (1952). When not to factor analyze. *Psychological Bulletin, 49,* 26–37. doi:10.1037/h0054935

Hamaker, E. L., Nesselroade, J. R., & Molenaar, P. C. M. (2007). The integrated trait–state model. *Journal of Research in Personality, 41,* 295–315. doi:10.1016/j.jrp.2006.04.003

Harris, C. W. (Ed.). (1963). *Problems in measuring change.* Madison: University of Wisconsin Press.

Hultsch, D. F., Hertzog, C., Dixon, R. A., & Small, B. J. (1998). *Memory change in the aged.* Cambridge, England: Cambridge University Press.

Kagan, J. (1980). Perspectives on continuity. In O. G. Brim Jr. & J. Kagan (Eds.), *Constancy and change in human development* (pp. 26–74). Cambridge, MA: Harvard University Press.

Lamiell, J. T. (1981). Toward an idiothetic psychology of personality. *American Psychologist, 36,* 276–289. doi:10.1037/0003-066X.36.3.276

Lamiell, J. T. (1988, August). *Once more into the breach: Why individual differences research cannot advance personality theory.* Paper presented at the 96th Annual Convention of the American Psychological Association, Atlanta, GA.

Lebo, M. A., & Nesselroade, J. R. (1978). Intraindividual differences dimensions of mood change during pregnancy identified in five P-technique factor analyses. *Journal of Research in Personality, 12,* 205–224. doi:10.1016/0092-6566(78)90098-3

Magnusson, D. (2003, Fall). The person approach: Concepts, measurement models, and research strategy. *New Directions for Child and Adolescent Development,* 3–23.

Maydeu-Olivares, A., & McArdle, J. J. (Eds.). (2005). *Psychometrics: A Festschrift to Roderick P. McDonald.* Mahwah, NJ: Erlbaum.

Mischel, W. (1991, April). *Finding personality coherence in the pattern of variability.* Lecture given at the meeting of the Eastern Psychological Association, New York, NY.

Molenaar, P. C. M. (1985). A dynamic factor model for the analysis of multivariate time series. *Psychometrika, 50,* 181–202. doi:10.1007/BF02294246

Molenaar, P. C. M. (2004). A manifesto on psychology as idiographic science: Bringing the person back into scientific psychology—This time forever. *Measurement: Interdisciplinary Research & Perspective, 2,* 201–218. doi:10.1207/s15366359mea0204_1

Moskowitz, D. S., & Hershberger, S. L. (Eds.). (2002). *Modeling intraindividual variability with repeated measures data.* Mahwah, NJ: Erlbaum.

Nesselroade, J. R. (1988). Some implications of the trait–state distinction for the study of development across the life span: The case of personality research. In P. B. Baltes, D. L. Featherman, & R. M. Lerner (Eds.), *Life-span development and behavior* (Vol. 8, pp. 163–189). Hillsdale, NJ: Erlbaum.

Nesselroade, J. R., & Boker, S. M. (1994). Assessing constancy and change. In T. Heatherton & J. Weinberger (Eds.), *Can personality change?* (pp. 121–148). Washington, DC: American Psychological Association. doi:10.1037/10143-006

Nesselroade, J. R., & Ford, D. H. (1985). P-technique comes of age: Multivariate, replicated, single-subject designs for research on older adults. *Research on Aging, 7,* 46–80. doi:10.1177/0164027585007001003

Nesselroade, J. R., Gerstorf, D., Hardy, S. A., & Ram, N. (2007). Idiographic filters for psychological constructs. *Measurement: Interdisciplinary Research & Perspective, 5,* 217–235.

Nesselroade, J. R., McArdle, J. J., Aggen, S. H., & Meyers, J. M. (2002). Alternative dynamic factor models for multivariate time-series analyses. In D. M. Moskowitz & S. L. Hershberger (Eds.), *Modeling intraindividual variability with repeated measures data: Advances and techniques* (pp. 235–265). Mahwah, NJ: Erlbaum.

Nesselroade, J. R., & Molenaar, P. C. M. (1999). Pooling lagged covariance structures based on short, multivariate time-series for dynamic factor analysis. In R. H. Hoyle (Ed.), *Statistical strategies for small sample research* (pp. 224–250). Newbury Park, CA: Sage.

Rosenzweig, S. (1958). The place of the individual and of idiodynamics in psychology: A dialogue. *Journal of Individual Psychology, 14,* 3–21.

Rosenzweig, S. (1986). Idiodynamics vis-à-vis psychology. *American Psychologist, 41,* 241–245. doi:10.1037/0003-066X.41.3.241

Salthouse, T. A., Kausler, D. H., & Saults, J. S. (1986). Groups versus individuals as the comparison unit in cognitive aging research. *Developmental Neuropsychology, 2,* 363–372.

Tucker, L. R. (1966). Learning theory and multivariate experiment: Illustration by determination of generalized learning curves. In R. B. Cattell (Ed.), *Handbook of multivariate experimental psychology* (pp. 476–501). Chicago, IL: Rand McNally.

Van Kampen, V. (2000). Idiographic complexity and the common personality dimensions of insensitivity, extraversion, neuroticism, and orderliness. *European Journal of Personality, 14,* 217–243. doi:10.1002/1099-0984(200005/06)14:33.0.CO;2-G

Wundt, W. (1897). *Outlines of psychology* (C. H. Judd, Trans.). Leipzig, Germany: Wilhelm Engleman.

Zevon, M., & Tellegen, A. (1982). The structure of mood change: Idiographic/nomothetic analysis. *Journal of Personality and Social Psychology, 43,* 111–122. doi:10.1037/0022-3514.43.1.111

Zhang, Z., McArdle, J. J., & Nesselroade, J. R. (2009). *Growth rate models vs. growth curve models.* Unpublished manuscript, Department of Psychology, University of Notre Dame, South Bend, IN.

Index

About the Editors

Peter C. M. Molenaar, PhD, is a professor of human development in the Department of Human Development and Family Studies at The Pennsylvania State University, State College. The general theme of his work involves the application of mathematical theories in the following fields of research: singularity theory (in particular, catastrophe theory) to study developmental stage transitions, nonlinear signal analysis techniques to map theoretical models of cognitive information processing onto dynamically interacting neural sources, ergodic theory to study the relationships between intraindividual (idiographic) analyses and interindividual (nomothetic) analyses of psychological processes, advanced multivariate analysis techniques in quantitative genetics and developmental psychology, adaptive resonance theory neural networks to study the effects of nonlinear epigenetic processes, and computational control techniques to optimally guide developmental psychological processes and disease processes of individual subjects in real time.

Karl M. Newell, PhD, is the Marie Underhill Noll Chair of Human Performance and head of the Department of Kinesiology at The Pennsylvania State University, State College. Dr. Newell's research interests lie in the area of human movement in general and motor learning and control specifically. His research focuses on the coordination, control, and skill of normal and abnormal human movement across the life span; developmental disabilities and motor skills; and the influence of drug and exercise on movement control. One of the specific themes of his research is the study of variability in human movement and posture, with specific reference to the onset of aging and Parkinson's disease. His other major research theme is processes of change in motor learning and development—the focus of this book.